POPCULTURED

Thinking Christianly About Style, Media and Entertainment

STEVE TURNER

IVP Books

An imprint of InterVarsity Press
Downers Grove, Illinois

InterVarsity Press
P.O. Box 1400, Downers Grove, IL 60515-1426
World Wide Web: www.ivpress.com
Email: email@ivpress.com

InterVarsity Press® is the book-publishing division of InterVarsity Christian Fellowship/USA®, a movement
of students and faculty active on campus at hundreds of universities, colleges and schools of nursing in the
United States of America, and a member movement of the International Fellowship of Evangelical Students.
For information about local and regional activities, write Public Relations Dept., InterVarsity Christian
Fellowship/USA, 6400 Schroeder Rd., P.O. Box 7895, Madison, WI 53707-7895, or visit the IVCF website at
<www.intervarsity.org>.

All Scripture quotations, unless otherwise indicated, are taken from the Holy Bible, Today's New
International Version®, TNIV® Copyright © 2001 by International Bible Society. All rights reserved.

Cover design: Cindy Kiple
Interior design: Beth Hagenberg
Images: Collage of plastic figures: CSA Plastock/Getty Images; Paparazzi: © Shaun Lowe/iStockphoto;
   Business man: © PhotoInc/iStockphoto; Wall Texture: © peeterv/iStockphoto; Blue jeans: © Natallia
   Yaumenenk/iStockphoto; Female fashion model: © Juanmonino/iStockphoto; Graffiti on a wall:
   © Hans Laubel/iStockphoto; Time Square: © Francisco Diez Photography/Getty Images; Surprised
   woman: © esolla/iStockphoto; Roller coaster: © Cristian Lazzari/iStockphoto; Internet connection:
   © Axaulya/iStockphoto; Music: © aldra/iStockphoto

ISBN 978-0-8308-3768-7

Printed in the United States of America ∞

Library of Congress Cataloging-in-Publication Data

Turner, Steve, 1949-
 Popcultured : thinking Christianly about style, media, and entertainment / Steve Turner.
  pages cm
 Includes bibliographical references and index.
 ISBN 978-0-8308-3768-7 (pbk. : alk. paper)
 1. Popular culture—Religious aspects—Christianity. I. Title.
 BR115.C8T875 2013
 261—dc23

                      2013006894

| P | 20 | 19 | 18 | 17 | 16 | 15 | 14 | 13 | 12 | 11 | 10 | 9 | 8 | 7 | 6 | 5 | 4 | 3 | 2 | 1 |
| Y | 30 | 29 | 28 | 27 | 26 | 25 | 24 | 23 | 22 | 21 | 20 | 19 | 18 | 17 | 16 | 15 | 14 | 13 |

Contents

Introduction

We've Been Popcultured

†

My church runs a course for new Christians called "Christianity Explored," which is designed to establish them in the faith. The evenings begin with a meal, followed by table discussions and a talk. Those who graduate usually go on to take a follow-up course called "Discipleship Explored," which takes them into deeper study of the Bible. I've been privileged to lead table discussions at both courses and found it constantly challenging to prepare myself for new questions from new people, many of them with almost no background in Christian theology.

My personal interest for many years has been popular culture, and after taking part in the courses mentioned I idly wondered what a course called "Exploring Popular Culture" would look like. I wondered this because I think family, friends, work and popular culture (or leisure activities in general) are where the rubber of our theology hits the road of our ordinary lives. Lessons learned from theology shouldn't (but often do) remain in the area of theory. They should be evidenced in the way we treat friends and neighbors, earn our money, watch movies, read books and listen to music.

For most of my life I've not only consumed popular culture but also I've helped make some and have interviewed many people from the worlds of music, film, comedy, fashion, television, art, poetry and

literature. At the same time I've tried to make sense of it all through a
Christian understanding. The twentieth-century Swiss theologian
Karl Barth reputedly told his students, "Take your Bible and take your
newspaper, and read both. But interpret newspapers from your Bible."
That accurately sums up what I have tried to do in my work.

Popcultured has been another part of that journey. Although it's designed to help others, it has also helped me because it has forced me
to stare hard at different aspects of popular culture, read extensively
and search the Scriptures for those nuggets of truth that may have
evaded me. Rather than starting with a fixed thesis (other than the
thesis that God has something to say about every area of life), I've
discovered new things as I've gone along.

The title playfully reflects what I think has happened to us. We may
not be so bold as to claim to be cultured, but most of us are to some
degree or other popcultured. Popular culture, or "pop culture" as it's
often referred to, suffuses our lives. The opening ceremony of the
2012 Olympic Games in London was testament to how much we now
identify ourselves by the popular culture we create and consume. In
1948 the opening ceremony London summer Olympics used only
military bands. The most spectacular event was a twenty-one-gun
salute and the release of seven thousand pigeons. In 2012, $42 million
was spent on a three-hour ceremony held together by different forms
of rock music and designed to impress the world.

In a popcultured age it made sense to have the evening designed by
a movie director, Danny Boyle, and to showcase the work of actors,
dancers, performance artists, sculptors, clowns, storytellers, comedians, musicians and DJs. There were references to the high culture of
Shakespeare and Elgar, but the emphasis was on pop culture: James
Bond and Harry Potter, the Beatles and the Sex Pistols, *Chariots of Fire*
and the inventor of the World Wide Web, Tim Berners Lee.

This has been the first book I've written whose chapters I've sent
out for review before finishing the manuscript. This was because I'm
aware that I'm not an expert in many of the areas covered and I needed
assurance that I wasn't way off-beam. That doesn't mean that my

mentors have approved everything in the book. All opinions, and therefore all mistakes, are mine alone.

My good friend Bobette Buster, who is a Hollywood story guru, script consultant, lecturer and screenwriter, read the whole book and then spent time discussing it page by page with me on Skype. I value the time she gave to this project. Jeremy Begbie, Thomas A. Langford Research Professor of Theology at Duke Divinity School and a renowned expert on art and theology, read the first three chapters and made kind and considered comments.

Rebecca Ver Straten-McSparran, director of the L.A. Film Studies Center, read my chapter on film and discussed her views with me over a meal and then by email. I completely reworked the chapter as a result of her wise and informed comments. Nev Pierce, editor-at-large for *Empire* magazine, also read the chapter and emailed me with useful suggestions.

My friend Mark Joseph, author and CEO of MJM Entertainment Group, and Robert A. Case, founding director of the World Journalism Institute in New York, read the chapter on journalism. I haven't yet met Bob Case in person, but he was kind enough to tell me that the Institute had my book *Imagine: A Vision for Christians in the Arts* on its reading list and that he thought my chapter was good because he agreed with it.

Cliff Richard, one of Britain's longest-serving pop stars, gave my celebrity culture chapter the thumbs-up, as did Patty Heaton, star of *Everybody Loves Raymond* and *The Middle*. Patty also shared with me some of her experiences of dealing with fame as a believer. Rosie Mc-Conkey of Siren Design, Angela Buttolph, editor-at-large for *Grazzia* magazine, and Ali Hewson, co-founder of EDUN Clothing and NUDE Skincare, read my chapter on fashion. I showed the chapter on sensation to Dave Carlson, executive director of Opera-Matic in Chicago ("bringing moving visual art to the streets") and to Willie Williams, U2's stage and lighting designer for the past thirty years (as well as for David Bowie, the Stones, Lady Gaga, REM and others). Both made valuable comments.

I got extensive feedback on the comedy chapter from renowned British stand-up Milton Jones, American writer and performer Susan E. Isaacs, and TV writer/producer Dean Batali (*That '70s Show, Buffy the Vampire Slayer*). Some of their comments were so pertinent that I ended up dropping them into the revised chapter.

The advertising chapter I showed to Tony Neeves, a man who forsook the world of commercials to work for charities and is now vice president of international development for Compassion International. I also showed it to Adrian Reith, producer of radio jingles and owner of The Jungle Group Ltd.

Kevin Kelly, cofounder of *Wired* magazine, author of *What Technology Wants* and founding board member of the WELL, perused my chapter on electronic technology and assured me I was on track (or maybe assured me I wasn't off-track). Photographers Chris Dyball from California and Donata Wenders from Berlin reviewed the chapter on photography and were both very reassuring with their comments. Steve Taylor, musician and now film director (*Blue Like Jazz*), gave me a report on the chapter that looks at how Christians are portrayed in movies and on TV.

At the end of each chapter I've listed questions suitable as discussion starters, relevant books and websites and some practical suggestions. The books and websites don't all represent my viewpoint, but they cover the same ground and might be worth researching. It was sometimes hard to suggest a plan of action because I was aware that my readers will range from people who are still at school to serious practitioners of the arts being discussed.

Howard and Roberta Ahmanson helped me by arranging a grant through Fieldstead and Company to buy me valuable research and writing time. They were similarly generous when I was writing my earlier book *Imagine: A Vision for Christians in the Arts*, and I salute their kindness and their faith in the arts and culture. They never asked to see a manuscript before publication and had no say whatsoever in the actual writing of the book.

My hope is that *Popcultured* will help those trying to navigate the sometimes choppy waters of popular culture with the aid of Christian truth. It's far from the final word on the subject, but I hope that it stimulates study, discussion and thoughtful consideration. Above all I hope it promotes understanding and enjoyment of the areas covered and that readers will feel excited about their potential both as consumers and creators.

1

Leisure Pursuits

Why We Should Care

†

There are a lot of books available that teach people the basics of the Christian life. There are resources that explain who God is to people who are merely curious about Christianity. There are courses on how to read the Bible, how to pray, how to explain the gospel to others, how to resist temptation and how to follow Jesus. There are classes that instruct people in the "deeper things" such as fasting, meditation, waiting on God and spiritual disciplines.

This book is different. It may involve reference to many of the above ideas and practices but it's essentially about how we can be faithfully Christian while participating in and perhaps even creating popular culture. In the third century the church father Tertullian famously asked, "What indeed has Athens to do with Jerusalem?" meaning, what has biblical faith got to do with secular learning, or what has the gospel to do with philosophy? Today we might ask, What have Hollywood, Silicon Valley, Madison Avenue, Burbank or Times Square got to do with Jerusalem? In other words, what has popular culture got to do with the Christian faith? I think it's an important question to ask for ten reasons.

The Divided Mind

The first is that *many Christians still ask the question assuming that the correct answer is "They have nothing to do with each other"* (which, incidentally, was what Tertullian expected and wanted to hear). They may say this because they believe in separation, that Christians should keep a distance from all that's "worldly." There are clearly many verses in the Bible that tell us to avoid bad company, to resist the devil and to retain a Christian distinctiveness. The issue is, how do we apply these commands in relation to popular culture? Many Christians over the years have concluded that the most effective way is to abstain. They've ignored fashion, refused to watch movies, kept their homes free of television and some have even banned novels and newspapers.

Or they may say this because they have divided minds. The divided mind has a spiritual side and an earthly side. The spiritual side is engaged on Sundays and during times of Bible reading and prayer. The earthly side is activated when pursuing leisure activities. There are Christians today whose consumption of popular culture is not markedly different from the consumption of their nonbelieving contemporaries, and, more worryingly, their views of what they've seen, heard or read likewise seem to be no different. They evaluate a band, computer game or film as "good" or "bad" using the same criteria as their secular counterparts.

The Christian with the divided mind and the Christian who believes that "come out from them and be separate" (2 Cor 6:17) means avoidance of popular culture are usually poles apart theologically—as far apart as an Amish farmer from Pennsylvania and an emerging-church worshiper from California—but they both result from the same process, an avoidance of discrimination. The separatist usually deals with popular culture by issuing a blanket ban; the divided Christian, by a blanket acceptance. They both avoid the hard task of being simultaneously critically and spiritually engaged.

Not to Be Taken Seriously?

The second reason to ask the question is because *people often make popular culture with the intent of altering perceptions.* I hear people justify uncritical consumption on the grounds that what they're watching, reading, playing or listening to is "just a laugh" or "shouldn't be taken seriously." They think that to evaluate what they're being fed involves too much effort and goes against the spirit of entertainment. They say that they don't want to be overly serious or get too "heavy." Some people believe that popular culture is best imbibed when the mind is fully switched off. They watch films as if the moving images had as much moral content and power as crashing waves or trembling leaves.

This attitude seriously underestimates the intelligence and the motivation of those who create popular culture. These creators aren't children doodling with crayons. Predominantly they are trained people with a deep knowledge of their chosen art form and its history. They tend to be highly opinionated people with a vision of the world that they are keen to express. There's something about the status quo that irritates them and they want to put it right. Sometimes they are people who enjoy subversion—reeling people in with wholesome looking entertainment and then zapping them with a message that runs counter to expectations.

Some directors, producers and writers are quite upfront about how they want their films or TV programs to change attitudes. They realize, for example, that dramas and soaps are more effective mind-changers than documentaries because viewers get involved in the internal conflicts of characters they've come to love. They recognize that the public is more effectively persuaded through emotions than intellect. Campaigning organizations often lobby the makers of soaps to include their concerns in future story lines in order to promote their message to a wider audience. *EastEnders* actor Michael Cashman planted the first gay kiss on British primetime TV in 1987, leading to a storm of protests. "Public taste has to be developed," was his explanation. "Public opinion has to be led. And television and the media are central to that."[1]

The great poet T. S. Eliot believed that the culture we consume just for fun, with no thought of grappling with heavyweight theses, has the most effect on us. He thought this was true precisely because of the fun element. When we think something is relatively frivolous we disable our critical alarm systems and thereby allow influences to enter undetected. George Orwell had a similar view. In his 1939 essay "Boys' Weeklies," which looked at British comics, he asked the question "To what extent do people draw their ideas from fiction?" His answer was, "Personally I believe that most people are influenced far more than they would care to admit by novels, serial stories, films and so forth, and that from this point of view the worst books are often the most important, because they are usually the ones that are read earliest."[2] The novelist Graham Greene believed that we are profoundly affected by the books we read as children: "Early reading has more influence on conduct than any religious teaching."[3]

Comedians recognize that laughter can soften an audience up and make it easier for people to entertain views they might normally reject or be offended by. George Carlin said, "Once you get people laughing they're listening and you can tell them almost anything." He expanded on this idea in a 1998 interview:

> Most of the time, when you talk to people about, let's call them "issues," okay? People have their defenses up. They are going to defend their point of view, the thing they're used to, the ideas that they hold dear, and you have to take a long, logical route to get through to them, generally. . . . But when you are doing comedy or humor, people are open, and when the moment of laughter comes, their guard is down, so new data can be introduced more easily at that moment.[4]

This realization doesn't imply that all readily available culture is insidious, just that it has a habit of bypassing our scrutiny because it gives us warm feelings. When we suspect that culture has an agenda, we are naturally more guarded. When we think that it's only there to tickle us, we roll over and start purring. The Bible, insistence on vigilance presupposes that we are vulnerable to spiritual corruption when not alert.

The Gift of Culture

A third reason is *popular culture is a great gift to us and we should therefore take it seriously.* It's impossible to imagine a human society without culture. It's a significant expression of our humanity that distinguishes us from animals. We could easily drink out of a plain clay pot, but our instinct is to shape and embellish it with color and pattern. A lot of what we refer to as culture is shaping and embellishing of this sort. We shape tales of events into stories, sounds into music. We embellish plain walls with murals and make our hair go in directions that nature never thought of.

Theologians talk of God's instructions to Adam to reproduce, farm the land and name the animals as the "cultural mandate." Indeed, the word *cultivate*, which we most commonly associate with plowing, weeding, sowing, pruning and harvesting, has the same root as the word *culture.* Our culture, at its best, is another way of tilling, planting, rearing and gathering in. We break up the hard soil of our rational minds, plant beautiful ideas, rear the imagination and gather in more fully rounded human beings.

Culture should enhance our lives. It very often serves to relieve us of the cold, hard facts we have to deal with in our working lives and delivers us into the world of fantasy, myth and dream. "Art washes away from the soul the dust of everyday life," said Picasso.[5] Poems and plays and paintings can show us connections between things that we would never have discovered through ruthless logic. Songs and music help to bring people together and make us aware of the vastness of what it means to be human.

Popular culture is also a healthy forum for debate. New ways of living are explored, new philosophies are floated and new attitudes are tested. It was largely through popular music—rock music in particular—that the alternative views of the 1960s were articulated and explored. The songs and the opinions of the musicians were analyzed, challenged and criticized in other media. Indeed it's hard to discuss the youth revolt of the decade without reference to artists like the Beatles, the Rolling Stones, Bob Dylan, Jimi Hendrix and The Who.

The Lord of All Life

A fourth reason is that *the Christian view is that Christ is the Lord of all life*. That is the definition of discipleship. He wants us heart, mind, strength and soul—the total package. That means that there is nothing we experience that Christ doesn't have a claim on and doesn't have something to say about. Yet sometimes we treat him as though he wouldn't really understand some areas of our modern lives, such as popular culture. How could the Ancient of Days possibly keep up? Without meaning to, we treat him like a deaf and partially sighted old man who is so out of touch with contemporary culture that we think we're doing him a favor by not bothering him for an opinion.

The fact is that if Christ is Lord of all of our lives, then there must be a Christian way to enjoy and make popular culture. We will never know the mind of Christ in its totality, but part of the adventure of discipleship lies in trying to discover as much of it as we can. I would love to sit with Christ and ask him what he thinks of the music of the Beatles, the films of John Ford or the art of Picasso. The Beatles made *Revolver*, but God made John Lennon, Paul McCartney, George Harrison and Ringo Starr. Picasso painted *Guernica* but God fashioned Picasso. I think that art can delight or offend God, but it can never surprise him.

The Bible has many injunctions to glorify God in all aspects of life. Paul wrote, "So whether you eat or drink or whatever you do, do it all for the glory of God" (1 Cor 10:31). Eating and drinking are two of the most basic survival requirements. Other than in the cases of dietary laws, the avoidance of gluttony, the feeding of the hungry and the receiving of bread and wine in the Eucharist, there would seem to be no obvious connection between meals and religion. Yet Paul thought that consuming food and drink could be done in a glorifying way, and therefore, we must deduce, it has the potential of being done in a less than glorifying manner. If the "whatever you do" is broad enough to cover food and drink, it's certainly broad enough to cover popular culture.

The Pervasive Influence

A fifth reason for asking the question is because *most of us spend a good proportion our lives having our thoughts prompted by popular culture.* Through the day we may watch the news on TV, check out social networking sites, buy new clothes, read a newspaper or magazine, read ads, tweet or text, or play an online game. In the evening we may watch a TV drama, soap opera, reality show or talent show, spend time on the Internet, read a book or listen to music. On the weekend we may watch a movie, go to a play, dance, skateboard or attend a concert.

Any guidance we have on living or thinking as a Christian has to take into account popular culture because we spend so much time in the sphere of its influence. It's hard to argue that the Bible is a source of guidance when dealing with such areas of life as money, marriage, family, relationships, work, worship and prayer but has nothing useful to say when it comes to culture.

What we call popular culture is a natural result of increased leisure time, higher earnings and more luxury. Britain's Office for National Statistics reported that in 2010 Britons were spending nine times as much on recreation and culture as they had done in the 1970s. Will Galgey, managing director of trends consultancy The Futures Company, commented, "It's a big shift from material goods to experiences . . . our consumption is about how to enhance our experiences even in the context of our own homes."[6]

This shift is borne out in personal experience. My grandfather worked on a farm as a teenager and went to bed exhausted at night. On Saturdays he had to walk a round-trip journey of twenty-four miles to sell cattle. His only entertainment was a German-made music box that rotated tin discs, an accordion played by his father and some cheap sensational newspapers of the late Victorian era. My parents had dance bands, magazines, movies, gramophones, comics and early forms of radio. I had TV (but not until I was a teenager), transistor radio, record players and paperback books. My children have had computers, the Internet, iPods, iPads, computer games, satellite TV,

DVDs and iPhones. In just over a century my family's consumption of popular culture has increased dramatically.

The filmmaker Paul Schrader has estimated that the average thirty-year-old media-savvy person today has seen around 35,000 hours of "audio-visual narrative," including everything from movies and soap operas to cartoons and YouTube clips. This person's father, at the same age, would have only seen 20,000 hours, his grandfather 10,000 hours, and his great-grandfather 2,500 hours. "We are inundated by narrative," he said of today. "We are swimming in storylines."[7]

When *Rolling Stone* polled its readers in 2010, it found that they spent 11.5 hours a week listening to music, 7.9 hours watching TV, 4.4 hours social networking, 3 hours reading magazines and 2.8 hours playing video games. That adds up to over a day a week immersed in popular culture. Almost 95 percent of those polled said that music was "extremely or very important" in their lives. When asked what form of entertainment they would keep if they could only keep one, 64.7 percent said "listening to music" and 17.1 percent said "watching TV."[8]

Signs of the Times

A sixth reason is that *popular culture can be a useful indicator of the Zeitgeist, the "spirit of the times."* Anyone wanting to be alert to changing attitudes and trends in belief would be wise to pay attention. It's a place where society airs its hopes and uncertainties. It's where people attempt to win others to new ways of thinking. It's where possible futures are tried out. Cultural studies pioneer Stuart Hall has said that popular culture is a site where "collective social understandings are created."[9] Fashion designer Alexander McQueen said of his work, "I'm making points about my time, about the times we live in. My work is a social document about the world today."[10]

The Canadian communications guru Marshall McLuhan recognized in the 1940s that the much-maligned mass culture of the day provided a unique insight into the collective consciousness. In his 1951 book *The Mechanical Bride: Folklore of Industrial Man* he analyzed the assumptions behind advertisements, newspaper layout, book of the month clubs, crime comics, strip cartoons, westerns, Tarzan, Superman and Coca-Cola. He said,

Our hit parade tunes and our jazz are quite as representative of our inner lives as any old ballad is of a past way of life. As such, these popular expressions, even though produced by skillful technicians, are a valuable means of taking stock of our success or failure in developing a balanced existence.[11]

The cartoonist Jules Feiffer once said, "To know the true temper of a nation's people, turn not to its sociologists; turn to its junk."[12]

The journalist who best understood this in the 1960s was Tom Wolfe, a New York-based observer who expertly highlighted the connections between changing belief systems and the way people were dressing, behaving, talking and consuming. Where previous generations of writers may have focused on the behavior and attitudes of royalty, the aristocracy or the social elite, Wolfe looked to popular culture because be believed that it was here that the most significant social changes were being revealed. What happened in the coffee bars and nightclubs today was going to affect America tomorrow.

In the introduction to his 1965 collection of journalism, *The Kandy-Kolored Tangerine-Flake Streamline Baby*, Wolfe challenged those who ignored popular culture or who thought it was a bit beneath them:

Stock car racing, custom cars—and, for that matter, the jerk, the monkey, rock music—still seem beneath serious consideration, still the preserve of ratty people with ratty hair and dermatitis and corroded thoracic boxes and so forth. Yet all these rancid people are creating new styles all the time and changing the life of the whole country in ways that nobody even seems to bother to record, let alone analyze.[13]

The contemporary American stock market analyst Robert Prechter asserts that popular culture ("popular art, fashion and mores") accurately reflects the dominant public mood and that the changes of mood anticipate financial trends. When the mood is buoyant, as it was in the 1920s and 1960s, confidence in the market goes up. When the mood is downbeat, as it was in the 1930s and 1970s, confidence in the market evaporates. Prechter therefore uses close analysis of "music, movies, fashion, literature, television, popular philosophy, sports, dance, automobile styling, sexual identity, family life, campus activities, politics and poetry" to help him make his predictions.

In his frequently quoted essay "Popular Culture and the Stock Market," Prechter says,

> If mass mood change is indeed the cause, and its manifestation a visible indicator, of coming social events, the evidence of mood change is the single most important area of discovery for those who wish to peek into the future of social events. In the world of popular culture, "trendsetters" and the avant-garde must be carefully observed since their ideas are often the expression of the leading edge of the public mood.[14]

Isn't it to be expected that Christians should have a similar appetite for gauging the public mood? One of the most frequently made criticisms of the church is that it's completely out of touch. While it isn't the job of the Christian community to mimic the secular world or to alter its message to conform to contemporary tastes, it is its job to be familiar with a culture's hopes and fears, to engage with it and to speak in a relevant way. Jesus challenged the Pharisees and Sadducees over their inability to read the times. He said, "You know how to interpret the appearance of the sky, but you cannot interpret the signs of the times" (Mt 16:3).

The church would have been far better prepared to meet the challenges of the 1960s if in the 1950s it had been reading the mimeographed magazines of the Beat generation poets, listening to the songs on the jukeboxes and paying visits to the coffee bars and jazz cellars of Paris, London, New York and San Francisco. Everything that was to come was already there in embryo form. The future was being rehearsed in popular culture. As Paul Simon reminded us in "The Sound of Silence," one place to look for prophetic utterances is on the walls of subways and tenements.

Insights into Minds

A seventh reason is that *because popular culture is a place of debate and negotiation, it gives us examples of how our contemporaries are thinking.* Surely in order to love our neighbors as ourselves we will give their views respectful and thoughtful consideration. The best biblical example of this approach is when Paul makes a speech on the Areopagus, a small outcrop of rock close to the Acropolis popular at the time for speakers and debaters.

It's significant that Paul headed to the place where the latest ideas were kicked about. He could have holed up in the house of a believer and asked them to invite guests over, but instead he went to the city's cutting-edge philosophy forum. Once there he looked around at the statues erected to various gods and read the inscriptions. He wanted to get a sense of the competing worldviews that were already familiar to his audience. In our language he wanted to gauge their mindset. When talking he made reference to what he'd seen and also quoted (favorably) from poets that reflected their views. He used the culture of the Athenians as a walkway to their imaginations.

We do well to know the popular culture of our times because there we have the stories, the poetry and the idolatry of our times. It makes sense to illustrate a point by appealing to dialogue from a film, lines from a song or comments from a popular culture icon, because they're familiar to the contemporary audience. These examples establish a common ground for discussion. The space in people's brains that would once have been filled with stories from the Bible and verses from hymns is now full of stories by screenwriters and lines from lyricists.

When we do this we also make the point that the message of the gospel isn't that everything you've known up to now is wrong and all your culture is worthless. Profound truths about all of life are available to all people. Think of the films, poems, novels, songs and music that have provided you with insights and you'll find that the majority will have been the work of people outside the Christian faith. God gives understanding to all people. The gospel rearranges many things we already know, supplies a different framework and adds a different conclusion. The philosopher Epimenides was right to say that in God we live and move and have our being (Acts 17:28), but Paul says that if this is so we shouldn't think of God as an idol made of gold, silver or stone.

Entering the Conversation

An eighth reason is that *unless we first pay attention to popular culture, we have little chance of successfully contributing to it.* To join in any conversation we first of all have to listen to it and familiarize ourselves with the argument and the language being used. When we're up to speed we can add to the debate. We know what the pressing issues are, we know what arguments have been put up so far, and we recognize the tone.

We've probably all experienced the embarrassment of someone trying to use popular culture without understanding the vocabulary. There were Christian "beat groups" in the early 1960s that adopted the instrumental line up of the Beatles but performed songs that were no more than speeded up hymns. They may have looked (almost) like the real thing, but they lacked authenticity because they weren't addressing the hot issues of the day or employing the accepted vocabulary of pop.

Truth Is Truth

A ninth reason is that *God can address us through popular culture.* He can use songs to encourage us, movies to deepen our understanding of ourselves, biographies to inspire us, television to educate us, journalism to inform us. We are able to pray in a more compassionate way because of news gatherers, marvel at creation more deeply because of nature photographers, feel less isolated because of songwriters, build more communities of like-minded people because of the Internet.

Truth is truth whoever may say it, and because people are made by God they can't help discovering and passing on truth. It may be mixed in with falsehoods—it's our job to work it out—but we must revere truth whenever we encounter it. Even people who announce that they hate God will pronounce truths because it's impossible for anyone to operate on 100 percent lies. We're free to disagree with God but we're not free to live outside his universe.

God will use these truths to nudge, sensitize, awaken and embrace us. I can think of a minister who was helped through a period of depression by the music of U2 and a journalist who came to faith as the direct result of a painting. The Beatles played a part in my own pilgrimage. This is not to suggest that songs should be elevated to the level of Scripture or that visual meditations should replace sermons and Bible studies, but simply to point out that if we ignore popular culture we could be ignoring a channel through which God makes himself known.

The actor Patty Heaton makes the point beautifully:

> As far as worshiping people for their talent—of course we musn't. But there are people whose artistic talent is so enormous that even if they are narcissistic or whorish or drug addicted or materialistic, their talent nonetheless points to the greatness of God, even if they cannot see it themselves. The beauty of Christianity is that we can enjoy the blessings God has bestowed upon nonbelievers. In the play/movie *Amadeus*, the Christian Salieri is tortured by Mozart's God-given talent, incensed that God would bless a whore mongering lush with such talent, while his pious self churns out the 1700s version of elevator music. God is no respecter of persons and blesses whomever he chooses. Fortunately we can all reap the benefit![15]

Cultural Theory

A tenth reason for Christians to ask the question is because *people who don't accept spiritual realities are responsible for most of the serious academic exploration of popular culture.* When the spiritual is neglected, "reality" is reduced to the drives for sex, power and money. I don't mean to infer that these people have got everything wrong. I've benefited from all their points of view, but I'm left feeling that some-thing vital has been overlooked. Structuralism believes it's all down to language and signs; Marxism reckons capital, class and ownership are the deciding factors; feminism thinks gender politics are crucial; queer theory looks for the sexual subtext; postmodernism pins every-thing on the collapse of grand narratives.

What seems remarkable (given our Christian heritage) is that none of the leading schools of cultural theory in the West start with a bib-lical view of humanity or even seem to consider a spiritual dimension, and none of the key theoreticians has been religious. If Christians got involved in such scholarship they could raise questions that aren't currently being asked and add a disquieting voice to the ongoing debate. It would be nice to think that future textbooks surveying all the cultural theories currently on offer would be forced to appraise distinctly Christian contributions.

These are some of the important reasons why I believe that Chris-tians should equip themselves to understand, enjoy and participate in popular culture. Correctly dealt with, I believe that popular culture cannot only enlarge our experience of what it is to be human but can strengthen our faith through reminding us of forgotten truths, chal-lenging our assumptions, forging connections with the world around us and forcing us to think about the practical application of our faith. Feeling the world as others feel it can be a healthy check on our temp-tation to be arrogant or self-righteous.

Questions for Reflection or Discussion

- Can you think of a song, film or TV program that changed your at-titude about something important?

- What examples of drama and comedy that had a background agenda can you bring to mind?

- What would you need to give up if you were to remove all pop culture from your life?

- Think of a time when popular culture brought much-needed relief or consolation to you.

- God requires that we love him with heart, mind, strength and soul. What activities do you associate with each of these dimensions?

- Calculate roughly how many hours a week you spend consuming some form of popular culture.

- What is the most significant form of popular culture in your life? Compare and contrast it with what preoccupied your parents and grandparents at the same age.

- Do you think it is accurate to say that pop culture gives us an insight into the most important concerns of the era we are living in?

- Can you think of attempts by Christians to use popular culture that have left you feeling embarrassed? In retrospect what was it about their attempt that made you feel that way, and what could have been done better?

- Bring to mind examples of popular culture that you believe God has used in your life, and try to understand what it was that made it effective for you.

Useful Books on Culture by Christians

Crouch, Andy. *Culture Making: Recovering Our Creative Calling.* Downers Grove, IL: InterVarsity Press, 2008.

Detweiler, Craig, and Barry Taylor. *A Matrix of Meanings: Finding God in Pop Culture.* Grand Rapids: Baker Academic, 2003.

Don't Stop Believin': Pop Culture and Religion from Ben Hur to Zombies. Edited by Robert K. Johnston, Craig Detweiler and Barry Taylor. Louisville, KY: Westminster John Knox Press, 2012.

Lynch, Gordon. *Understanding Theology and Popular Culture.* Hoboken, NJ: Wiley-Blackwell, 2004.

Morrow, Jonathan. *Think Christianly: Looking at the Intersection of Faith and Culture.* Grand Rapids: Zondervan, 2012.

Romanowski, William. *Eyes Wide Open: Looking for God in Popular Culture.* Grand Rapids: Brazos, 2007.

————. *Pop Culture Wars: Religion and the Role of Entertainment in American Life.* Downers Grove, IL: InterVarsity Press, 1996.

Turnau, Ted. *Popologetics: Popular Culture in Christian Perspective.* Phillipsburg, NJ: P&R, 2012.

Websites Dealing with Issues of Christianity and Pop Culture

Plugged In: www.pluggedin.com
Two Handed Warriors: www.garydavidstratton.com
Bully Pulpit: www.bullypulpit.com
Dick Staub: www.dickstaub.com

Five Suggestions for Action

- Join or form a group where you can discuss what you're watching, reading or listening to.

- Be aware of what people are consuming by reading the top-ten lists of bestselling records, downloads, books and movies.

- Look out for and read interviews with prominent culture creators so that you become familiar with their views of the world.

- Read a wide selection of reviews so that you can choose your culture carefully.

- Check out free lectures, debates and performances that are frequently listed in local events magazines and websites.

2

Popular Culture

Defining the Term

†

I wonder what you first think of when you hear the word *culture*? You may think of rarefied pursuits where you have to sit quietly and reverently while supposedly being turned into a better person— "getting a bit of culture." You may think of a whole way of life such as when people speak of "European culture" or "ancient Aztec culture." You may think of ministries of culture, people of culture, cities of culture or the "culture" section of a magazine or newspaper. You may even think of phrases such as "a culture of intimidation" and "gang culture," or the title of the influential book *Culture Wars*.

The Nazi leader Hermann Goering was allegedly fond of the quote "When I hear the word 'culture,' I reach for my gun." Comedian Bob Hope once quipped that the definition of culture was "Being able to describe Rita Hayworth without using your hands." To the nineteenth-century writer Matthew Arnold, culture was nothing less than "the study and pursuit of perfection."

It's a problematic word because it has so many possible meanings. In 1872 the British Association for the Advancement of Science came up with seventy-six topics that could be considered under the heading of "culture." In 1938 the "Outline of Cultural Materials" defined 79 divisions of culture and 637 subdivisions. In the 1950s two American anthropologists, Alfred Kroeber and Clyde Kluckhohn, came up with over 160 definitions of culture in their book *Culture: A Critical Review of Concepts and Definition*. No wonder that the British cultural critic Raymond Williams referred to culture as "one of the two or three most complicated words in the English language."[1]

It's a fifteenth-century word with origins in the Latin *cultus* (from the verb *colere*), which described tilling the land. Cultus had associated meanings of protection, nurture, adornment and devotion to a god. We retain some of these meanings in our words *cultivate*, *culture* (as in "bacteria culture") and *cult*. So culture was thought of as something that played a part in cultivating people. There was the idea that in some way we were like hard soil that needed breaking up before being planted with good seeds.

The quotes attributed to Goering, Hope and Arnold actually acknowledge this definition. The Goering quote has been sourced to a play written by a Nazi where a character is arguing that learning is a waste of time because only violence can change the world. The actual line is "When I hear 'culture' . . . I release the safety catch of my Browning." Culture, with its metaphorical tilling and planting, is a slow route to change. The gun is far quicker. The quip by Bob Hope assumes that if you have culture you will have enough descriptive words available to you, and enough appreciation of Rita Hayworth's skills as an actor, to avoid reducing her to a physical shape. Arnold thought that culture, like religion, could improve people.

Getting Cultured

We're all familiar with this idea that culture is good for us. We may be bored with the art museum or find the opera a bit difficult to follow, but we are encouraged to believe that it's turning us into better people. We may not be able to dance to Beethoven, but we can learn to appreciate him. A play by Shakespeare is not as fast moving as a soap opera, but the hard work of trying to understand him should pay off in unique insights into human nature. When we talk of someone being cultured, we mean that they've had a wide exposure to the best things in life. Young aristocrats in the eighteenth century would travel through Europe on what became known as the "grand tour" in order to become cultured. They would learn how to dance, draw and fence, explore ancient ruins, visit art museums, speak another language, study architecture and bring home foreign treasures that could decorate their vast country mansions.

This was the idea of culture put forward by Matthew Arnold in his influential book *Culture and Anarchy* in 1869. His title declared his thesis. He saw culture as the only way of preventing society sliding into chaos, anarchy and barbarism. He was writing a decade after the publication of Charles Darwin's *The Origin of Species* and therefore may have been worrying about the apparently thin line separating humans from chimpanzees, apes and gorillas. Culture was Victorian humanity's protection against animalism.

Arnold believed that culture contained "the best that has been thought and known." He argued that it could be used to improve people. He didn't want it to displace religion but nevertheless considered that it performed a religious role. It's perhaps no coincidence that the great museums and galleries of the Victorian era had cathedral-like qualities that to this day encourage people to walk round them in hushed reverence. "In determining generally in what human perfection consists, religion comes to a conclusion identical with that which culture . . . reaches," Arnold wrote. "Religion says: The kingdom of God is within you; and culture, in like manner, places human perfection in an internal condition in the growth and predominance of our humanity proper, as distinguished from our animality."[2]

Although Arnold didn't coin the terms *high culture* and *low culture*, he created the climate for such a distinction. He defined rather than described the sort of culture he thought would preserve civilization, but it was clear that "the best that has been thought and known" was going to include Shakespeare and Tolstoy rather than music hall routines and "penny dreadfuls" (cheap, sensationalist newspapers). Arnold wanted culture to be offered to all, but the nature of that culture was going to be defined by an educated elite and would naturally reflect its background, class and taste.

Culture High and Low

We are all inheritors of this distinction between high and low culture. The work of Mozart and Michelangelo would be high culture. The work of rapper Jay-Z and cartoonist Gary Trudeau would be low culture. Over the past half century there has been a move toward eradicating these distinctions by making high culture more accessible to the masses and by recognizing that some low culture is as profound and artistically well executed as some high culture. Some classical musicians (Nigel Kennedy) have adopted a very pop approach to their careers, while some pop musicians (Paul McCartney) have composed in a classical style for orchestras. The great operatic tenor Luciano Pavarotti performed at rock concerts, and contemporary operas have been written about pop cultural subjects such as tabloid talk show host Jerry Springer (*Jerry Springer: The Opera*, 2003) and model Anna Nicole Smith (*Anna Nicole*, 2011).

Yet despite the increased flexibility, popular culture still primarily occupies the status of low culture. It has been said that popular culture is what you're left with once high culture has been decided on. In Arnold's day if you had subtracted classical music, serious drama, opera, poetry and the literary novel, you would have been left with a folk culture that had been declining since the Industrial Revolution, and the beginnings of the emerging mass culture. The earliest mentions of "popular culture" are descriptions of the entertainments of what were then referred to as the "lower classes."

Folk Culture and Mass Culture

Folk culture, or traditional culture, may have involved commerce (writers paid for broadsides, singers paid for their performances), but it was made to fulfill an existing need rather than to create the need itself. Nursery rhymes were made up to amuse children, ballads were composed to pass on news, dances were developed to mark rites of passage, mystery plays were created to reinforce church teachings. It was characteristic of folk culture that the originators were anonymous. The material was passed on and added to by others over time.

Folk culture was generally regarded as being more authentic than the later mass culture because it conveyed more genuine feeling, had a purpose other than making money for the creator and owed its longevity to genuine broad appeal rather than skillful marketing. This search for authenticity continues in popular culture today; indie music versus commercial pop, art house movies versus Hollywood blockbusters, literary fiction versus airport novels. Some people continue to demand what they consider to be "real" and reject what they consider to be "candy floss," "pap," "production line" or "disposable."

Popular culture constantly veers between authentic personal expression and commercial exploitation. This doesn't mean that culture intended to be authentic is automatically better than culture designed purely to make cash. Commercial survival can be a useful creative stimulus just as the desire to be credible can be an excuse for laziness and self-indulgence. Berry Gordy founded Motown Records in Detroit with the express intention of making music in the same way that the Ford Motor Company made cars. Writers worked office hours, musicians played for session fees and songs were assigned to artists during board meetings. This was production line pop. Yet the work of Smokey Robinson and the Miracles, Stevie Wonder, Marvin Gaye, the Four Tops, the Supremes and the Temptations was of high quality and has endured. The Motown song factory produced classics.

Mass culture was the result of advances in technology. The invention of the printing press was the first step. The Bible became the first mass-produced object. Then, during the nineteenth century came photography, electricity, sound recording and motion pictures. Words, sounds and filmed images, both still and moving, could be distributed widely. The public now no longer needed to be in earshot of the musician to hear the music or in view of the actor to see the drama. Reproduction enabled artists to reach more people than ever before.

The phrase *mass culture* developed negative connotations. It sounded impersonal and bland. It could appear to be something imposed on society from the top down. It has largely been superseded by the more neutral term *popular culture*. This was culture that was popular, that reached a large percentage of society and that required no specialist knowledge to appreciate.

Popular Culture

What is included under the umbrella of popular culture? It can vary from expert to expert. I've read rewarding popular culture essays on everything from family Christmas card photos and the (literal) dreams of pop fans to the meaning of the moustaches and work shirts adopted by male homosexuals in the 1970s. The point about such studies is that they take apparently inconsequential behavior, art or style and reveal them as indicators of profound shifts of attitude.

In the 1920s the arts critic Gilbert Seldes began writing about comic strips, motion pictures, musical comedy, vaudeville, radio, popular music and dance. This was innovative at the time because the art forms he was evaluating weren't generally considered to be worthy of serious criticism. It was like having a restaurant critic review a Big Mac and fries.

In his 1924 book *The Seven Lively Arts* Seldes dealt with Charlie Chaplin, Irving Berlin, George Gershwin, Florenz Ziegfeld, Al Jolson and Krazy Kat as though they were the equals of Chopin, Schubert and Hamlet. Seldes summed up his intentions in this way:

> My theme was that entertainment of a high order exists in places not usually associated with Art, that the place where an object was to be seen or heard had no bearing on its merits, that some of Jerome Kern's songs in the Princess shows were lovelier than any number of operatic airs and that a comic strip printed on newspulp which would tatter and rumple in a day might be as worthy of a second look as a considerable number of canvasses at most of our museums.[3]

A decade later, and in a similar way, George Orwell wrote essays on such aspects of British culture as tea drinking and picture postcards. In the 1940s Marshall McLuhan began studying such phenomena as movie posters, self-help ads, press photographs, pulp fiction, high street fashion, magazine covers and superheroes as a way of understanding the collective mind. He made provocative comments such as "Advertising is the greatest art form of the twentieth century" and "Art at its most significant is a distant early warning system that can always be relied on to tell the old culture what is beginning to happen."[4]

University study of popular culture typically began when literature courses widened the scope of permissible material to include magazines, ads and bestsellers. Later these courses embraced film and television. Almost half a century on from the founding of the innovative Birmingham Centre for Contemporary Cultural Studies at Birmingham University in England, it's commonplace to encounter popular culture being dissected using the analytic tools of literary theory.

The Birmingham Centre was established in 1964 by Richard Hoggart, whose study of working-class culture in *The Uses of Literacy* (1957) had created a groundbreaking book. Using the skills he'd picked up studying literature at Oxford under the influential literary critic F. R. Leavis, he trained his attention on the minutiae of his own background, discovering meaning in jokes, ads, sayings, newspapers, magazines, radio, television and popular songs.

In 1967, Dr. Ray Browne founded the *Journal of Popular Culture* in America. While lecturing at Bowling Green State University in Ohio, Browne began incorporating genre fiction such as detective novels, westerns and romances into the syllabus, and realized that a separate course (and, later, a separate department) was required to do them justice. Today the Center for Popular Culture Studies focuses on "those aspects of national and international culture that have the most impact on a majority of the population." An obituary for Browne in the *New York Times* tried to explain the extent of what could be considered under this rubric:

> Popular culture casts a wide net. It takes in dime novels, tabloid newspapers and TV weathermen; the Monkees, the Muppets and "The Love Boat"; T-shirts and G-strings; baseball cards and tarot cards; infomercials, Chatty Cathy dolls and needlepoint pillows;

Bob Hope, Tiny Tim, Archie Bunker and Erica Jong; Tupperware, cream pies and Spam (both kinds); hood ornaments, Harlequin romances, "Leave It to Beaver" and a great deal else.[5]

Most of what is distinguished as popular culture could be classified under the headings of "popular arts," "design," "mass media," "recreation" and "lifestyle." What seems to define it is that in contrast to high culture it's relatively cheap, readily available and requires no previous education in order to understand and enjoy it. Exposure to the great films of Hollywood may enhance your viewing experience as you recognize certain allusions made by the director, but it's not a requirement for movie pleasure. Similarly, knowledge of the history of rock, pop, soul and rap will help you pick up on nuances in popular music, but a preschool child can dance to a Michael Jackson record. Let's look at these categories.

Pop Culture Categories

The popular arts. The popular arts are what people most readily think of when thinking of popular culture. The *Encyclopaedia Britannica* defines them as "Any dance, literature, music, theatre or other art form intended to be received and appreciated by ordinary people in a literate, technological advanced society dominated by urban culture." The popular art of the Simpsons is part of popular culture as is *Star Wars*, U2, *Friends*, *Glee*, break dancing, street theater, political cartoons, musicals, stand-up comedy and *Sex and the City*.

Design. Design is involved when creating clothes, haircuts, branding, typefaces, interiors, ads, websites, computer games, gardens, landscapes, towns, cities, magazine layouts as well as everything from jet airliners to cars and buildings. The celebrated New York designer Milton Glaser (who is responsible for the "I ♥ NY" design) has created book covers, in-store displays, posters, buttons, slogans, magazines, murals, restaurant interiors, supermarket labels and many logos. Writing about him in 1999, journalist Peter Hamill said that Glaser had spent his professional life "changing the way we see."

Designers, most of whom we don't know by name, literally shape the world we live in. Their visions of the way things are or the way things should be can have an effect on generations to come. It's almost impossible to imagine Paris without the long, straight boulevards designed by Georges-Eugène Haussmann in the nineteenth century, Coca-Cola without the familiar cursive script introduced by Frank Mason Robinson, or the America of the 1950s without the car tail fins introduced by General Motors' design chief Harley Earl.

Mass media. The mass media, including radio, TV, Internet, newspapers and magazines, provides one of the primary ways we receive news about contemporary events, but it also plays a role in creating some of these events. In one newspaper before me today there is a story about Prince Harry wearing "a pair of light brown desert-style boots," and the paper predicts this news will "prompt a global rush for his footwear." If there is a rush, it will be because the paper predicted it. Elsewhere in the paper there are nine big stories about magazines, apps, pop music, movie stars and television. The media fascinates the media.

Recreation. Straightforward recreation is responsible for some specific forms of popular culture ranging from computer games and children's toys to amusement parks and sporting events. The mid-twentieth-century British seaside preference for ice cream, deck chairs, saucy postcards, buckets, spades, Punch and Judy shows, handkerchief hats and end-of-pier entertainment was part of popular culture just as Disneyland and Disney World, with their utopian visions and fake danger, are in the early twenty-first century.

Lifestyle. Finally, *lifestyle*, a word that wasn't coined until 1939, reflects the growing emphasis on individual choice and the coordinating of all our preferences into a statement of who we are. One definition of *culture* is "a whole way of life," and there are certain ways of life that are as much a part of popular culture as such artifacts as records. This has been particularly true of youth subcultures where music and fashion played a defining role. When Tom Wolfe befriended hippies in San Francisco and mods in London, or Hunter Thompson went riding with the Hell's Angels, they produced books that gave insights into tribes of young people who expressed their disassociation from the dominant culture through such symbols as hair length, clothes, modes of transportation, music choice, language and interior design.

Lifestyle journalism also observes apparently small changes in behavior likely to herald a more general trend. When writer David Blum noticed that his friends were opting for pizza nights in front of the TV rather than evenings out on the town, he wrote a story titled "Couch Potatoes" (1987) for *New York* magazine and introduced a new phrase into our vocabularies (as he had done two years earlier with the phrase *Brat Pack*, used to describe a group of young Hollywood actors). Tom Wolfe had done the same thing in the same magazine with his report on the unusual relationship between revolutionary Black Panthers and New York's social elite in a piece he called "Radical Chic" (1970) and then with his influential zeitgeist essay "The Me Decade" (1976).

Pop art. I should briefly distinguish popular culture from "pop art" and the "pop arts," both of which can be a part of popular culture but neither of which is synonymous with it. Pop art was an art movement first defined in 1956. The pop arts, spoken of in the mid-to-late 1960s, referred to arts that were inspired by or dependent on pop music such as album cover design, concert posters and promotional films for records.

Pop art was a movement in the visual arts where trained painters and sculptors looked to popular culture for inspiration. Roy Lichtenstein based paintings on American comic book art; pop music, wrestling and cigarette cards inspired Peter Blake; Andy Warhol created modern icons based on such things as commercial products (soup cans) and movie stars (Marilyn Monroe); Richard Hamilton made collages from newspaper headlines, catalog images and advertising slogans. The fact that "serious" artists were revaluing what had previously been considered throwaway culture gave new dignity to such things as packaging, branding, comics, ads, confessional magazines and even pornography.

Pop art in turn influenced the pop music it had once paid homage to when musicians created work that in a similar way referenced popular culture, such as The Who's album *A Quick One* that referenced advertising, Roxy Music that caricatured past images of rock 'n' roll, and the Beatles who incorporated into their songs the words of a circus poster ("Being for the Benefit of Mr. Kite"), newspaper headlines ("A Day in the Life," "She's Leaving Home"), comic books ("The Continuing Adventures of Bungalow Bill") and jingles ("Good Morning Good Morning"). Significantly, four of the songs just mentioned are from *Sgt. Pepper's Lonely Hearts Club Band*, the cover of which was designed by Britain's leading pop artist, Peter Blake.

The term *pop arts* is almost redundant today (as is *rock culture*), but in 1972 it meant enough for art critic and musician George Melly to write *Revolt Into Style: The Pop Arts in Britain*. Over half of his book was devoted to pop and rock music, the rest to commercial visual art (book covers, posters, album art), fashion, pop movies and TV, rock radio, and pop literature (oral poetry, underground magazines, pop journalism).

Melly thought the main difference between popular culture and the pop arts was that popular culture emerged naturally and accepted prevailing values, whereas the pop arts were created knowingly by a more educated elite and tended to embody an attitude of protest. "Popular culture was unconscious, or perhaps unselfconscious would be more exact, whereas pop culture came about as the result of a deliberate search for objects, clothes, music, heroes and attitudes which could help to define a stance."

Culture for All

In this book I am not offering a fresh definition of *popular culture*. The expressions that I have chosen to investigate—film, television, advertising, comedy, fashion, magazines, newspapers, spectaculars, photography, the Internet and celebrity culture—are accepted as being part of popular culture by all specialists in the area. The products are generally mass-produced, predominantly consumed during leisure hours, overwhelmingly created for financial gain, don't require a specialist education in order to be appreciated and are usually capable of being enjoyed by a broad, nonelite audience.

I'm conscious of areas that I've left out—graphic novels, cartoons, video games, sports events, slang, rock music, rap, graffiti, body art, dancing and so much more. This is partly to do with space. If I had covered these in the same detail, the book would have been twice as long. However, I believe that the principles I have used in these chapters can easily, and fruitfully, be applied to what I've had to leave out.

It may seem a long way from Matthew Arnold's "study and pursuit of perfection" to comic books, pop groups and Andy Warhol's soup cans, but it's all a part of understanding what popular culture is and how we came to be where we are today. It's all a part of making sense of the time and place that God has chosen to place us.

Questions for Reflection or Discussion

- What do you think of when you hear the word *culture*?

- Does the concept of culture intimidate, excite or bore you?

- Is pop culture a waste of time?

- In Maslow's well-known "hierarchy of needs," creativity is deemed to be something we can only concentrate on once such basic needs as safety, love, belonging and esteem are dealt with. Does this mean that popular culture is a luxury rather than a necessity?

- Do you think that Mozart is better than pop, or that Shakespeare is better than the latest TV soap opera? Why or why not?

- Is the division between high culture and pop culture one of quality or one of social division (high culture being for the well educated and wealthy, pop culture for the less educated and poor)?

- Do you look for "authenticity" in the culture you consume? Do you like things to be "gritty" and "real"? If so, why do you think this is?

- Can mass-produced culture have any lasting value, or does its genius reside in the very fact that it's designed to be disposable?

- Think of your favorite piece of contemporary design (clothing, logo, graphics, car body, building) and articulate what it is that appeals to you and how you think that appeal was achieved.

- Think of a group of people in your culture that is distinguished by clothing, hairstyles and language. What are the defining marks of those who belong? What satisfaction do you think members get from identifying with a subculture?

General Books About Culture

Arnold, Matthew. *Culture and Anarchy*. London: Smith, Elder, 1869.

Hoggart, Richard. *The Uses of Literacy*. London: Chatto & Windus, 1957.

McLuhan, Marshall. *The Mechanical Bride: Folklore of Industrial Man*. New York: Vanguard, 1951.

Melly, George. *Revolt into Style: The Pop Arts in Britain*. London: Allen Lane, 1970.

Seldes, Gilbert. *The Seven Lively Arts*. New York: Harper, 1924.

Storey, John. *Cultural Theory and Popular Culture*. London: Pearson Education, 2003.

General Websites Exploring Popular Culture

Popular Culture Department of Bowling Green State University: www .bgsu.edu/departments/popc

Popular Culture Association and American Culture Association: www.pcaaca.org

Smithsonian Center for Folklife and Cultural Heritage: www.folklife .si.edu

The American Folklore Center at the Library of Congress: www.loc .gov/folklife/archive.html

English Folk Dance and Song Society: www.efdss.org

Five Suggestions for Action

- Find the lyrics of your favorite music act online and read them in order to detect recurrent themes and prevailing points of view.

- Familiarize yourself with an art form that you think you're least likely to enjoy.

- Pick up every free magazine that you find on your hall floor, on train seats and in sidewalk newsracks. Read them to give you windows on worlds that may otherwise have passed you by.

- Record your responses to films, books and records in notebooks. Moleskine produces journals specifically designed for such reports: www.moleskineus.com/moleskine-passion-books.html.

- Buy a specialist magazine you wouldn't normally buy on design, PR, advertising, travel, photography, the leisure industry, architecture, fashion or catering.

3

Working It Out

Some Biblical Parameters

†

One of the problems faced by anyone trying to develop a Christian understanding of popular culture is the fact that the Bible doesn't recognize it as a separate category. This is partly because the children of Israel lived in a theocracy where popular culture would have been synonymous with religious culture and partly because a large percentage of what we would today classify as popular culture has only been made possible by electricity. Most of the art forms we deal with were not in existence at the time of the Old or New Testaments.

Yet the foundations for culture are established very early on in the Bible: gardening and naming in Genesis 2, farming and clothes making in Genesis 3, city building and harp and pipe playing in Genesis 4, shipbuilding in Genesis 6, altar building in Genesis 8, fruit growing and wine making in Genesis 9, brick baking in Genesis 11, tent making in Genesis 12. In the description of the building of the tabernacle in Exodus we get the most detailed information about artistic embellishment from the precise measurements, preferred types of wood and the use of gold, silver and precious stones.

The first artist named in the Bible is Bezalel who is specifically "filled . . . with the Spirit of God, with wisdom, with understanding, with knowledge and with all kinds of skills" (Ex 31:2-3). His gifts al-

lowed him to work in gold, silver and brass; to carve wood; to cut and
set stones; to engrave and to embroider. Although his gifts were to be
used to build a place of worship, it established the principle that God
enjoys beauty, design and proportion. God wanted to be remembered
in a special way in a building that was the product of contemporary
popular culture.

By the time of the New Testament the Jews were living in territory
ruled by the Romans. Their lives revolved around work, housekeeping, the preparation and consumption of food, celebrations, conversations and the life of the synagogue. As with my grandfather
almost two thousand years later, there wasn't a lot of time left over for
entertainment. The artistry of musicians, dancers and storytellers
would have been employed at parties and feasts. In common with
societies in developing areas of the world today, popular culture
played a role in knitting the community together, marking significant
transitions and remembering their history. It wasn't something divorced from the daily routine of life. When the prodigal son comes
home, the father dressed him in "the best" robe (Lk 15:22) and put a
ring on his finger. He then threw a party that involved "music and
dancing" (Lk 15:25).

Contemporary musician Emmanuel Jal grew up in a village in
Sudan, and what he told me about the place of music in his country
is probably true of all folk cultures: "You know how it is in Africa," he
said. "Music is for everything. When there's a party, there's music.
When there's a wedding, there's music. When a leader is visiting,
there's music. There is music for when a baby is welcomed into a
family. There is music to comfort those whose hearts are broken."

Jesus made an interesting reference when he compared the current
faithless generation who had ignored John the Baptist and was now
ignoring him to "children sitting in the marketplaces" who call to
their friends and say,

We played the flute for you, and you did not dance;
    we wailed, and you did not mourn. (Mt 11:16-17 NRSV)

This alluded to a game played by Jewish children in the first century. It's an indication of the fundamental nature of rituals and games, and by the tone of the comment we can assume that Jesus approved of this game and had played it.

Paul and Pop

Paul came into the closest proximity with popular culture as we know it, but nowhere gave advice on how to approach it beyond the broad principles governing engagement with the world at large. The cities he visited such as Rome, Ephesus, Corinth, Athens and Philippi had shops, marketplaces, public baths, forums, theaters, arenas and circuses. Roman citizens of the era enjoyed playing games, listening to poetry recitals, exercising, bathing, taking part in competitive sports and attending gladiatorial matches and chariot races. There's no mention of Paul participating in these things, although he alludes to boxing, wrestling, exercising, running and winning sporting prizes when comparing the spiritual life to physical competition.

One possible reason that Paul makes no mention of these things may have been that he was a missionary, teacher and pastor, not a cultural commentator, and focused on his speaking engagements and offering pastoral advice. Another reason could be that some of these entertainments were brutal and profoundly un-Christian (such as gladiatorial combat), and others were built around the worship of false idols. Clearly, as we have already discovered, he read the poets known to Athenians but there is no record of his thoughts on Greek or Roman theater.

But the lack of specific instruction regarding popular culture is no different from the lack of instruction on, for example, medical ethics. Our understanding of how to behave has to emerge from overarching biblical principles. I can only conclude that God likes us to work for our insights because the Bible could easily have been delivered as a manual or rulebook but is instead a mixture of literary forms written by many different people over many years.

Key Questions

We can start by considering what the key questions about popular culture might be and then see if the Bible offers any guidance. The initial question should be, "Is popular culture a good thing in itself?" Until we know the answer, we can't proceed. Imagine if someone asked what a Christian brothel would be like and the answer was given that Bibles should be left by each bedside and the whole place be characterized by fairness, courtesy, generosity and love. This answer is only ridiculous because we haven't asked the first question, Are brothels good things in themselves? It's impossible to develop a Christian approach to popular culture if popular culture is something we should be shunning.

The Bible unhesitatingly approves of culture. It could be said one of our main tasks on earth is to make culture. Our basic demand for food and drink leads to farming, gardening, cookery, restaurants, taverns, shops and recipes. These activities then require farming implements, work clothes, transport, barns and pans. Because we never want to stick with basics, it leads to pottery, ceramics, glassware and decoration. Meals become times of celebration, feasting, sharing and friendship building rather than mere fueling stops. The simple need for nutrition leads to the formation of culture.

Our basic demand for warmth leads inevitably to clothing, which leads to fashion. And fashion involves design, coloring and printing. Our basic demand for shelter leads to building, architecture, town planning, plumbing and carpentry. Our basic demand for communication requires words, stories, papyrus, pens and ink. The exercise of our primal needs necessitates the building of a culture. Jesus made things out of wood. Paul made tents. David wrote poetry. Noah built a boat.

The Benefits of Culture

The next question to ask is, "How does culture benefit us?" There have been Christians down the ages who have spoken as though any reliance on culture for our pleasure or education is a failure to rely on God. They've said, "Why should I need these cheap amusements when

I should be relying on God totally for everything? Only nonbelievers need these things because their lives are so empty without God."

This argument fails to understand the ways in which God supports and fulfills us. It presupposes that we're only delighting in God during the moments when we're doing overtly "religious" things. Yet we directly experience the benevolence of God through the things he gives us as well as in quiet moments of reflection or worship. Sunshine and rain provide blessings. God shows us his love not merely through warm inner feelings but through family, friends and (sometimes) strangers. God sustains us not just through Scripture but also through eggs, bread and milk. He brings us healing not just through the laying on of hands but through surgical procedures, drugs, exercise and physiotherapy.

Culture is one of the ways God stimulates our intellects, soothes our troubled minds, reveals the wonder of life, gives us insights into the feelings of others, softens the blows of misfortune, provides memory triggers, challenges our assumptions, trains our eyes to see, reveals to us both beauty and ugliness, exalts our spirits, delights our senses, makes us laugh and reveals aspects of his character.

We're all familiar with the story of Christ's temptation. When the devil challenges him to turn stones into bread he says, "One does not live by bread alone, but by every word that comes from the mouth of God" (Mt 4:4 NRSV). It's easy to take this to mean that all we need is the Bible, but this is not what is being said. We need both bread and Bible. If the devil had offered Jesus the Bible, Jesus may well have said, "Man shall not live on Bible alone, but on bread."

Those who live by popular culture alone are depriving themselves, but so are those who live by Bible alone. We become more balanced, useful, enriched, holistic Christians when we take advantage of culture. Just as we don't use the example of the glutton to deter us from eating, we shouldn't use the example of the secularized reprobate to deter us from culture. The men and women who have helped me most in my Christian life have been people who treasured the Bible but who also had a healthy enjoyment of culture. Most of the men and women I've seen who have had a destructive effect through church ministry have been Bible-alone people.

One of the ways in which we punish people is by depriving them of culture. That's how essential it is to our being. We put them in undecorated rooms and make them wear plain clothes that eliminate all sense of individuality. We limit their access to media. If they're really bad we cut off all social contact and put them in solitary confinement. Of course there have been Christians who've been imprisoned alone and who've witnessed to the fact that God was with them, but this is not how we were meant to live. I wonder if the phrase "it is not good for the man to be alone" has a more general application in addition to the immediate application about marriage.

Handle with Care

Once we've accepted that culture is good and that God intends it as a means of nurturing us, we are left with questions about how to handle it with care. This was not a question that Adam had to ask before the fall. Back then culture presented only goodness. God made the animals, and Adam cared for them and gave them names. He went into the culture-making business with God. Following the fall culture had the potential to increase the distance between humans and God. We can even put culture in God's place. Cain, the fugitive killer of Abel, becomes the first city builder. The first mention of bricks and mortar comes during a description of the building of the tower of Babel, a human construction intended to bring people closer to heaven (Gen 11:1-9).

We can be tempted to make culture our religion. A lot of people in the arts say, "Painting is my religion," or "Music is my religion." They don't necessarily mean that painting or music answers the questions that religion answers but that these things inspire them, consume them and animate them in the way that they imagine religion does for its adherents. They may also mean that these arts dominate their lives, that everything else is subservient to them. Even people who make no great claims about art being their religion actually have lives that are centered on such activities as gaming, clubbing or television. In the nineteenth century the poet Shelley wrote, "I burn with impatience for the moment of Christianity's dissolution,"[1] and "there is a great and spiritual force to put in its place. Poetry is something divine. It is the centre and circumference of all knowledge."[2]

Theology of Leisure

Priorities are an issue. Popular culture is generally enjoyed during our leisure time and the question to raise is—how much time should we have left over once our commitments to friends, family, church, work, the poor have been fulfilled? Many of the criticisms made by the Puritans about sports, fairs, card games and even novel reading were not because they were implicitly evil but because they wasted time that could have better been spent on spiritual improvement. Their maxim "Idle hands are the Devil's workshop" acknowledged that it was when "at a loose end" that people were most susceptible to temptation.

German sociologist Max Weber pointed out in his classic study *The Protestant Ethic and the Spirit of Capitalism* that American affluence was made possible through a commitment to industry and a suspicion of idleness. He summarized the belief of the people he was writing about in this way:

> Waste of time is thus the first and in principle the deadliest of sins. The span of human life is infinitely short and precious to make sure of one's own election. Loss of time through sociability, idle talk, luxury, even more sleep than is necessary for health . . . is worthy of absolute moral condemnation. It does not yet hold, with Franklin, that time is money, but the proposition is true in a certain spiritual sense. It is infinitely valuable because every hour lost is lost to labor for the glory of God.[3]

The Puritans encouraged the keeping of journals so that every moment could be accounted for and all actions evaluated. Activities that were frivolous were discouraged. They cited Paul who wrote, "Be careful then how you live, not as unwise people but as wise, making the most of the time, because the days are evil" (Eph 5:15-16 NRSV).

Yet not all relaxation is a waste of time. It can be taking stock, drinking in our environment or simply delighting in being alive. The word *recreation*, which we often associate with mindless abandon, was coined to mean putting ourselves back together—re-creating ourselves. The old proverb says, "All work and no play makes Jack a dull boy," meaning that the person who only knows how to work is incomplete. Jesus had three years to complete his appointed task, and yet he had time to simply walk along the shores of Lake Galilee, to eat with friends or to talk to his disciples.

> A poor life this, if full of care
> We have no time to stand and stare.[4]

In his poem "Biography" the English poet John Masefield argued that when his life would be assessed by future obituary writers and biographers, they would note only the hard work and the career achievements, but that to him the most important moments were the ones that no one ever saw: the days spent watching the ocean, walking in his favorite hills or listening to the songs of birds.

> Best trust the happy moments. What they gave
> Makes man less fearful of the certain grave,
> And gives his work compassion and new eyes.
> The days that make us happy make us wise.[5]

In the 1950s the German Catholic philosopher Josef Pieper, author of *Leisure: The Basis of Culture*, argued that it's what we create or consume in our "spare time" that defines our culture. We work at what we have to, but we play at what we want to. Therefore, it's how we play that tells us more about our true desires than how we work. "All that is good in this sense, all man's gifts and faculties are not necessarily useful in a practical way; though there is no denying that they belong to a truly human life, not strictly speaking necessary, even though he could not do without them."[6]

Powers and Principalities

Because we are fallen, popular culture is also a sphere for what Christians call "spiritual warfare." It is no longer an unadulterated blessing. This is why Christians need to practice discrimination, to "test everything" as Paul instructs the Thessalonians and to "hold fast to what is good" (1 Thess 5:21 NRSV). As has already been said, the things we read, listen to and watch for pleasure have ways of shaping our attitudes without our even being aware of the changes. The first time we see a film with people behaving in ungodly ways and getting rewarded, we may be disturbed. The second time less so. By the tenth or eleventh time we may be so unmoved that we start to accept what we see as normal. Our indignation has been progressively muted.

Most people don't change their minds about important moral issues because of a blinding revelation or an unassailable argument, but because of acclimatization, frequently orchestrated by the media. It just gets too hard to hold on to your convictions when they are constantly ignored or mocked. Malcolm Muggeridge, a prominent British journalist in the middle of the last century, used to give the illustration of a frog and boiling water. If you put a frog near boiling water it will immediately react by leaping away from it. However, if you pop a frog into cold water and slowly boil it, there will be no sign of struggle and it will eventually be boiled to death. It crosses the barrier between safety and danger unaware of the change.

It's not hard to understand the attractiveness of popular culture to the devil. It's an opportunity to have your product—sin and rebellion—placed in the context of pleasure, in front of an audience of billions. Why bother niggling people individually when you can niggle one or two and their views can be transmitted around the world? It's said that the devil cherishes the influence of creative people because he has no innate creativity himself. He can only destroy and therefore has to piggyback on the talents of others. Muggeridge said in 1975 that television "had provided the Devil with the greatest opportunity he ever had in human history."

We can't afford not to be alert when consuming popular culture in the same way that ordinary citizens can't be complacent on the home front during a time of war or threatened invasion. "Discipline yourselves, keep alert. Like a roaring lion your adversary the devil prowls around, looking for someone to devour" (1 Pet 5:8 NRSV). There is a recurring temptation to think that the devil is merely a character from medieval myth and not a living being with influence and intention. Describing as a work of the devil anything we disapprove of is an extreme to avoid. It's almost impossible to say with certainty when something is specifically devilish and when it's just the work of sinful humans. But the opposite extreme—there is no devil, or the devil is inactive in popular culture—is equally as bad.

Thought Life

The secular world rarely considers the effect of popular culture on our thoughts. The only time it shows concern for the thought life is when bad thoughts lead to bad actions—such as when someone becomes a racist through being exposed to racist literature, or a killer mimics a scene from a violent film. The Bible presents the different idea that what we think is judged alongside what we do. It's possible to keep the law and yet have an immoral mind. Our thoughts are as much a part of our moral character as our actions. "People look at the outward appearance, but the LORD looks at the heart" (1 Sam 16:7).

Often people will defend unsavory entertainment because they say it hasn't led them to do anything bad, but this doesn't take into account the content of their minds. We can remain meek and mild yet have a brain swirling with the most poisonous images. When Jimmy Carter was running for U.S. president in 1976, he gave an interview to *Playboy* in which he was asked whether he had committed adultery. In his answer he said that he had committed adultery many times in his heart. The secular media scoffed at this because it hardly seemed like a moral infringement, but Carter was of course picking up on a Bible truth that it's possible to commit sins in the privacy of our heads, sins known only to God.

Quite often bad thought lives do affect behavior. A twenty-three-year-old man writing in a newspaper about his addiction to online pornography credits his erratic sex life and inability to form long-term relationships to his viewing habits. So far he has cheated on all of his real girlfriends. "I'm convinced this is because using Internet porn is a form of cheating—after all, I'm lusting after the body of a stranger rather than my girlfriend—and that once you've grown accustomed to this online infidelity, real-life cheating becomes much, much easier."[7]

Sometimes we have to sit through some bad stuff in order to get to the good stuff. That's as true for the Bible as it is for Shakespeare. If one long film were made of the Bible there would be sex, violence and mass destruction, along with miracles, harps and lambs lying down with lions. The point is to have the good things as our benchmark, to want to meditate on the sweet and awe-inspiring rather than the hateful and destructive. "Finally, brothers and sisters, whatever is true, whatever is noble, whatever is right, whatever is pure, whatever is lovely, whatever is admirable—if anything is excellent or praiseworthy—think about such things" (Phil 4:8).

Christians sometimes expose themselves to dangerous stuff just to show how resilient they are. It's the spiritual equivalent of tightening your six-pack and challenging someone to deliver a swift punch: "See! It didn't hurt." But we can't always tell at the time how things will affect us in the long term. Images we saw decades ago can rise to the surface of our consciousness without our being aware of where they came from. The biblical proverb asks,

Can a man scoop fire into his lap
    without his clothes being burned?
Can a man walk on hot coals
    without his feet being scorched? (Prov 6:27-28)

Vigilance

Dealing with popular culture demands more effort of a Christian because his or her nonbelieving counterpart feels no obligation to remain alert and vigilant. The unbeliever is not concerned about giving an account of his or her thoughts and words to God. Most people are content to "go with the flow"; they gladly allow themselves to be shaped by events, changes in the philosophical undercurrent and the influence of popular culture. They are content to be carried along like people caught in a crowd surge and unable to determine their own direction, content to be going somewhere and in apparently good company. For many people being up to date in their thinking is a virtue rather than an indication of how malleable they are.

The Christian doesn't have the option of being passively educated by culture. Writing to the Romans Paul says, "Do not conform to the pattern of this world, but be transformed by the renewing of your mind. Then you will be able to test and approve what God's will is—his good, pleasing and perfect will" (Rom 12:2). The word *world* here can be translated "age." J. B. Phillips paraphrased this as, "Don't let the world around you squeeze you into its own mould." There is an acknowledgment here that the "world," the spirit of our particular era, will shape us, unless countered by the force of a renewed mind. And it takes something as powerful to resist it. Our natural condition is to be a child of our time.

This suggests that we can't be careless about our consumption of popular culture. We have to respect its capability to shape our opinions and decorate our minds, and need to work at being transformed in order not to be overwhelmed. The fact that you are reading this book can be part of that process. We can't expect the culture that is trying to fashion us to reveal the secrets of how it is fashioning us. The world will tell us that nothing untoward is happening to us. We are being overanxious. We are being too intense. We are victims of Christian paranoia.

We need help from other Christians to see how to make sense of popular culture using a biblical outlook. We live in a good age to do so because the last half a century has seen the development of scholarship in this area. There are magazines and websites that review films, books and music from a Christian perspective. These will naturally include authorial biases, but we can at least begin to build up a sense of how God may view the culture we are surrounded by. Discussion groups, book reading groups and debates can also help because we need to hear the insights of other believers, and it's good to be in an environment where views are challenged.

Spirit of Discernment

Discrimination requires careful evaluation. There has been a Christian tendency to want to mark things as either good or bad without acknowledging that popular culture, like the visible church, is a mixture of good seed and weeds (Mt 13:24-30). It's not always easy to distinguish or to separate one from another. This is not only true for a whole art form but for one painting, song or poster. It's far easier to openly accept everything or condemn everything.

Some things are technically of a high quality but totally false in what they say. Other things are technically good but partly true and partly false. Confusingly, some things may be totally true but artistically awful. Is a poorly executed movie that clearly tells the truth of salvation to be deemed good or bad? Are we tempted to call it good just because we agree with the premise? What about a powerfully delivered song with excellent musicianship that has a false message in its lyric? *Good* or *bad*? Are we worried about giving praise to something that shows the writers and performers to have integrity but that offends us? Surely, if they were to sing something that was true but yet they didn't personally believe it, we could accuse them of hypocrisy.

It may at first appear a daunting task to try to understand popular culture with the eyes of faith, but it should be a thrill. This is a significant area of life where we can test and strengthen our beliefs and where we can contribute to the marketplace of ideas through everything from conversation to culture making. We won't always get it right, but we can certainly guarantee to get it wrong by refusing to participate.

Most Christians are familiar with the parable of the talents as reported in Matthew 25. Three servants are given money (talents) to look after in their master's absence. Two of them use their money to double their capital, but the third servant keeps his safe by hiding it in the ground. He risks no loss, but as a result makes no gain. The parable has numerous applications, which must be as Jesus intended, and has been a cornerstone belief in the Protestant work ethic.

Faithful Servanthood

Let's apply it to the subject of this book. God entrusts culture to us— the ability to create it, enjoy it and critique it. The faithful servant does all three. By *create* I don't mean that we all shoot films or write books, but that we all make culture by dressing ourselves, designing our homes, developing our Facebook pages and in many other ways. By *critique* I don't necessarily mean writing a review or presenting a paper, but by sharing our opinions in casual conversation or formal discussions.

What does the unfaithful servant do? The unfaithful servant that Jesus describes is characterized by fear. Rather than put a foot wrong he decides not to move. In terms of culture that would be someone saying that they had turned their face from it because they were afraid that they'd be tainted, that God would disapprove, that it was a waste of time, that they'd make a mistake or that their faith couldn't withstand the engagement. The response of the unfaithful servant in the parable is to hide the talent. In terms of culture that would be someone either not developing their ability to create, therefore keeping it hidden, or not developing their capacity to enjoy and critique, therefore hiding *from* it.

Throughout the rest of the book I will look at particular areas of popular culture to see how we can understand them with the advantage of biblical truth. I hope that it will make you a better consumer, creator and critic and encourage you not to hide.

Questions for Reflection or Discussion

- Can you think of ways that popular culture has improved your life?

- Have you ever harbored the thought that the highest form of spiritual life would be one in which you didn't need to have any contact with pop culture?

- Do you imagine that there will be culture in the renewed heaven and earth?

- Think of ways in which you've seen culture replace religion in people's lives.

- Do you think that we are more vulnerable to temptation when in a leisure mode?

- How do you distinguish between much-needed relaxation and wasting time?

- Can you think of times when culture has "heated up" (to use the illustration of the frog boiling to death when the temperature of the water is increased only gradually) without people really noticing it?

- There have been times when Christians have attributed new developments in popular culture to the direct influence of the devil. Do you think they've ever been right?

- Is it too scrupulous to try to monitor our thought lives?

- What areas should we consider when contemplating whether a cultural expression is good or bad?

Christian Attempts to Understand Culture

Carson, D. A. *Christ and Culture Revisited*. Grand Rapids: Eerdmans, 2008.

Cobb, Kelton. *The Blackwell Guide to Theology and Popular Culture.* New York: Wiley-Blackwell, 2005.

Eliot, T. S. *Notes Towards the Definition of a Culture.* London: Faber & Faber, 1948.

Kuyper, Abraham. *Lectures on Calvinism.* Grand Rapids: Eerdmans, 1931.

Machen, J. Gresham. *Christianity and Culture.* L'Abri, Switzerland: L'Abri Fellowship, 1969.

Niebuhr. H. Richard. *Christ and Culture.* New York: Harper & Row, 1951.

Pieper, Josef. *Leisure: The Basis of Culture.* London: Faber & Faber, 1952.

Tillich, Paul. *Theology of Culture.* New York: Oxford University Press, 1959.

Van Til, Henry R. *The Calvinistic Concept of Culture.* Grand Rapids: Baker, 1959.

Websites Dealing with Issues of Christianity and Culture

Culture page of popular Patheos site: www.patheos.com/blogs/bible andculture

"The Other Journal: An Intersection of Theology and Culture" from The Seattle School of Theology and Psychology: www.theother-journal.com

Essay "The Apostle Paul and Culture" by Lutheran pastor (and now seminary president) Paul Wendland: www.wlsessays.net/files/WendlandCulture.pdf

Lectures given by John M. Frame in 2001 at Pensacola Theological Institute: http://reformedperspectives.org/newfiles/joh_frame/Frame.Apologetics2004.ChristandCulture.pdf

Critique of H. Richard Niebuhr's *Christ and Culture* by Peter R. Gathje: www.religion-online.org/showarticle.asp?title=2641

Five Suggestions for Action

- As you read through the Bible in your normal studies, note references to the popular culture of the time. Consider what the contemporary equivalents would be.

- Share insights and recommendations with people on your church leadership team. Many of them would love to be made aware of current trends but often don't have as much time (or money) as we do to pursue their interests. If your pastor is out of touch, you must bear some responsibility.

- If you're on Facebook, provide links to interesting articles and films on YouTube that you think your contacts would benefit from reading or watching.

- Become acquainted with any groups in your area where Christians are studying the relationship between faith and movies, books, music or the arts in general.

- Discernment should be enjoyable, uplifting and rewarding. Avoid the extreme of overanalyzing and seeing dangers of contamination in everything but also the extreme of simply going with the flow.

4

Cinematic Art

The Story of Stories

†

No one disputes that movies are part of popular culture. Although you can get more out of a film if you've studied cinema, no background knowledge is necessary to enjoy it. Film supplies more widespread cultural references than any other art form. There's more widespread recognition of an illustration from *Titanic* or *Terminator* than from a poem by Billy Collins, a novel by Philip Roth or even a parable told by Jesus. The activities of great cinematic characters such as Forrest Gump, Darth Vader, Jack Sparrow, James Bond and Hannibal Lecter are, in general, better known than the activities of John the Baptist, Paul of Tarsus or the woman at the well. One pastor says that 80 percent of his meaningful conversations with non-Christians are made possible by the doorway opened up by discussion of film: "It's such a natural point of connection."[1]

Think how many times we hear someone explaining an emotion, situation, landscape, moral dilemma, belief system, atmosphere, character trait or outlook by referencing a film or a scene from a film. Movies provide a shared reference point. A good illustration of the pervasiveness of film is the fact that in the 2001 census for England and Wales almost 400,000 people registered their religion as "Jedi," a reference to the beliefs of the Jedi Knights in *Star Wars*. Censuses in Australia, New Zealand, Canada, Ireland and the Czech Republic had also seen people declare themselves as followers of the Jedi Code.

Film is an important cultural realm where philosophies of life are tested, behavior rehearsed, values questioned, injustice exposed, fears confronted, history reexamined and possible futures imagined. In her 1950 book *Hollywood the Dream Factory* anthropologist Hortense Powdermaker observed, "Movies are successful largely because they meet some of modern man's deepest needs."[2] More recently, screenwriting guru Robert McKee, who has been running well-attended screenwriting courses around the world for over thirty years, argued that storytelling has replaced philosophy, theology and science as our main source of information about life's meaning. "The world now consumes films, novels, theatre, and television in such quantities and with such ravenous hunger," he wrote, "that the story arts have become humanity's prime source of inspiration, as it seeks to order chaos and gain insight into life."[3] In 1993 George Lucas (*American Graffiti*, *Star Wars*) said of the motivation behind his work as a storyteller, "I'm trying to figure out what we are, what life is, and what are some of the truths that lie beneath the surface."[4]

The questions Christians generally ask about film fall into two categories, depending on whether the questioner is primarily a consumer or a creator. Those who go to the movies want to know what they can watch in all good conscience and the best way of understanding what they see. Those who make movies want to know what stories they should be telling that will be both consistent with their faith and commercially viable.

The Power of Story

Both sets of questions acknowledge the perpetual power of story. From the days when humans sat around campfires listening to tales of animal hunts and territorial exploration up to the age of contemporary movie watching, we have always been fascinated with stories that have beginnings, middles and ends and that draw us in so powerfully that we empathize with characters, feel the emotional impact of crises and are temporarily swept up into the action. The child in bed at night doesn't say, "Tell me some interesting facts" but "Read me a story."

Some commentators believe that history's most successful stories share common traits that tell us something about who we are. Why, for example, are we drawn to stories that tell of someone's crisis, their desire to restore balance to their lives and their eventual rescue by a savior figure? Is there something printed in our DNA that spells out the story of creation, fall and redemption, and ensures that we recognize that pattern reproduced in drama?

Over the past forty years Hollywood writers and directors have become conscious that they manufacture contemporary myths, and as a result have become interested in the power of mythology. They have asked, "What can ancient myths teach us about important truths and how can we use those truths to fashion new stories?" In his influential book *The Writer's Journey*, the story analyst Christopher Vogler asks, "Where do stories come from? How do they work? What do they tell us about ourselves? What do they mean? Why do we need them? How can we use them to improve the world?"[5]

Vogler, who has helped guide the screenplays of such films as *Fight Club*, *Black Swan*, *The Wrestler* and *The Lion King*, applied to film the ideas of mythologist Joseph Campbell and analytical psychologist Carl Jung to see if a consistent pattern indicative of timeless truths would emerge. What he found was "a beautiful design, a set of principles that govern the conduct of life and the world of storytelling the way physics and chemistry govern the physical world. It's difficult to avoid the sensation that the Hero's Journey exists somewhere, somehow, as an eternal reality, a Platonic ideal form, a divine model."[6]

The Hero's Journey

The concept of the "hero's journey" came from Jung and was developed by Campbell in his books *The Hero with a Thousand Faces*, *The Power of Myth* (with Bill Moyers) and the four volumes of *The Masks of God*. Vogler applied these findings to the traditional three-act film. In the first act, he discovered, the hero is usually found in the "ordinary world" but soon after is called to take part in an adventure (think *Harry Potter and the Sorcerer's Stone, The Wizard of Oz*). There is an initial refusal of the call, then a meeting with a mentor figure who helps the hero deal with apprehensions before crossing the "first threshold." The journey has begun (think *Star Wars*).

Act two is taken up with conflict as the hero pursues the goal (think *Lord of the Rings*). There are tests and trials. Enemies emerge to create blocks and diversions. Then comes the greatest of all battles. The hero faces an ordeal in the "inmost cave." It could be a literal cave, cellar or dungeon, but is more likely to be the cave of the soul, the deepest part of the person (think *Toy Story 3*). This is a test of spirit and courage. If the hero overcomes, a reward will be gained. The third act sees the hero take the road back. There is a final battle followed by a resurrection (think *Romancing the Stone*). The hero then returns home with "the elixir" that brings healing to the family, community, tribe, country or even the world (think *It's a Wonderful Life*).

The lives of many great Bible heroes fit this pattern. Even the life of Jesus fits it. He doesn't refuse the call to the ministry at the time of his baptism, but he does cross the threshold, face tests, find allies and create enemies. Gethsemane is the site of his "inmost cave," the place where he asks if his suffering can be spared. His final trial is the crucifixion itself, which is followed by a real resurrection. The elixir he brings to the world is salvation from sin, the promise of eternal life and, ultimately, a renewed heaven and earth.

Redemptive Movies

Films that follow this pattern can be called films of redemption. They don't tell *the* story of redemption, but they offer microcosms of that story. The *Star Wars* films of George Lucas drew conscious inspiration from the works of Joseph Campbell. Lucas wanted *Star Wars* to "tell an old myth in a new way." In 1997 the National Air and Space Museum of the Smithsonian Institution in Washington, D.C., mounted an exhibition called "Star Wars: The Magic of Myth." Exhibition curator Mary Henderson wrote, "*Star Wars* fulfills the basic function of myth: to open our hearts to the dimension of mystery in our lives and to give us some guidance on our own hero's journey."[7]

We seem to be wired to respond to stories of people being transformed, of savior figures that rescue and of goodness that triumphs over evil. We're wired to believe in the supremacy of purpose over futility, love over hate, truth over falsehood. We're wired to believe that struggle brings reward. We're wired to hope for an eventual happy ending.

Can you imagine trying to pitch the idea for *The King's Speech* to a studio or a financial backer? "I've got this great idea. A member of the British royal family overcomes a speech impediment." Yet the film had universal appeal. Why so? Because it was a redemption story. The "ordinary world" of Albert, the Duke of York (played by Colin Firth), is the life of the royal family and marriage to the woman he loves. The "call to adventure" comes unexpectedly. When his brother King Edward VIII suddenly abdicates, he is next in line to the British throne. It's a role he never imagined having to take on. Then comes the struggle. He is expected to lead and inspire his nation, especially when it is drawn into war, but he faces the ordeal of being unable to speak effectively in public due to a stutter. He wants to fulfill his duty but has deep-seated concerns about his worthiness.

Along comes a mentor figure, a savior, in the form of a maverick Australian speech therapist Lionel Logue (played by Geoffrey Rush), who uses unconventional methods to cure him. The bulk of the film is taken up with the battle to iron out the impediment, and when he manages to get his words out without faltering we feel his salvation, followed by his resurrection. The British public, aware of what their king has surmounted, feels uplifted and rewarded. It feasts on the elixir. Through overcoming this obstacle he has boosted the morale of the British people. It's a personal and national triumph. Both king and kingdom can become emboldened.

Many films from all genres follow this pattern. The world of the main character is upset just as the Garden of Eden is disturbed by the entry of the serpent. Nothing can be the same again. The protagonist's aim is to bring back hope. There will come a point when it appears that there is no hope to be had. As when Christ was on the cross, it looked as though the whole redemption plan had been destroyed. But the very worst that could happen turned into the best that could happen. This is the ultimate reversal. The death of the Savior produces the life of the church. What the devil assumes will be the final blow turns out to be the key to his own destruction.

In the final act of the film the hero begins the journey home, bearing the fruits of the struggle. Most importantly, the situation at the end is not just a return to the status quo. It's even better, just as the kingdom of heaven is better than the Garden of Eden because there is no temptation or possibility of rebellion when God reigns and Satan is chained.

Christian Realism

Although the redemption story is what we were made to respond warmly to, the reality is that not everyone will be redeemed and we therefore also carry the alternative story that the journey we set out on will end in frustration, despair and damnation. If you were to film the story Jesus told of the rich man and the beggar at his gate from the perspective of the beggar, it would be a classic redemption story. If you were to film it from the point of view of the rich man, it would be a story ending in resentment, regret and torment.

Christian realism would accept that not everyone lives out a redemption story and not all paths lead to glory. It is cheap sentimentality to pretend that all stories have a happy ending. Non-Christian realism frequently tells this story too. Life, for some people, is a bad joke, a "tale told by an idiot, full of sound and fury, signifying nothing" in Shakespeare's memorable phrase. Many films appear to end abruptly or unsatisfyingly, because life, in the view of the filmmaker, has no ultimate consummation. Stanley Kubrick, director of films such as *Dr. Strangelove*, *A Clockwork Orange* and *2001: A Space Odyssey*, told *Playboy*, "The most terrifying fact about the universe is not that it's hostile but that it is indifferent. . . . However vast the darkness, we must supply our own light."[8]

Messy Redemption

Christian realism would also accept that even in the case of redemption not every redemption story happens in an orderly, timely
way. Some of us, Paul says, are saved "even though only as one escaping through the flames" (1 Cor 3:15). Many of the things we have
relied on will be incinerated by God's judgment. Other people move
forward only to slide back. So stories can be redemptive in theme but
a bit messy at the same time. A good example of this is Lars Von
Trier's film *Breaking the Waves*, which ends with undeniable redemption, but one that is reached in unexpected ways that challenge
the viewer to rethink concepts of goodness, moral purity and love of
God's Word.

Some people only want to watch "positive" films, forgetting that
life is not unrelentingly positive and also that some "negative" portrayals serve to accentuate the positive. This is true in the Bible. The
negativity of most of Ecclesiastes doesn't make us want to become
nihilists. It makes us crave meaning and purpose because we are repelled by the frustrations of godlessness. So too with films like *Col-
lateral*, *The Book of Eli*, *Lord of the Flies* and Ingmar Bergman's *The
Silence*. The perceived absence of God usually brings resignation
rather than celebration.

Sometimes art made by nonbelievers to show that life is futile
and meaningless propels us in the opposite direction because it
makes us think, *No! This cannot be true. We deserve much more than
this*. The paintings of Francis Bacon and the plays of Samuel
Beckett had that effect on me. So too did films like *The Graduate*,
Alfie and *Blow-Up*. In the final scene of the original *Alfie*, Michael
Caine stands with his back to the Thames and adds up what he's
gained from his life of womanizing. Not much, he concludes. He
has a lot of material things, but he knows he has treated people
badly. "I ain't got me peace of mind," he says to camera. "And if
you ain't got that you ain't got nothing. . . . So what's the answer?
That's what I keep asking myself. What's it all about? Know what I
mean?"

Family Values?

When it comes to making, rather than just watching, movies, Christians who want to integrate their faith with their art are frequently hampered by a limited vision of the possibilities available. Many of them are genuinely keen to make a difference but don't know the best way to achieve this. They tend to look only at four main possibilities: family films, biblical epics, heroes of the faith, or movies with scenes of repentance and conversion.

Family films are attractive not only because there is an expectation that they will pass on good, wholesome values, but also because they are blissfully free of some of the big dilemmas facing Christians in Hollywood. Family films, because of their intended market, don't involve obscenity, nudity, drugs, extreme violence or the positive portrayal of antisocial behavior. The films produced by the likes of Disney and Pixar help develop the imaginations of children, provide memorable experiences that bind generations together, encourage values of tolerance, love and respect, and produce an oasis of entertainment that is free from bitterness, nastiness and despair.

The movies we see as children are formative. Bruno Bettelheim, in his groundbreaking study *The Uses of Enchantment*, argued that children are able to resolve anxieties and dilemmas through story. They provide an opportunity to endorse behaviors and attitudes that most reasonable adults agree on. They enable us to enjoy a period of our lives when everything seems possible, a time before most of us experience death, tragedy and disappointment. Because of the way that Jesus dealt with children, Christians have been at the forefront of education, childcare, Sunday schools and children's literature.

However, making family entertainment can sometimes be used as an excuse by creative people fearful of grappling with the darker, more complex side of life. It's difficult to deal honestly and realistically with adult experiences of life without acknowledging that people lie, cheat, swear, fornicate and even murder their neighbors. It's not the admission that these things exist that can corrupt but the portrayal of them as admirable, pleasurable or inconsequential.

Epically Biblical

Biblical epics present themselves as the ideal material for the Christian moviemaker. What could be a better expression of faith than the re-telling of a Bible story? Yet the opportunities to do so (for the general market) are very limited, and as Western society has become less bib-lically literate the appetite for them has decreased. The *Greatest Story Ever Told*, made in 1965, had made only $8 million by 1983, less than 20 percent of what it needed to break even. *King David*, directed by Bruce Beresford in 1985, cost $21 million to make and made only $5 million back from the box office. The summary offered by Wikipedia sounds accurate: "Growing secularism and diversity in North America and Europe, along with the ever increasing importance of the interna-tional market, meant that the Biblical epic was no longer guaranteed to appeal to a large section of the audience."[9]

Closely allied to the biblical epic is the movie about the man or woman of faith such as Eric Liddell in *Chariots of Fire*, C. S. Lewis in *Shadowlands*, Sister Helen Prejean in *Dead Man Walking* and Arch-bishop Oscar Romero in *Romero*. Interestingly, none of the films just mentioned were written or directed by Christians (although *Romero* was financed by Catholics). Great story has always been at the center, and each of these films was driven by crisis and transformation, and just happened to center on Christians.

Too often Christians look at biopics as a way of presenting the gospel in a dramatic and interesting way, but the viewing public cares nothing for these beliefs as beliefs. They only become interesting if they are a natural part of a compelling story. A fantastic story about a nonbeliever will probably contain more attractive truth than a boring story about a saint. The moviemaker who is a Christian needs to trust the power of truth to come through in a screenplay that is truthful about all it touches on.

A Sanctified Ending

The fourth attractive possibility is the film where a conversion takes place. For many people this is the ultimate way they think Christians can transform movies. The story would typically be of someone getting deeper and deeper into sin (preferably drug addiction or violence rather than greed or self-righteousness), realizing the folly and emptiness of his or her ways, hearing the gospel in a compressed John 3:16 type of way, repenting and having his or her life changed so that the person becomes noticeably happier and more fulfilled.

There are many perils in such a format. One is that in movies the life of sin inevitably has much more appeal than the life of righteousness. Imagine if seventy minutes into *The Hangover* all of the main characters repented and became clean-living, honest and stable people. The laughs would stop. The audience would rather see five missionaries try to convert Las Vegas and end up as alcoholics than five alcoholics going to Las Vegas and ending up as missionaries.

A second problem is that conversion is an intimate transaction between the individual and God. Although the results can be dramatic, the exchange most often isn't. In real life we can only be sure that it has taken place in someone's life when we see the results: "By their fruit you will recognize them" (Mt 7:16). In film there isn't time to show fruit. A nasty person suddenly turning nice seems corny. If the conversion is the climax of the film, we have no way of telling whether it was genuine or fake. It may just be an easy way of pulling together loose ends.

The best movies featuring Christian characters (such as those mentioned previously) haven't been ones that have shown dramatic conversions but ones in which people who were already Christian have had to confront a challenge to their faith. Eric Liddell has to risk losing an almost certain gold medal in order to be faithful to his understanding of the sabbath commandment. C. S. Lewis has always confidently written and spoken about suffering and pain, and then has to confront the death of his wife. Oscar Romero is compelled to challenge his government, knowing that this will make him a target for assassination.

The Story of Stories

Christians involved in film should consider how story is used in the Bible. It's been estimated that around 40 percent of the Bible is narrative. One of the most effective ways of promoting truth and wisdom is by using stories. "You shall not commit adultery" could have been enough to let us know God's view on the subject of unfaithfulness, but the law on its own can be very flat and not engaging. The story of David and Bathsheba draws us in. We recognize ourselves. We learn that even someone as great and godly as King David wasn't immune to temptation. We see how his casual gaze, held too long perhaps, turned to lust, and how the lust led to murder. We also see the consequences of his sin on the rest of his life. The story of Jesus and the woman at the well draws us in, as does the story of Joseph resisting the overtures of Potiphar's wife.

There are several types of Bible story, each used for a different purpose. The first type of story is myth. This is often misunderstood to mean a story about something that never happened. Myth can be this, as with the stories of Greek gods, but it can also mean stories of things that possibly happened but around which have accrued fictional amendments and additions (King Arthur, Robin Hood) or stories that are entirely true (the sinking of the Titanic) and symbolize a value or an era. What all myths have in common is that they embody values and teachings, often about the origin of a society or the ideal way to live, or they stand as lessons about the consequences of breaking rules.

There are theologians who believe that the Genesis story of creation has elements of mythology. They are not saying that God didn't create the world but that the necessary complexity was reduced to better communicate the essentials to prescientific, preliterate people. It is a vitally important story because it tells us where we came from, why we're here, who we are and what state we are in. The true story of the Israelites forty years in the wilderness assumes the significance of myth because it tells Jewish people important details about how they became the chosen people and how they were led to the Promised Land.

One of the most important cinematic myths has been the Western. Cowboy movies reassured Americans about the value of the pioneer spirit, self-reliance and the conquest of nature. They illustrated notions of the perfect community ruled by a law enforcer, usually a sheriff, and the importance of the gun in quelling evil and administering justice. They also, unfortunately, promoted imperialism and racism, because the original inhabitants of the land (Native Americans, then referred to as Indians or redskins) were viewed not as people with entitlements but as impediments to expansion.

Christians have myths about how the faith arrived in their country or continent, or how their particular denomination was founded. These are important stories that God would have us celebrate and pass on to new generations. The Jewish people reinforced their national identity by constantly retelling the story of their bondage in Egypt, their escape from Pharaoh, their wandering and their final entry into the "land of milk and honey."

A second type of Bible story is history, showing how God dealt with Israel and highlighting the lives of special people. Cinema frequently revisits significant historical figures from the days of Spartacus and Cleopatra to Mahatma Gandhi, Lawrence of Arabia, Michael Collins and JFK. Often history is manipulated to fit the demands of a two-hour story, but nevertheless attention is drawn to important events in a vivid way and new life is generally breathed into books that are more accurate.

Prophetic Film

A third style of Bible story is prophecy and the prophetic act. Special messengers sometimes acted out stories to convey to people how God felt about their behavior. Isaiah went naked and barefoot to illustrate what would befall the Ethiopians and Egyptians. Jeremiah stuffed his unwashed underwear in the cleft of a rock and retrieved it when moldy to show how God would humble the pride of Judah. Ezekiel showed Jerusalem what would happen to it by shaving off his hair and beard, dividing it into three equal piles, burning one pile, slashing a second pile with his sword and letting the third pile be blown away by the wind.

Contemporary filmmakers can't claim to be speaking a direct word of God in quite the same way, but there is a tradition of film that effectively says, "The logic of carrying on living in this way or believing in these ideas will be this kind of disastrous society." This is not to be confused with films like *Minority Report* or *Blade Runner* that are merely set in the future and speculate about certain political or technological developments. The truly prophetic film carries a warning. It graphically enacts probable consequences.

Gattaca, made in 1997 by writer/director Andrew Niccol (later to make *The Truman Show*), speculated on a future where genetic screening was used not only to prevent the births of the deformed and diseased, but those who weren't deemed useful to society and its tasks. The hero of the film wants to be an astronaut but can only be accepted by stealing someone else's identity because he slipped through the screening process and doesn't have the right documentation.

One of the most prophetic films of the past forty years was *Network*. It starred Peter Finch as a deranged news anchor, Howard Beale, used by his employers to boost ratings by having his own show on which to vent his anger. This necessitated preying on public fears and whipping up populist resentment through chanting, "I'm mad as hell, and I'm not going to take this anymore." They eventually had him assassinated on live TV. This was a film warning of the dangers of prioritizing ratings over truth, of making news a branch of entertainment. It anticipated such future trends as "tabloid TV," "reality TV," "infotainment" and "shock jocks."

When *Network* came out in 1976, critic Vincent Canby of the *New York Times* called it "the satirist's cardiogram of the hidden heart."[10] In 2000, when Roger Ebert included it in his list of great movies, he said it was "Like prophecy. When Chayefsky [playwright Paddy Chayefsky] created Howard Beale, could he have imagined Jerry Springer, Howard Stern, and the World Wrestling Federation?"[11]

Parable

A fourth kind of biblical story is the one most associated with Jesus, the parable. Whereas myths comfort and reinforce, parables disturb and disarm. The intended response to a parable is perplexity followed by illumination as the hearer sees him- or herself in the story. The Welsh theologian C. H. Dodd defined parable as "a metaphor or simile drawn from nature or common life, arresting the hearer by its vividness or strangeness, and leaving the mind in sufficient doubt about its precise application as to tease it into active thought."[12]

Some of the parables (the pearl of great price, the lost coin) are mere illustrations to amplify the meaning of a concept. Other parables, the ones that are perhaps best known (such as the prodigal son, the good Samaritan), have depths of their own that warrant constant study and interpretation. They involve more than one character, a dramatic arc and a resolution. We may speculate as to whether the prodigal son is a returning backslider or a new convert, but we all take the point that God welcomes the repentant sinner. We may speculate as to whether the priest and the Levite who bypassed the man attacked by robbers were obeying ceremonial laws, hurrying to worship or fearful of being lured into a trap, but we all take the point that loving our neighbor means helping anyone in need regardless of our attachment to them by blood, tribe or religion.

Parables allow us to see ourselves in a dramatic context and therefore to know in advance the ultimate judgment on our action. In the stories of the prodigal son and the good Samaritan, the people expected to be good behave in bad ways and the people expected to be bad end up doing good. Our expectations are confounded. At different times in our lives we may have been each person in both parables.

Many films use techniques similar to those used in the parables. Very often writers take a story about something in the past that provides a commentary on a contemporary event once we become aware of the parallels. It would have seemed too obvious and heavy-handed to use the contemporary event to make the point. Giving an audience the opportunity to make its own discovery bestows it with dignity. Films like *Avatar* and *The Hunger Games* are widely welcomed as "parables of our times," although few can agree on the interpretations.

The Crucible, originally written by Arthur Miller as a play in 1952, is ostensibly about the Salem witch trials of the 1690s but was actually in part a comment on Senator Joseph McCarthy's pursuit of American communists in the 1950s. Miller's aim was to highlight the parallels and to make the point that McCarthyism was just an update on seventeenth-century witch hunts. The story was strong enough to stand on its own, but at the time it was written it had the effect of forcing viewers to reflect on a current issue.

In other instances entirely fictional contemporary stories are created that yield their greatest benefit when seen as commentary on society. *Being There*, the 1979 film starring Peter Sellers, tells the story of a simple gardener whose homespun wisdom and observations on plant life are mistakenly taken to be spiritual, political and economic insights. He becomes so influential that he is called in to advise the president of the United States and, when the president dies, to replace him. It was a comment on television, politics, innocence and human gullibility.

The Bible's use of stories shouldn't limit us to those forms only or lead us to assume that if we use those forms we have to use them for the same ends as the Bible authors. For example, a myth doesn't have to be one that explains the rise of Christianity, because we each have several other identities besides our identities as children of God, all of which are important. We're each part of a particular family and may want to investigate and tell that story. We're part of a country and also a region in that country. As a writer I also have a literary ancestry consisting of people whose work has been vital to mine. There are many stories that have led to our story, and we should feel free to both explore and celebrate them.

To take another example, if we create parables, they don't always have to be parables that liken something to the kingdom of God. We may create a parable about environmental destruction, celebrity culture, neighborliness, dehumanized sex or many other issues that concern us. Besides having specific intended applications for his followers, the parables that Jesus told have broader social applications about the desirability of love, forgiveness, thrift, importunity, justice, vigilance and hard work.

Telling the Truth

Moviemakers (along with journalists, poets and many others in popular culture) are not primarily called to preach the gospel but to tell the truth. When I write a biography, my aim is not to find something in the subject that would warrant explaining the life, death and resurrection of Christ, but to tell the truth, as far as it's possible to ascertain with naturally limited resources, about one person's actions, thoughts, relationships, beliefs and heritage. The truth, if it's told well, will always endorse some aspect of the gospel. If you're truthful about an unrepentant sinner, it will act as a warning. If you're truthful about a struggling believer, it will act as inspiration.

Often Christians fail in art projects by trying to tell all of the truth every time. The result is that they overburden the medium they're working in. No single painting, poem, song or film can tell the whole truth. We're finite and don't know the whole truth. We should stick with the truths that are relevant to the issue under discussion and not try to pull in larger, overarching truths that have no immediate bearing. But at the same time we shouldn't skimp on truth we know for fear of being unpopular. Bono once said that rock 'n' roll had been very good at telling the story of what Johnny got up to with his girlfriend in the back of a car. What it wasn't accomplished at, and what he wanted U2 to achieve, was telling the story of what happened next. Movies are a great medium for following up the consequences of actions, but these knock-on effects have to be believable.

Art, Not Propaganda

Film is best suited to art, not propaganda. There is a place for propaganda. For instance, if you are trying to communicate a message that unwashed hands spread disease, it's necessary that the audience understand what you're telling it. It would be no good making an interesting drama where the main characters happen to wash their hands once or twice. But movies are not information films. People go to see great stories well told. Mark Joseph, who has advised on the marketing of several films with potential in the "faith community," has said, "The right to send a message or teach a lesson is earned first by being entertaining. If it's not entertaining it will bomb. No amount of earnestness will save it."[13]

Because films can be summarized as being about something or other, people often conclude that the writer begins with a thesis and the drama grows out of it. The opposite is almost always true. A writer is attracted to a particular story because it encapsulates a deeply held belief, but it's often not until the writing's over that the point is discovered. *Blood Diamond* is seen as a film commenting on injustice in the diamond mining industry, but screenwriter Charles Leavitt said that his initial interest was in character.

> I feel something for these characters. I'd like to go into a movie theater and see these characters. . . . I don't look in terms of themes. I put myself in a darkened theater and imagine the story I'm trying to tell and how am I going to keep someone interested who's paid 10 dollars to sit in the theater and watch this.[14]

Asked how he was able to make a point without beating an audience over the head, he said, "I've found that the only way you can make a strong point is by *not* beating an audience over the head with it. When movies try too hard to manipulate, it just goes over an audience's head. I respect the intelligence of an audience. Less is more with me."[15]

Arthur Miller had been fascinated by the Salem witch trials since he was a child, but he'd rejected writing about them because he didn't think he was capable of getting to the minds of either the witches or those judging them. He was too rational. "But gradually, over weeks, a living connection between myself and Salem, and between Salem and Washington, was made in my mind," he wrote in his autobiography *Timebends*. "I knew that to simply will a play into existence was to insure a didactic failure. By now I was far beyond the teaching impulse; I knew that my own life was speaking here in many disguises, not merely my time."[16]

The best art seems to be a work that forces its way into existence; a story that has to be told. The meaning is something that makes itself known during the writing or maybe even afterwards. It's an organic process. You neither start with a meaning and then build a story to illustrate it, nor start with a story and then graft a meaning onto it. Much bad Christian art is made by Christians who see themselves as dispensers of answers to life's great problems. They begin with conclusions rather than questions. When art struggles to make sense of information and experience, it's more likely to draw fellow strugglers in. Joan Didion wrote, "I write entirely to find out what I'm thinking, what I'm looking at, what I see and what it means."[17]

Enrichment

The goal of a film should be enrichment or enlightenment, not conversion. Enrichment means that the viewers leave the film feeling better off for having seen it; maybe they feel heartened or enlarged, maybe just less stressed or more at peace. Enlightenment means viewers understand more about themselves, other people or the world. Maybe the film has exposed some evil they weren't aware of or some blessing they'd previously ignored. All conversions enrich and enlighten but not all experiences of enrichment and enlightenment are conversions.

When filmmakers deliberately make films in order to convert people, they inevitably fail to enrich or enlighten. As a member of the audience you can tell that the director has no interest in the story or the art of film. Everything has been put in the service of changing your mind. This usually results in characters that are only there to represent a particular point of view. They have no depth, no unpredictability and they're not real enough to make us care what happens to them.

Being Human

Finally, films are best when they deal with our humanity rather than our Christianity. A truly human film will embrace our faith, but films of faith rarely embrace our humanity. The late art critic Hans Rookmaaker made a powerful point when he said that Christ didn't die in order that we could go to more church meetings but that we should become fully human. What he meant was that God's ultimate goal is not to make us more religious but to complete our humanity. What we call religion is the means to this completeness but it's not the goal. The end product is that we should be the kind of people he envisaged at the dawn of creation.

What this means is that we can be on the side of any film that encourages us to be more fully human or that denounces dehumanization, any film that promotes truth or exposes lies, any film that expands our understanding of life or awakens our sensitivity, any film that displays true excellence and delights the imagination.

Questions for Reflection or Discussion

- Think of times when you've found the best way of describing something has been to use the example of a particular movie or scene from a movie.

- Do you think Robert McKee is correct to say that movies have become an important source of information about life's meaning in contemporary society?

- Does the major story told in the Bible easily fit the model of downfall, struggle, setback and eventual redemption, or does it have to be forced to fit?

- Which film is more redemptive—*The Sound of Music* or *Fight Club*?

- Would you prefer to see a biblical epic or the latest Hollywood blockbuster? Why?

- What do you consider to be the most sensitive and fair portrayal of a Christian in a mainstream movie and what made it so?

- What is the difference between art and propaganda?

- Should we ever decline to see a movie on moral grounds?
- Which mainstream movies do you think a film-making Christian would be proud to have made?
- Name a movie that you believe has been genuinely prophetic in that it pointed out a flaw in society and challenged viewers to behave differently?

Books Devoted to a Christian Understanding of Movies

Behind the Screen. Edited by Spencer Lewerenz and Barbara Nicolosi. Grand Rapids: Baker, 2005.

Geivett, R. Douglas, and James S. Spiegel. *Faith, Film and Philosophy: Big Ideas on the Big Screen.* Downers Grove, IL: InterVarsity Press, 2007.

Godawa, Brian. *Hollywood Worldviews.* Downers Grove, IL: Inter-Varsity Press, 2002.

Jewett, Robert. *Saint Paul Returns to the Movies: Triumph Over Shame.* Grand Rapids: Eerdmans, 1999.

Johnston, Robert K. *Reel Spirituality: Theology and Film in Dialogue.* Grand Rapids: Baker Academic, 2000.

Kuritz, Paul. *The Fiery Serpent: A Christian Theory of Film and Theater.* Enumclaw, WA: Pleasant Word, 2007.

Overstreet, Jeffrey. *Through a Screen Darkly.* Ventura, CA: Regal Books, 2007.

General Books on Story

Bettelheim, Bruno. *The Uses of Enchantment.* New York: Vintage, 1977.

Booker, Christopher. *The Seven Basic Plots: Why We Tell Story.* New York: Continuum, 2004.

Campbell, Joseph. *The Hero with a Thousand Faces.* New York: Pantheon, 1949.

Egri, Lajos. *The Art of Dramatic Writing.* New York: Simon & Schuster, 1946.

McKee, Robert. *Story*. New York: HarperCollins, 1997.

Moyers, Bill, and Joseph Campbell. *The Power of Myth*. New York: Doubleday, 1988.

Tierno, Michael. *Aristotle's Poetics for Screenwriters*. New York: Hyperion, 2002.

Vogler, Christopher. *The Writer's Journey: Mythic Structure for Storytellers and Screenwriters*. Studio City, CA: Michael Wiese Productions, 1992.

Websites Looking at Movies from a Christian Perspective

Hollywood Jesus: www.hollywoodjesus.com
Godawa's MovieBlog: www.godawa.com/movieblog
Looking Closer: www.lookingcloser.org
Christianity Today: www.christianitytoday.com/ct/movies/
Patheos Movies: www.patheos.com/Movies

Five Suggestions for Action

- Read a broad section of reviews and always take into account the life perspective of the reviewer.

- Read interviews with actors, directors and screenwriters so that you are aware of how they view what they have accomplished.

- Try to see movies with friends whose views you respect.

- If you are a maker of films, become as technically proficient as you can and listen to the conversation going on between movies and the public so that you become aware of which stories you could tell that are most appropriate for the moment.

- A reviewer once said that the big taboo in movies today was intimacy, rather than sex. If you are a filmmaker think of other taboo subjects about which a Christian has a lot to say.

5

Journalism

Reading Between the Lines

†

When writing the last chapter, I composed the sentence "Act two is taken up with conflict as the hero pursues the goal." I was going to write, "as the hero pursues *his* goal" but I stopped myself. You will automatically know why. We have all become conscious that if we use the personal pronoun *he* to represent all people, we are assuming male supremacy. Not only are we assuming it but by unthinkingly using the pronoun we are perpetuating it.

Feminist thinkers have done an excellent job of making us aware of buried assumptions. We all now feel uncomfortable with old ads that assumed that the wife was in the kitchen and the husband was at work, and with stories where boys took on tough challenges while the girls made sandwiches, or with language that hides or denigrates women. When I come across a Christian author from the early part of the twentieth century speaking about "the Christian man" when what is meant is "the Christian," it leaps out at me and raises the question, what about the Christian woman? in a way that it wouldn't have leapt out at anyone in 1935. Back then it just seemed normal. Now it seems abnormal.

So, what has changed? Feminists pointed out that there was a male bias that was so ingrained that it affected the very structures of communication. It was difficult to think about gender equality because our language didn't allow it. They then argued that our behavior reflected the way we thought. If they had examined my example of "the Christian man," they would have shown that by perpetuating the idea that the truly great Christian was a "man of God" rather than a "man or woman of God" (or a "person of God"), women were relegated to the margins. If we never hear the phrase *woman of God*, we're likely to conclude that no such possibility exists.

Personal assumptions are difficult to detect precisely because they are assumptions. They are also difficult to detect because many of them are supported by the unexamined axioms of popular culture. When our beliefs are bolstered by the culture around us, we think everything is normal. Nothing jars. Nothing contradicts. Feminists skillfully educate us in the art of reading between the lines. They show us that it isn't defiantly antifemale statements that keep women in their place but culture that simply assumes male dominance. Andrew R. Cline, associate professor of journalism at Missouri State University, says, "Language cannot be neutral; it reflects and structures our ideologies and worldviews. To speak at all is to speak politically."[1]

Understanding Bias

One of the most powerful ways that popular culture affects people is through unexamined assumptions. The only way that we can resist such a molding effect is to become acutely aware of how assumptions are incorporated and what those assumptions are. I want to look at popular journalism to show how views of the world can be buried deep in the text.

Journalists ostensibly strive for fairness, accuracy, completeness and balance, but there are conscious and unconscious decisions that often hinder this. Even though writers try to resist bias, the media has biases that are inbuilt. Andrew R. Cline points out that magazines and newspapers are naturally biased toward sales, immediacy, the values of the owner, deadlines, the visual, bad news and stories that have clearly defined protagonists and antagonists. Picture editors are biased toward attractive faces and famous people. Often papers are openly biased toward a particular political party.

Editors and writers display their bias from the get-go by what they include and exclude from their publications. This in itself involves assumptions about what is important, and will in turn influence the values of the readership. Popular down-market newspapers generally don't devote much space to foreign policy but a lot to celebrity. This leads its readers to believe, at a subconscious level at least, that what happens in a pop star's bedroom is more significant than what happens in a back street in Mogadishu, or that the lives of a few hundred actors living comfortably in Los Angeles have more value that the lives of millions of undernourished children around the world. Readers may even come to use celebrity as a measure of their worth or the physiques of models as the standard by which to judge the desirability of their bodies.

The magazine *Men's Health* advertises itself as "The Magazine Men Live By" and promises coverage of everything that "today's man needs to feel fitter, healthier and happier." However, good as the magazine is at dealing with the body, it totally ignores the soul. Its implicit assumption is that spirituality has no place in the outlook of "today's man" and it shares this view not by ranting against the spiritual but by ignoring it. The magazine thereby creates the impression that real masculinity is down to what you earn, how you look, what you spend, how you feel and how successfully you can conquer women.

I wouldn't expect *Men's Health* to present gospel messages, just as I wouldn't expect *Christianity Today* to teach me how to build up my pectorals. These things are outside its editorial scope. But a magazine that has as its declared aim the *total* well-being of a man could surely address issues that involve spirituality even in its loosest definition, just as motivational speaker Stephen R. Covey included it in such books as *The 7 Habits of Highly Effective People*. It is otherwise very comprehensive in what it covers, listing on its website fitness, weight loss, health, food, nutrition, meals, sex, relationships, gear, style, grooming, travel and wealth. By excluding the spiritual *Men's Health* promotes the purely material as normal, as all that needs to be considered when pursuing happiness and well-being.

What's the News?

The earliest American journalism was committed to faithfully re-cording "publick occurrences" as they might appear to the mind of God. The first Boston newspaper, published in 1690, came out monthly, but special editions would be printed in the case of extraor-dinary events. The assumption here was that there were not enough events classifiable as "news" to fill a more regularly published paper. We now have twenty-four-hour TV channels and daily newspapers that have to be filled with stories regardless of significance. This creates the temptation to manufacture news, exaggerate the impor-tance of events, create controversy where none previously existed or to make news out of the news-gathering process. There are more ce-lebrities today not because there are more accomplished people but because the media needs an ever-larger parade of recognizable faces to report on. A news anchor can't announce, "I am sorry, but there was no news today."

In the early years of newspapers there was a belief that the editors and writers were engaged in recording a world that was a battlefield between God and the devil. In his account of James Gordon Bennett, founder of the *New York Herald*, the Victorian historian James Parton commented, "The skilled and faithful journalist, recording with ex-actness and power the thing that has come to pass, is Providence ad-dressing men."[2] The story is told of a Baptist clergyman before the Civil War who would each day request his morning paper and before sitting down say to his servants, "Be kind enough to let me have it a few minutes, till I see how the Supreme Being is governing the world."

In his stimulating book *The Image* Daniel Boorstin argued that once this divine perspective was lost, journalism changed from re-cording events in order to increase understanding to manufacturing them to increase excitement. He contrasted Parton's attitude with that of Arthur McEwen, the first editor of the San Francisco *Examiner*, who defined news as "Anything that makes the reader go, 'Gee whiz!'"[3] Boorstin was convinced that people had come to expect more drama and innovation from the world than was actually there, and that this had led to the creation of what he termed "pseudo events." These were happenings devised expressly to be covered by journalists, events that wouldn't have taken place if there had been no opportunity for media coverage. Boorstin was writing long before the advent of reality TV, but it's a form of entertainment that proves his point. The events covered by reality TV are pseudo events that create pseudo stars (people whose only achievement is to have been filmed) whose lives off-screen then create further pseudo events.

Priorities

Aside from choosing which stories to cover, the editors and writers choose how much space to give a particular topic and where to place it. The layout and positioning of a piece communicates its importance. Traditionally newspapers lead with hard news and international news, and follow up with domestic news. Subjects like sports, travel, food, show business and the arts are positioned toward the back of the paper or even in a separate supplement. This accurately reflects the fact that happenings on the world stage are more likely to affect us in the long term than a nice meal or a good film. TV news usually begins with national or international news and then signs off with an amusing story designed to leave viewers feeling a warm glow.

The drift toward what has been called "infotainment" means that the trivial is often put side by side with the important, the merely amusing next to the life-affectingly serious, as if they were equally significant. A wardrobe malfunction by Janet Jackson is made to look as worthy of our attention as a decision taken to invade a country. One daily paper that I buy always has a photo-led show business story on its front page, to the right of the headline news, as if international events were like cabbage (not very tasty but vital for good health) and entertainment was dessert (pleasing to the palate but maybe not good for the skin). A similar thing happens with Web news feeds. Major world events are bundled in with voyeuristic trivialities.

Washington Post journalist Carl Bernstein, famed for his role in breaking the Watergate story in the 1970s, said,

In this culture of journalistic titillation, we're teaching our readers and our viewers that the trivial is significant, that the lurid and the loopy are more important than real news. We do not serve our readers and viewers; we pander to them. . . .

We are in the process of creating, in sum, what deserves to be called an idiot culture. . . . For the first time in our history the weird and the coarse are becoming our cultural norm, even our cultural identity.[4]

How religion is dealt with in magazines and newspapers differs not only from country to country but from region to region. In some places it would be normal to refer to faith and God in an editorial. In others, religion is relegated to its own special place at the back of the paper or the foot of the page. Tabloid newspapers tend not to have religion correspondents. Again, as with the *Men's Health* attitude to spirituality, this is the product of an assumption, the assumption being that religion is a special interest like gardening or chess rather than a whole way of living and thinking that affects every department of life.

In Britain BBC radio has an important daily current-events program called *Today* that is invaluably informative and attempts to set the agenda for the day's news. It is vital listening for politicians, editors and opinion formers. At 7:45 a.m. there is a 2-minute-and-45-second slot called "Thought for the Day" in which a religious figure "reflects on a topical issue from a theological standpoint." This is not to attract listeners, but is because of the BBC's obligations to religious broadcasting. The ring-fenced nature of the spot conveys the message that religion is divorced from real life—like an old castle, it no longer plays a useful role in our lives, but we wouldn't really like to see it pulled down—and the title suggests that theology is something that happens in the privacy of our minds. A "thought for the day" is pondering rather than doing. Journalists and correspondents, the other contributors to the program, don't deal in mere "thoughts" but in hard facts and tough questions. The assumption here is that for facts we look to journalism, but for nice thoughts we turn to religion.

The Bible doesn't tell us how to produce radio programs or edit newspapers, but it has a lot to say about priorities. In our sinful condition our values are distorted. For example, we respect the rich and powerful, and look down on (or avoid looking at) the poor and weak. We don't remedy the situation by despising the rich and worshiping the poor, but by valuing the humanity of all. We need to see the ordinariness of those who are glamourized and the glamour of those considered ordinary. The *Guardian* newspaper of London prints obituaries of lesser-known people alongside those of people who've achieved a lot in public life, and they act as reminders of how glorious these unseen, and often unsung, lives can be.

From a biblical perspective the body is important but spiritual development is more important, quite the reverse of the *Men's Health* perspective. The body will decay and disintegrate, and the best we can hope for is to delay the process. The creation of new bodies, the promise of almost every fitness magazine, is actually a job God has already got in hand. But while our bodies run down, our spirits can be strengthened. Physically most of us will end up like babies, but spiritually we can become giants. "Physical training is of some value, but godliness has value for all things, holding promise for both the present life and the life to come" (1 Tim 4:8).

Embedded Values

A further way that journalism uses assumptions is in what it highlights and therefore deems valuable in the people that it covers. Because interviews and profiles appear to consist only of facts and direct quotations, we assume that they are values free. However, the priorities of the writer will be evident at every point, for it's the writer who chooses the questions to ask (and therefore determines to some extent the answers given), selects the quotes that appear most appropriate, organizes the material to emphasize certain points and then frames the whole event.

The worldview of an interviewer shapes the course of an interview. One great newspaper interviewer of the 1970s, although an atheist, always asked his interviewees what he called "the God question" because he believed (rightly, in my opinion) that what people felt about God (or God's absence), death and the afterlife, almost always revealed something interesting about a subject's hopes, fears and values. If "the God question" is asked, it can open up avenues of thought that would otherwise remain untouched. Alternatively, if an interviewer made "the sex question" or "the money question" the core of the interview, then, not surprisingly, the resulting quotes would mainly be about sex or money.

Once an interview has been conducted, the writer has further choices to make based on further assumptions. Five or six thousand words of transcript have to be boiled down to a few hundred words of journalism, including observations and commentary. Something has to go. In fact, a lot has to go. A writer could include only the most controversial or entertaining quotes, or possibly only the quotes that make the subject look good or bad. A good writer will want to present a balanced and honest portrait that gives the readership enough information to form an opinion.

Besides the direct quotations of the interviewee, every profile will have the opinions of the writer (unless it's a Q&A interview with no introduction). This can come from direct comment but also, more subtly, from what is tacitly approved of. In his book *The Christian Mind*, Harry Blamires gives the example of an innocent-sounding letter of recommendation sent from a master at one school to the housemaster at another. The pupil being recommended happened to be Guy Burgess, later to become a notorious double agent during the Cold War along with Kim Philby and Donald Maclean. The letter read in part, "It is refreshing to find one who is really well-read and who can become enthusiastic or have something to say about most things from Vermeer to Meredith. He is also a lively and amusing person."[5]

Blamires argued that the statement contained what he termed "accidental self-revelation." Burgess was not being singled out for having well-informed views but simply for having "something to say." This had become a commendable value in itself. "The essential triviality of this idea is noteworthy," wrote Blamires. "Does it matter whether one is becoming enthusiastic over what is important or over what is petty? Does it matter what one has to say about most things represents a balanced, sound, wise judgment?" Burgess was praised for being lively, amusing and enthusiastic, another set of assumptions about what is good. "Hitler was enthusiastic," retorted Blamires. "He also had something to say about most things. So what? Are we not concerned with what people are enthusiastic about, with the truth or falsity of what they say about most things? Is there no value in having nothing to say about many things?"[6]

Even the most apparently harmless tributes are full of values and judgments. Consider how many interviews begin by drawing attention to the subject's wealth, professional achievements, looks, power and number of sexual partners. These are almost always listed in a way that assumes we will be impressed and that the more of each of these that the subject possesses the more worthy they are of our respect and the more valuable are their opinions.

Consider this subhead in a woman's magazine: "She packed marriage, a baby, divorce and an Oscar nomination into her twenties. Now, at 32, Kate Hudson is in love and pregnant again. But that doesn't mean she's settling down."[7] The whole emphasis is on what can be "packed into" a life. The assumption is that it is an achievement to cram events into your life, regardless of the moral quality or the social impact. "Settling down" is presented as something negative (you can't pack things in if you're settled). Love leading to pregnancy is OK, but love leading to commitment is unadventurous. We're clearly meant to cheer at Kate Hudson's ability to move on.

A newspaper subhead, this time for a profile of singer Katy Perry, says, "The singer escaped a strict Christian childhood to find fame."[8] Here it's taken for granted that "strict" Christianity is something to escape from and that fame offers some form of relief or that "strict" Christianity and fame are incompatible. Would the same newspaper write of someone "escaping" from a rigorously academic family or a passionately committed political family? Would it ever write about someone "escaping" the clutches of fame and money to find personal salvation? The attitude of the statement presupposes that "strict" Christianity is a form of imprisonment and that fame is a form of blessing.

A magazine interview with Natalia Vodianova begins by telling us that the Russian model lives in a converted mill house and has six cars parked in the driveway, indications that "this is no ordinary country-dweller, but an empress with an empire." We are told that Vodianova has "a personal fortune of $45 million" and that she is ninth on *Forbes* magazine's "Supermodel Rich List." She is, the magazine carries on, "widely regarded as one of the most beautiful women in the world." Her beauty is so powerful that "it has spread from person to person like laughter, getting things done in ways that we unbeautiful people could never manage."[9] In a world that values health, beauty, wealth, power, excitement and fulfilling sex above everything else, this model has achieved sainthood. And as if to offset the carbons released by her high living she organizes charity events.

In a similar way a profile of reality TV celebrity Kim Kardashian in *Cosmopolitan* starts with her looks ("her make-up is immaculate"). We then learn that she is "committed" to her appearance. The use of the word *committed*, a word normally used to describe dedication, fidelity and sacrifice, makes it seem that Kardashian has a solemn duty to look good and that she is doing it out of a higher calling rather than because of vanity. Anyway, her "commitment" is made that much easier because "she converted one bedroom in her house into a closet and another into a hair-and-makeup room."[10]

In both stories "success" is equated with beauty, wealth, work, busyness and being in love. This same assumption about the fulfilled life lies behind a lot of contemporary journalism. Vodianova is summarized as a "flawless, faultless woman." Kardashian "prides herself on" her ability to "move on and get better after making mistakes." Both articles are illustrated with photographs of the subjects posing as models, accompanied by credits for hairdressers, makeup artists and clothing retailers.

In the same issue of the magazine that featured Vodianova was a four-page interview with a prostitute who'd slept with a well-known athlete when his wife was five months pregnant. She was photographed as a model alongside listings of where to buy her underwear, makeup and skirt. The write-up was "nonjudgmental." The girl thought the athlete's wife deserved to be cheated on because she'd put up with previous infidelities. She could make up to £3,000 a weekend as a prostitute and this had allowed her to move into a "leafy suburb." Her aim was to write a book and have a sex advice column, for the reason, "I want to use my experience and use my brain."[11] Stories like this imply that it doesn't matter how fame is acquired just as long as you acquire it. Once famous, everyone is treated with same degree of respect.

Loaded Words

Another way that simple words can convey assumptions is when we rely on the connotation rather than the denotation. *Well built, fat* and *obese* may all have the same meaning, but the connotation of *well built* is entirely different to the connotation of *obese. Well built* connotes "statuesque" or "generously endowed," whereas *obese* connotes "chunky" or "blubbery." If we want to create a favorable impression of someone, we'll say that they're quite "well built." If we want to create an unfavorable impression we will use "fat" or "obese."

This is pertinent to written-up interviews because a writer can prejudice us against the subject by the use of a word with negative connotations. "'I'm not in favor of government regulation,' said the politician" is neutral. "'I'm not in favor of government regulation,' said the obese politician" may be true but the adjective is designed to plant suspicion. If the politician can't control a personal weight problem, how could he or she control a community or a state? "'I'm not in favor of government regulation,' said the beaming politician" may also be true, but this time the aim is to assure the reader that the politician is in control and at peace.

Usually the words are less obvious and physical. If a writer likes someone's values, he or she might describe the person as "highly principled." If the writer doesn't, the person could be a "self-styled moralist." If the "highly principled" person refuses to budge on an issue, he or she is "determined." If the moralist is similarly tenacious, he or she is "stubborn." If the writer likes the religion the subject espouses, the person can be "spiritual." If not, he or she can be a "fanatic." Phrases such as *found God* or *got religion* are almost always used pejoratively to make it seem that the convert has done something completely irrational.

Accurately reported quotes can be undercut by accompanying verbs, nouns and adjectives. The "tireless campaigner" will be listened to with respect, whereas the "belligerent activist" can be dismissed as an eccentric. The "freedom fighter" has courage, whereas the "terrorist" is a coward. We warm to people who "smile," but not to those who "smirk." Our reception of a quote will be affected by whether the speaker "said" it, "screamed" it, "muttered" it or "shouted" it. If a writer is unsure of the veracity of a statement, he or she can always insert "claimed" in the place of the usual "said" ("God speaks to me every day," claimed the minister) and it hints at suspicion. The wisest of statements can be made, but if it is packaged within negative sounding words we're more likely to reject it.

I once read an interview with a creationist in a newspaper well known for its liberal/humanist leanings. I can't recall any of the actual quotes but I remember that the creationist was eating a dessert as he spoke and that this detail had clearly been used to subtly undermine his credibility. We know that it's possible to speak profound truths while eating a toffee pudding but the juxtaposition of the somewhat lowly, and sticky, activity with the high flown ideas created an incongruity that succeeded where cleverer demolition jobs might have failed.

In 2012 a British judge sentenced a woman to eight years in prison for self-aborting her child at thirty-nine weeks. Two months later a front page headline appeared in the *Guardian*: "Abortion case judge linked to conservative Christian group." The group in question was the Lawyers' Christian Group, a fellowship organization to which 2,500 Christians in the legal profession belong to. The use of the word *link* made the relationship sound sinister, which I presume was the intention. "Links" are normally things uncovered by investigators. Pedophiles and terrorists have "links." It suggests something furtive and concealed. "Abortion case judge belongs to Christian fellowship" sounds nowhere near as threatening.

It's not wrong to have assumptions. This book is full of them. I assume the existence of God. I don't try to prove it. Life would be impossible without assumptions. A Christian is not someone free of them but (hopefully) someone who knows where his or her assumptions derive from, someone who believes there is an absolute truth even though they don't always see it clearly and sometimes misrepresents or misunderstands it. Asking an interviewee whether he or she believes in God assumes that this is an important question, more important than asking whether the person believes in ghosts or the Bermuda Triangle. Editing an interview assumes that some statements are more pertinent or interesting than others. Making judgments about an interviewee—whether the person is arrogant or humble, happy or sad, stimulating or boring—assumes that there is some correspondence between observations made through our senses and reality.

The purpose of this chapter is not to invalidate the use of assumptions but to point out how to spot them so we can avoid being subconsciously manipulated or subconsciously manipulative. The Christian view is that there is an objective truth about any situation. This doesn't mean that we always find it, but it does give us the motivation, courage, humility and determination to search it out. We may only approximate the truth, but at least we know that there is a truth to be approximated. We may only produce a shadowy outline of what is actually there, but at least we know something is there. We are not just drifting on a sea of chatter and personal opinion.

To see the world as God sees it is an exciting pursuit to be engaged in. It's highlighted for the journalist because at its most noble, journalism is about discovering truth and exposing lies, but it should be the same for anyone claiming to be a follower of Jesus. We are all the time trying to align our feelings and observations with those of God. We are all the time trying to ensure that his assumptions become ours.

Questions for Reflection or Discussion

- Every age has its assumptions. What do you think are the major assumptions of our age?

- Is it possible to avoid having a bias when we write?

- Compare the benefits of working as a reporter for a religious TV channel, where you are expected to put a Christian spin on the news, and working for a major network, where you are expected to be "objective."

- Cut an interview from a newspaper or magazine and underline the adjectives. What qualities does the writer highlight and present as being admirable?

- Do you think there is any value in writing to a newspaper to challenge the veracity of something it published?

- Identify some of the ways that newspapers, magazines and websites promote assumptions without flagging up their beliefs in an explicit way.

- Newspapers and news channels are often criticized for focusing on bad news. Can you imagine what they would be like if they only focused on good news?

- The public doesn't have a high regard for journalists when it comes to their honesty and respect for truth. Do you think this reputation is deserved or is it a cliché?

- To what extent does the media set the agenda for what people consider to be the important issues in their culture?

- If Jesus were to guest edit the *New York Times,* what changes would he make?

Books on Journalism by Christians

Blind Spot: When Journalists Get Religion Wrong. Edited by Paul Marshall, Lela Gilbert and Roberta Green-Ahmanson. Oxford University Press, 2008.

Kennedy, Jon R. *The Reformation of Journalism: A Christian Approach to Mass Communication.* Nutley, NJ: Craig Press, 1972.

Olasky, Marvin. *Telling the Truth: How to Revitalize Christian Journalism.* Wheaton, IL: Crossway, 1996.

Pippert, Wesley. *An Ethic of News: A Reporter's Search for the Truth.* Washington, DC: Georgetown University Press, 1989.

Schmalzbauer, John. *People of Faith: Religious Conviction in American Journalism and Higher Education.* Ithaca, NY: Cornell University Press, 2002.

Speaking the Truth: Monographs from the World Journalism Institute. Compiled and edited by Kimberly Collins. New York: World & Life Books, 2008.

General Books on Journalism

Evans, Harold. *Essential English for Journalists, Editors and Writers.* London: Pimlico, 2000.

Mencher, Marvin. *News Reporting and Writing.* New York: McGraw Hill, 1997.

Tell Me No Lies: Investigative Journalism and Its Triumphs. Edited by John Pilger. London: Vintage, 2005.

Zinsser, William. *On Writing Well.* New York: HarperCollins, 1976.

Some Websites for Christians in Journalism

The World Journalism Institute (New York): www.worldji.com

Christians in Journalism (London): www.cij.org.uk

Washington Journalism Center: www.bestsemester.com/wjc

"Challenges and Opportunities for Christian Journalism" by Arne H. Fjeldstad: www.ocrpl.org/?p=18

Five Suggestions for Action

- Read a newspaper you're likely to disagree with as well as one you're likely to agree with so that you're always aware of both sides of important debates.

- Familiarize yourself with the political and philosophical leanings of the major newspapers and TV channels, and also the interests of their owners.

- Take advantage of online access to major newspapers around the world so that you can build a global perspective.

- See if you can publish a story that is widely known within the Christian community but completely unknown outside of it. If you are a writer, you could write it up yourself. If you are not a writer, you could tip off a reporter or a newspaper that you know.

- If you are a journalist, interpret the church to the world and the world to the church. Also, interpret the church to the church and the world to the world. Tell the truth at all times, glory in goodness and expose evil.

6

Celebrity Culture

The Game of the Fame

†

When I was working on a rock magazine in the early 1970s, aspiring singers and songwriters would try to persuade me to see them in concert or hear playbacks in a studio. One of the most persistent was a young man living in Beckenham, Kent. I liked his songs and on May 5, 1971, I went to his home for a meal. He met me at the station in a battered old sports car. He had shoulder-length hair, was unshaven and wore jeans. We spent several hours together and had a great time. His name was David Bowie.

Just under a year later, on April 20, 1972, I went to see him in a small theater in Harlow, Essex. We met up before the show. He was completely transformed. His hair had been colored and cut short. He was wearing white satin trousers tucked into boxing style boots. He had consciously decided to develop an image that would change him from an admired performer into a superstar. His manager, Tony De-Fries, said that he was determined that he would become one of those legendary performers known simply by mention of their surname: Sinatra, Chaplin, Dylan, Brando.

I interviewed him again a week later and then saw him in concert in Croydon, Surrey, in June and at the Royal Festival Hall in London in July. By this time he was certainly a star, performing songs from his new album *Ziggy Stardust and the Spiders from Mars*. Journalists from around the world were on hand to mark his arrival as a name to reckon with. The curious thing was that although I knew him and had seen from close quarters how he'd created this character, I was still mesmerized by it. I became interested in the way that he'd managed to make something apparently extraordinary out of something ordinary.

Part of the way he built his image was by rationing personal information in a way that stirred interest. The public would only get to see the bits of David Bowie that Bowie wanted them to see, and these glimpses would be aggressively managed. He became increasingly hard to get to. Interviews were limited. Only one official photographer was allowed at concerts so that his visual impression could be carefully controlled. He would appear at events flanked by bodyguards, not because he needed protection but because the sight of someone with security implied importance. When in Harlow I mentioned to him that I'd been reading *The Hidden Persuaders* by Vance Packard, a book about advertising techniques, and *The Selling of the President* by Joe McGinniss, an account of how Richard Nixon was made more palatable to the American public in the 1968 election. Bowie had read both books and commended me on my choice of reading.

The McGinniss book was particularly pertinent because it quoted extensively from memoranda that passed between Nixon's chief image-makers and was virtually a guide to celebrity creation. One of Nixon's advisers, Ray Price, made a distinction between what was being promoted and the actual person. "It's not what's there that counts," he wrote. "It's what's projected. And carrying it one step further, it's not what he projects but rather what the voter receives. It's not the man we have to change, but rather the received impression."[1]

The advice that would have excited Bowie came from Nixon's speechwriter William Gavin, who wrote,

> People are stirred by the legend, including the living legend not by the man himself. It's the aura that surrounds the charismatic figure more than it is the figure itself that draws the followers.

Our task is to build that aura. Attention begets attention. People who wouldn't look twice at something happening in the street will if they see a crowd gathered to watch. People pant over movie stars in person not because they're inherently any more interesting than the person next door, but because they're a focus of public attention, of adulation. They're events, happenings, institutions, legends: see the legend in the flesh, it's something to tell the neighbors about.[2]

Bowie went on to build his career out of a series of rapidly changing images and styles of music, becoming an inspiration to generations of image-conscious rock stars. Celebrity and image are nothing new. In Greco-Roman times it was emperors, philosophers, military leaders and kings who were well known to the people. Actors, gladiators and charioteers also became famous and wealthy, although the term *fame* was used only of people whose reputations lived on long after they were dead. Fame was the lasting impression, not the instant impact. In more recent centuries novelists, vaudeville performers and musicians have been celebrated.

It seems natural that a select group of people becomes widely known in any society and age and that their gifts, powers and talents are applauded and even imitated. But in order to understand the power of celebrity in our own age, and to distinguish celebrity culture from a culture that happens to have celebrities, we need to look at what it takes to become well known, what role the famous then play, and what the nature of contemporary celebrity tells us about the spiritual condition of our age. Additionally, as Christians we should ask whether celebrity creation is consistent with the biblical view of being equal before God and compare the qualities of a celebrated person today with the qualities that God esteems.

Occupation Celebrity

In today's world celebrity is viewed as something approximating an occupation. There are people whose faces and comments fill the gossip magazines whose talents we can't quite pinpoint. All we know is that they are famous, they earn money because of it and they have more power than the average person. What, for example, is Paris Hilton's job? She's important enough to put her name to brands and to be an important opening-night guest, but what is her actual talent? Why is she celebrated? What has she achieved? What is Ozzy Osbourne's skill? Is he a great vocalist or composer? Does he write lyrics that make life easier to understand or that amuse? Is he a great communicator? Why is it that millions of people watched TV programs that followed him and his family as they went through their daily routines? What does Kim Kardashian do?

One condition of contemporary celebrity is that it doesn't matter what gets you there as long as you arrive. The central thing is to be gazed at covetously by millions of people. When you are a celebrity you can use the power to endorse products, enjoy financial freedom and gain access to people and places beyond the reach of the noncelebrity. By the time someone is in this bracket, the public may have forgotten how the fame was first acquired. There are people who are famous simply because of a previous association with someone famous. Liz Hurley is best known as the ex-girlfriend of actor Hugh Grant, David Guest as the former husband of singer Liza Minnelli.

TV talent shows and reality shows attract contestants who often want to ascend to international fame without having to tread the lower rungs of obscurity, apprenticeship, hard knocks and rejection. They don't see artistic or personal proficiency as their goal, but fame itself. What once was a byproduct of hard graft and talent has become the whole point. At one time stars were so-called because they shone out above all others, but then in the late 1960s all performers began to be referred to as stars, and becoming a "film star" meant the same as becoming an actor who worked in cinema, and becoming a "rock star" the same as becoming a singer or a member of a band. This required a new term for those who really excelled, so Andy Warhol and others encouraged the use of the term *superstar*.

Stardom has now become so ordinary that millions of people think they are capable of achieving it. People see "being a star" as a legitimate job description that requires nothing more than lucky breaks. A British survey conducted in 2009 with five- to eleven-year-olds found that their top three future occupations were sports star, pop star and actor. Twenty-five years previously the top three were teacher, banker and doctor. As Rachel once said in the TV series pilot of *Glee*, "Nowadays being anonymous is worse than being poor."

Being unknown is regarded as a sin for which stardom is the only cure. The tears of many failed talent-show contestants are shed because they see salvation slipping away from them. They believe they are validated only if they are famous, and so when fame eludes them they feel crushed. Pop star Jarvis Cocker noted that, "Becoming famous has taken the place of going to heaven in modern society. That's the place where your dreams will come true. It's an act of faith now. They think that's going to sort things out."[3]

Magazines perpetuate this view by discussing fame as though it is always an undiluted blessing and that it always equals success. The truth is that success in most areas of normal life and most occupations does not result in fame, and fame for many people does not bring success. In fact, fame very often destroys people's ability to be successful in other departments of their lives. Consider how many famous people fail as fathers and mothers, husbands and wives, neighbors and friends, and how many of them lose the ability to control selfish desires.

In 2004 Mel Gibson released *The Passion of the Christ*, a film that would become one of the highest grossing movies of all time. A married man with seven children, good looks and an incredibly successful career, he seemed to be someone able to combine a devout faith (he is a traditionalist Catholic), a happy family life and the rewards of fame. Two years later he announced his separation from his wife of twenty-six years. In 2009 he was caught drunk driving and then poured racist abuse on the arresting police officers. The same year he was photographed with another woman who in 2010 took out a restraining order against him. In a very short time he had gone from being a poster boy for Christian filmmaking to a Hollywood bad boy of the highest order. When his wife finally divorced him in 2011, he had to pay a $400 million settlement. Possibly some of these things would have happened anyway, but one can't help but think that fame and its rewards encouraged his collapse.

Fame and Celebrity

One of the main differences between the contemporary celebrity and the famous person of old is that fame used to be the result of greatness. In his book *Life: The Movie* Neal Gabler reports, "Traditionally fame had been tied, however loosely, to ability or accomplishment or office. Celebrity, on the other hand, seemed less a function of what one did than of how much one was perceived."[4] Daniel Boorstin, writing in *The Image*, argues that our interest in celebrities goes back to a time when we believed that human greatness was an indication of a flash of the divine. "Two centuries ago when a great man appeared, people looked for God's purpose in him," he wrote. "Today we look for his press agent."[5]

Another difference is that celebrities now use the fact that they are well known to involve themselves in areas of life where they have no recognized expertise. Since Ronald Reagan became president of the United States and Arnold Schwarzenegger became governor of California it has been customary to ask actors whether they're considering running for office. Why should we think that a skill in remembering lines and pretending to be someone else prepares someone for political leadership, unless that's all we demand of our politicians? It's highly dangerous to think that someone who's able to win fans through looking good or developing believable characters would automatically be able to lead a state or a nation.

Because the media is predisposed to report on almost anything a celebrity says, celebrities wield an opinion-shaping power disproportionate to their wisdom, knowledge and maturity. Political parties look for celebrity endorsements to give them credibility and introduce their policies to people who wouldn't normally listen. This is reckoned to have started with the 1920 presidential election when Warren Harding enlisted the help of some early stars of film, including Douglas Fairbanks, Al Jolson and Mary Pickford. In 1960 John F. Kennedy was supported by singers Sammy Davis Jr and Dean Martin, and famously had Marilyn Monroe sing for his birthday at a Democratic fundraiser in May 1962. More recently Barack Obama was praised by Bruce Springsteen, Oprah Winfrey, George Clooney and Tom Hanks. When Britain had a referendum in 2011 on an alternative voting system, the campaign to accept the change was spearheaded by four celebrities made up of two broadcasters, an actress and a musician.

Causes gain more publicity if they have celebrities willing to campaign for them. This is again based on the premise that the public will listen to famous people rather than experts or professional fundraisers. Not only do charities get more exposure through being associated with celebrities but also celebrities get more exposure by working for charities. There are PR companies who will marry celebrities to high-profile causes appropriate to the image they want to cultivate for themselves. The website www.looktothestars.org lists 1,754 charities that have the support of 2,735 celebrities. The most popular causes are children (with 1,683 celebrities), health (1,468) and AIDS (941). The least popular are depression/suicide (57), fair trade (39) and emergency services (13).

Celebrities also like to campaign on issues that are close to their hearts. Elton John has probably done more through interviews to promote gay marriage and gay parenting than any amount of campaigning by pressure groups. In the 1960s the debate about recreational drugs was taken to the public more through musicians than pharmacologists, neuroscientists or health care professionals. When actor George Clooney was arrested during a protest outside the Sudanese embassy in Washington in 2012, the story made front pages and TV headlines around the world, and drew attention to attacks on civilians by the government of Sudan.

Increasingly celebrities are moving into areas of the media that were traditionally the domain of professional authors or reporters.

Television travel programs once presented by seasoned travel correspondents now focus on the experiences of comedians and actors. At
the time of this writing, every book but one in the *Sunday Times* list
of bestselling hardback nonfiction is either by or about a celebrity.
Celebrities are invited to review books, write opinion pieces (often by
dictation to a real journalist), produce television programs, appear on
chat shows (or run chat shows), author diet and exercise books, and
even to become "guest editors" of newspapers and magazines.

A relatively short time ago celebrities were only thought to have
relevant things to say about their particular area of expertise, but now
their opinions on all matters are valued. The Twitter revolution has
meant that even their most mundane observations can be instantly
spread around the world. At the time of writing this book the ten
people with the most followers on Twitter are seven singers (six of
them female), one actor, one reality TV show participant and the president of the United States.

It seems right that some people become better known than others.
Many famous people are justly celebrated because they are highly accomplished at what they do or have entertaining and pleasing person-
alities that make them ideal guests on TV or radio shows. I count
myself privileged to have met so many people who've been skilled as
comedians, songwriters, actors, cartoonists, artists, novelists and
poets. It's always a thrill to spend time with someone who is undeniably gifted and to learn firsthand how they view the world and what
they've done to develop their raw talent.

We tend to feel warm toward people who've brought us pleasure
through their work. Entertainers appeal to us because we think our
joy would be deepened if we could make contact with the person at
the source of that pleasure. How else can we explain the desire people
have to talk to, touch or get an autograph from a famous person?

Getting Things into Proportion

So how should we approach celebrity as Christians? We need to
maintain our perspective. Because someone can write memorable

songs, tell gripping stories or design wonderful clothes doesn't mean that they are worthy of reverence or deference. We can respect someone who has a basic gift that they have subsequently developed, but we shouldn't glorify them as though they had invented the gift itself. We can compliment a woman on her creative use of makeup, but we can't thank her for her fine bone structure or her long legs, because they came direct from God.

When I interview famous people I think of them as equals in that they have been gifted and have used that gift to the best of their ability, just as I believe I have. Their gift may be more highly valued than mine—people will pay an excellent ball player more than they'll ever pay an excellent poet or journalist—but it's no more valuable. It's said that when the Caesars took part in Triumphs—parades after particularly great battlefield victories—a slave would run behind the victor's chariot as the crowds cheered and whisper into Caesar's ear, "Remember that thou art mortal." It's a potent reminder of the potential of celebrity to divorce us from reality.

I also have to bear in mind that most professions don't produce celebrities. Music does, but teaching doesn't. Film does, but nursing doesn't. Who knows the best accountant in the world or the best street sweeper? Many professions are absolutely vital to our well-being (shop assistant, garbage collector) but have no glamour attached to them. Models and actors talk of how challenging their work is, but although they may work long hours the end product not only provides them with money but also attention, respect and praise. People who work with autistic children or cancer patients hardly ever even get their names in the papers.

The question of whether we should ever make fame a life goal is less straightforward that it may first appear. Instinctively the Christian wants to reject it. After all Jesus said, "All those who exalt themselves will be humbled, and those who humble themselves will be exalted" (Lk 14:11). However, there are some professions—like acting or performing music—where fame is not only a measure of how many people you are reaching but of how long your career will endure. Additionally, applause, good reviews and awards are the equivalent of end of term reports for people in the arts. Artists constantly need affirmation in their work.

As a writer I accept that being known by as many people as possible is an important part of my job. I need to promote myself. I need to have confidence in the books I write and to be able to say without fear of displaying sinful pride, "This is worth reading. It's good." I need to do things that draw attention to me. I need to be photographed and written about. I even need to sign autographs! It's possible, I believe, to do these things without being enslaved by the idea of fame. It's possible to do them without believing that they make me any more important than anyone else. I still get a kick out of seeing my name on the spine of a new book, but at the same time I don't kid myself that it is leading to immortality. Salvation comes not by being known by the crowds, but being known by God.

Patty Heaton, best known as the star of the long-running TV show *Everybody Loves Raymond*, makes the point that perspective is needed:

I have found that there is a certain amount of compartmentalization that must take place to maintain the balance. I love wearing a beautiful gown, getting blinded by the flash of camera lights, and winning awards! It's fantastic, and I wish everyone could experience it! But God was gracious to me in His timing— he withheld all of it from me until I was married and had a family. That life-changing experience cemented in me what was truly important, and freed me to fully enjoy any success that came along, knowing that I would trade it in a heartbeat for my kids. It's been like stepping onto a roller coaster, whooping with the thrill of the ride, then getting off, turning to the family and saying "That was fun! What do you want to do next?"[6]

The Rise of the Celebocracy

Celebrity has created a new aristocracy. A century ago working-class and middle-class people took their cues from the wealthy. It was the fashions and lifestyles of the upper classes that fascinated them, and the newspapers would report regularly on the goings on of the various lords, ladies, barons and princesses who sailed between Europe, America and the Far East. Now the celebrity class sets the trends. When an aristocrat has this sort of influence today, it's not because of breeding but because of celebrity. Princess Diana was admired more for her style, poise and looks than for her royal lineage. Princess Anne never had that sort of attention.

At the time of the Gospels it seems that "the rich" occupied the strata where we have placed celebrities. They were the ones most likely to be envied, emulated and pandered to. Jesus never taught anyone to despise them, but he did make the point that it was difficult for these people to enter the kingdom of heaven. Why would this be? It can only have been because their wealth and everything that went with it created an obstacle. They were relying on their status, on how other people perceived them, and were therefore less likely to rely on something or someone else.

The rich back then, like celebrities today, would be preferred as guests at feasts. They added glamour and style. They turned a meal into a talking point. Maybe some would only come to the feast if they thought some rich people were going to be there. Yet when Jesus talks of a feast he suggests that rather than the "rich neighbors," his listeners should invite "the poor, the crippled, the lame, the blind" (Lk 14:13). He turns the accepted hierarchy on its head. He puts the people who typically couldn't even get on the guest list in the seats of honor, while the VIPs are turned away.

Boorstin points out that that one of the major differences between the famous people of the past and the celebrities of the modern age is that fame often didn't even arrive in the famous person's lifetime. It was something bestowed on them by future generations. Celebrity, on the other hand, could be achieved in an instant (and could also be lost in an instant). Now we have the power to manufacture fame, it doesn't matter if the person in question is great or not. Fame once had to be earned; now it can be bought or manufactured.

In 1967 the British journalist Malcolm Muggeridge wrote,

In the past if someone was famous or notorious, it was for something—as a writer or an actor or a criminal; for some talent or distinction or abomination. Today one is famous for being famous. People who come up to me on the street or in public places to claim recognition nearly always say: "I've seen you on the telly!" It is very rare indeed for them to recall anything one has said, and even when they do they more often than not get it wrong. They are the viewers, one is the viewed.[7]

Heroic Qualities

It's said that you can tell the deep values of a culture by the people it chooses as heroes. If a culture values self-sacrifice it will honor self-sacrificial people. If it values peace it will value peacemakers. Some of our contemporary heroes are truly worthy men and women who've worked for peace, justice, equality and freedom, but many of them are mere celebrities looked up to because of their looks, wealth, sexual prowess and access to the "good things of life."

Christians are not immune to the cult of celebrity. Evangelists and church leaders can become stars with all the trappings of stardom, and often all the sins as well. They dress, act, live and make money like stars. Some of them use their stardom as proof of God's blessing. At the same time attempts are often made to turn stars into evangelists on the mistaken assumption that the power that has convinced people to buy records or see films will be able to convince people to follow Jesus. But so often the image that has made the celebrity is only a partial truth (or a complete fabrication); it's the "aura" that Nixon's image makers discussed and therefore how can something illusory be used to persuade people of ultimate reality?

The Bible doesn't decry fame as such. The Jews very deliberately kept alive the names of the great. They built memorials to them, passed on stories of their exploits and sang songs about them. Joseph became famous because of his rescue (Gen 45:7), Joshua for his leadership

(Josh 6:27), Solomon for his wisdom, prosperity, proverbs and songs (1 Kings 4:31; 10:7), David for his military victories (1 Chron 14:17), Mordecai for his trustworthiness (Esther 9:4), Jesus for his preaching and healing (Mt 4:24). Even God speaks of his reputation as "fame" (Is 66:19). Paul commends the Thessalonian church for being an example to churches in Macedonia and Achaia (1 Thess 1:7).

It's not fame that is the issue but what the fame is for and how we use its influence. Fame should never be employed to arouse the sort of worship that only God deserves or to delude people into thinking that the famous person is intrinsically of more value than others. When Paul and Barnabas came to Lystra the locals mistook them for gods. A modern PR adviser would regard this as a coup, the ultimate creation of an aura. But the two first-century missionaries disabused the Lystrans saying, "Friends, why are you doing this? We too are only human, like you" (Acts 14:15).

The Virtuous Person

A key question for Christians to ask is what qualities deserve to be celebrated and how do these differ from what we now see being celebrated in popular culture? Virtues are scattered throughout the Bible, but it's instructive to look at the description of a "virtuous woman" in Proverbs 31, and the expectations of a man wanting to become a church overseer in 1 Timothy 3. The woman is praised for her strength, wisdom, dignity, industry, kindness and trustworthiness, among other things. The man needed to be temperate, sober minded, orderly, hospitable, gentle and a good husband and father. Contrast these with the qualities highlighted in two randomly selected contemporary celebrity magazines: (of women) "sassy," "headstrong," "chic," "stylish," "stunning," "cool," "toned," "powerful," "successful," "glamorous," "confident"; (of men) "super-fit," "fun," "handsome," "hunky," "playboy," "heart-throb," "stud," "fun."

Not only does celebrity tend to inflate peoples egos, but the public also wants celebrities that have inflated egos because it makes them watchable. Humility and self-control don't make good stories, but arrogance and recklessness do. People want their stars to be larger than life. They want them to do things that they dream of but don't have the courage, money or opportunity to do. The media will happily report on stars whose lives are spiraling out of control, whereas someone exhibiting the seven cardinal virtues would be considered to be boring.

It is difficult to be both famous and humble because everything in the experience of fame vies against humility. How is it possible to obey the command "Do not think of yourself more highly than you ought" (Rom 12:3) while being deluged with approval, attention and fan worship? How is it possible to be humble and count others better than yourself (Phil 2:3) when engaged in self-promotion? The best way of dealing with fame is with a healthy skepticism. Being known by a lot of people can be destructive; it encourages someone to lose perspective of their true significance, but it can be helpful if it provides an audience that can be inspired, connected with each other or urged to do good things.

When asked about his work to relieve Africa of the burden of debt in 2006, Bono said,

> It's an opportunity for us in the West to show our values, because a lot people are not sure we have any—to show what we are made of, to see a continent in crisis and demonstrate what we can do. I see it as an opportunity for me to put this ridiculous thing called celebrity to some use. Celebrity is ridiculous and silly and it's mad that people like me are listened to—you know, rap stars and movie stars. You know, rather than nurses and farmhands and others. But it is currency. Celebrity is currency, so I wanted to use mine effectively.[8]

Questions for Reflection or Discussion

- Is it right that some people become famous? Is there anything intrinsically wrong about fame?

- Is it possible to distinguish between fame and celebrity?
- In what easy way can fame be seen as a secular form of salvation?
- Can you think of instances where fame appears to have destroyed someone's life?
- Have you ever met a famous person? Describe your feelings beforehand, during the meeting and afterwards.
- Do celebrities make good advocates for causes?
- Do you think that a famous person who has become a Christian is likely to bring about more conversions than an unknown but highly articulate pastor?
- Do social networking sites encourage us to develop an image and court a minor type of fame through "likes" and "friends"?
- Should "Christian celebrity" be an oxymoron?
- What do you think Bono meant by "Celebrity is a currency," and was he right?

General Books on Fame, Image and Celebrity

Boorstin, Daniel J. *The Image: A Guide to Pseudo-Events in America.* New York: Vintage, 1962.

Borkowski, Mark. *The Fame Formula: How Hollywood Fixers, Fakers and Star Makers Created the Celebrity Industry.* London: Pan, 2009.

The Celebrity Culture Reader. Edited by P. David Marshall. London: Routledge, 2006.

Gabler, Neal. *Life: The Movie—How Entertainment Conquered Reality.* New York: Vintage, 2000.

Rojek, Chris. *Fame Attack: The Inflation of Celebrity and Its Consequences.* London: Bloomsbury, 2012.

A Christian Perspective

Ward, Pete. *Gods Behaving Badly: Media, Religion and Celebrity Culture.*
Waco, TX: Baylor University Press, 2012.

Five Suggestions for Action (If You're Already Famous)

- Take fame with a pinch of salt. It can disappear as quickly as it arrived.

- Don't lose contact with your old friends. They will keep you grounded and remind you of who you really are.

- Share your blessings with as many people as you can.

- If fame is a currency, spend it wisely.

- Don't allow yourself to be exploited by churches and Christian organizations. Just because you're well known doesn't mean you're wise, spiritually mature or called to preach.

7

Fashion

The Language of Clothes

†

As I sit in my study writing this chapter, I am wearing a pair of blue jeans. My reason for wearing jeans is entirely practical. They're warm, durable, relatively inexpensive and don't crease like suit trousers. If coffee spills or ink drips, it doesn't really matter. If the bottoms fray, no one cares. Because I work at home I'm not on display. As long as I'm respectable enough to answer a knock at the door, I'm respectable enough.

Yet jeans have played another role in my life. When I bought my first pair of Levi 501s from a boutique in Carnaby Street in 1965, it was because I wanted to make a fashion statement. They were then the most expensive clothing item I'd ever bought. I didn't want just a pair of blue jeans but a pair of Levi jeans because I wanted other people to notice the label and admire my taste. I didn't consider practicalities. I was buying them so that I would be identified as a mod, the latest British youth subculture.

It then became fashionable not only to have Levi blue jeans but also to fade them. This was long before they could be bought pre-faded. This was to give the jeans character, to convey the impression that both you and the jeans had been through (and survived) some tough and interesting times. Theories abounded about soaking them in brine, cleaning them with domestic scrubbing brushes, wearing them in the bath to shrink and thrashing them with sticks. The person with the faded jeans was more respected than the person with the nice new dark-blue jeans that hadn't been "worn-in."

The next stage was ripped jeans. During the early 1970s it became cool not merely to have jeans that were losing their color but were also losing their threads. The most character-filled jeans were the ones with giant tears in the knees. Then came various patches that could be used to cover the emerging holes. The point of patches was not to merge with the denim but to be very pronounced, often made from entirely different material. They were displayed like medals. Neil Young was so proud of his patched jeans that he featured them prominently on the back cover of his 1970 album *After the Goldrush*.

Clothing as Communication

The point I'm making is that clothing has always operated on two levels simultaneously. On one level we simply need clothing for protection, warmth and modesty. We will often choose clothes by considering how long they will last, whether they can be repaired, whether they're appropriate for the season or climate, and whether they're comfortable. On another level we need clothes that communicate messages because we use clothes to let people know how we feel about ourselves, what we aspire to, what we believe in and, ultimately, how we feel about the world around us and our status in it. As James Laver says of clothes in his book *Style in Costume*, "They are nothing less than the furniture of the mind made visible."[1]

When teenagers began to adopt jeans in the 1950s, they weren't just looking for something serviceable, although jeans were both functional and adaptable. They were taking an item of clothing developed in the 1870s for working people (mostly lumberjacks, farmers, cowboys and railroad workers) and recontextualizing it as leisure wear for students. There was an element of rebellion in what they were doing. People who could afford not to endure the hardships that required the protection of what was described as "riveted menswear" were choosing to identify with the proletariat. A similar thing had happened to suntans in the 1920s. Prior to Coco Chanel returning from the French Riviera with accidentally browned skin, a suntan was considered to be the sign of the poor person who had to work outdoors, whereas lily-white skin was the privilege of the rich who could afford to remain at home. Today, a suntan lets people know how much leisure time you can afford and pale skin how little you can afford.

Blue jeans got a tremendous boost from the film stars Marlon Brando (*The Wild One*, 1953) and James Dean (*Rebel Without a Cause*, 1955). Brando had already caused a fashion revolution after his appearance in *A Streetcar Named Desire* (1951), where he wore a T-shirt. Again it was a case of taking a lowly garment and elevating it. Older people who had grown up believing that blue jeans were for manual labor and T-shirts were to be worn under top shirts were alarmed at the trend because it felt like an attack on propriety.

However, jeans and a T-shirt rapidly became the uniform of the American young. In his book *Civilization: The West and the Rest* historian Niall Fergusson argues that blue jeans are the perfect example of how capitalism conquered the world. They not only became symbolic of American popular culture, along with rock music, but also were feared by countries behind the Iron Curtain who thought that once their young people adopted them they would no longer be happy with communist ideology. Today blue jeans are the most ubiquitous item of clothing in the world.

The bleaching and premature aging of denim, besides creating a badge of honor and giving jeans a story, was also a snub to clean and neat conformism. How strange that the richest young people in the richest country in the world would deliberately try to create the impression of poverty and wretchedness by turning expensive jeans into damaged goods with rips and tears! In a similar way to the case of the suntan, it was now only the relatively well off who could afford to damage their Levis.

Social Indications

Because clothes are expressive of how we feel about the world and ourselves, they have always acted as a barometer of the mood of the times. Nothing illustrates the Victorian ethos better than the clothes they wore. They tended to be dark, sober, practical, dignified and sexually muted. The advent of the pill, the rise of relativistic thinking and the popularity of recreational drugs in the 1960s brought psychedelic fabrics, unisex clothing, hipsters, tight jeans and the miniskirt. An age devoted to hard work, thrift and self-control developed austere clothing. An age devoted to leisure, conspicuous consumption and carefree abandon developed clothing that was gaudy and frivolous.

An interesting study could be carried out on the rise of tattoos and piercings over the past forty years. How did these markings, once the preserve of sailors, soldiers, deviants, criminals and bikers, spread to the middle classes? Part of the answer has to be that the traditional resistance to these practices, which owed a lot to the Judeo-Christian teaching that the body belonged to God, has weakened at the same time that paganism has gained luster. Rather than having God's mark on them, which is what circumcision meant for the Jews, they want their own mark. A tattoo or a piercing says, "I am claiming ownership of my body. Don't invade me or try to control me."

Among devotees of body modification talk about piercing and tattooing is often semireligious. Apparently the top five reasons for getting pierced are to forge self-identity, to achieve a higher state of consciousness, to fulfill a spiritual need, to achieve group affiliation or disaffiliation, and to enhance sexuality. According to a tattooist named Woody quoted in the *Guardian* in 2010:

A tattoo gives you something to live for. . . . A tattoo offers you something personal and fun and exciting in a world that can be drab and grey. People's souls are crying out for that. Tattoos are great for finding out more about yourself, for meeting people, for getting up in the morning and thinking "Look at that! A work of art in progress."[2]

Without getting into the morality of tattooing (I found one Christian website where it was argued that the prohibition against cutting and marking the body in Leviticus 19:28 extended to face painting and writing phone numbers on the back of the hand!), it's a historical fact that pagan cultures have encouraged markings on the skin, whereas Jewish and Christian cultures have forbidden it. When this changes it signifies not just a mere change in taste but also an underlying change in views about the body, sacredness and human autonomy.

Designs on You

Most of us buy clothes simply because we like them. When we're in the clothing store we are not considering philosophy, sociology or history. However, the designers of the clothes we rifle through are familiar with these areas of knowledge. They will have studied at an art school or fashion college and will know that alterations in public taste are intimately connected to ideological shifts. They will study costumes from other eras and cultures but will also find inspiration in other art forms and in the burning issues of the day. The hairdresser Vidal Sassoon, for example, famous for introducing geometrical haircuts for women, was inspired by the German Bauhaus art movement of the 1930s and postwar British architecture. Alexander McQueen's influences ranged from historical books and German puppetry to cult films and Charles Darwin's *The Origin of Species*. Vivienne Westwood, who pioneered the punk fashion of ripped T-shirts and bondage trousers, studied deviant literature and fetish catalogs. Her philosophy of fashion at the time was "Clothes should be a way of kicking society where it hurts."[3]

Designers are often compelled by political, social and moral agendas. Their private lives—who they associate with, what relationships they're in, how they seek pleasure—will affect their whole outlook. It was designers involved in drugs who developed a fashion style known as "heroin chic." In 1996 the *Los Angeles Times* described collections by Alexander McQueen and Helmut Lang as exhibiting "morning-after-a-rough-night-out style and the seductive nature of death."[4] It's no surprise that designers who inhabit the netherworlds of deviant sex will find inspiration in the imagery of androgyny, pornography and prostitution. McQueen said, "My collections have always been auto-biographical, a lot to do with my sexuality and coming to terms with the person I am—it was like exorcising my ghosts."[5]

Mary Quant, who named the miniskirt in 1964, saw the fashion as an expression of a significant shift in sexual morality. In her view the skirts communicated the message "I'm very sexy. I enjoy sex. I feel provocative, but you're going to have a job to get me. You've got to excite me and you've got to be jolly marvelous to attract me. I can't be bought, but if I want you, I'll have you."[6]

We should at least be aware of how ideas are communicated through fashion and of the thinking behind the design of clothes. We should be alert to our own motivations for choosing what we wear. Creating an impression is an important and natural consideration. We want others to believe that we're clean, trustworthy, design conscious, dynamic, energetic, up to date, serious or casual. To go to a first interview dressed in shorts and sandals, unless applying to be a lifeguard, would be a mistake, just as sunbathing in a tuxedo would be a mistake. Appropriateness is important. In the same way, to create the impression that we're wealthier than we are, or even more switched-on than we are, would be a mistake. It's possible to deceive through clothing. Some might argue that the whole point of clothing is to deceive—to make us look taller, thinner, sexier and more affluent than we really are!

The Naked Truth

The Christian starting point has always been that clothes are necessary, even if only a loincloth. The Bible story of Adam and Eve covering their nakedness after succumbing to temptation is not an easy one to interpret. It appears to say that bodily shame is a result of the fall, yet if there was no one else present to lust after the first couple or for them to lust after, and they were (literally) made for each other, how could any inappropriateness take place? Some commentators believe that the nakedness described was of a moral and spiritual nature, and that after sinning their guilt made them feel so exposed that they needed a covering that only God could provide. Critics have cited the passage as a source of self-loathing about the flesh, arguing that Christianity teaches us that we would be better off without bodies and bodily appetites.

Yet the Bible states that the body is marvelous, so marvelous that the Son of God took on a human body and that this body was resurrected following his death. According to the psalmist we are "fearfully and wonderfully made" (Ps 139:14). The Song of Solomon pictures two lovers admiring each other's bodies. Clothes are not to conceal something that we should be embarrassed about but to provide dignity and modesty for something we should be proud of. Nakedness itself isn't bad. Priests had to take care not to expose their genitals when officiating by wearing special undergarments, but David, when alone, danced seminaked before God (2 Sam 6:14) and Peter apparently stripped down when out fishing on Galilee (Jn 21:7).

Yet there are parts of our bodies that are not for sharing with everyone. The Old Testament often speaks of "seeing" someone's nakedness as a euphemism for sexual intimacy. The implication is that when you are naked you are making yourself vulnerable and are appearing in front of someone in absolute openness and honesty. There is acknowledgment of this even in a deeply secular society where it is considered wrong to expose yourself in public, touch someone "inappropriately" or spy on someone undressing. If sex is nothing more than a basic appetite like eating, and our bodies are not objects of shame, why then do we safeguard certain areas? Why is *privates* a euphemism for genitalia? Why do changing rooms have doors?

There have been Bible followers who've argued that nakedness was next to godliness. The Adamites of the second to fourth centuries believed that by shedding their clothes they were returning to the innocence of the Garden of Eden prior to the fall. There has been a trend in recent years to disconnect nakedness from any sense of inappropriateness. Films such as *The Full Monty* and *Calendar Girls* attempted to make it seem innocent, playful and inconsequential. The American photographer Spencer Tunick set up large nude spectacles in public places. In 2003 he photographed 500 nudes in the London store Selfridges and a crowd of 7,000 in Barcelona. Such artists argue that shame is a social construct, most specifically a product of Christian theology, and the way to get rid of the shame is to remove the fig leaf. The more often this happens, the less shame is felt. Tunick says that his subjects "become abstractions that challenge or reconfigure one's views of nudity and privacy." New York artist Jeff Koons married a porn star known as La Cicciolina in the 1990s and created super-realistic photographs and sculptures of them making love under the title "Made in Heaven." He claimed that the goal of his work was "to remove guilt and shame. There's no judgment. There's just acceptance."

It's a paradox that when we're stripped of our clothes in public we lose rather than gain our identity. Naked we are just "a man" or "a woman" without anything to communicate our individuality, tastes or style. When the Nazis herded Jews into the gas chambers they took away their clothes as a final act of humiliation. Removing people's clothes against their will is almost always degrading. As C. S. Lewis observed, "Nudity emphasises common humanity and soft-pedals what is individual. In that way we are 'more ourselves' when clothed."[7]

Dressing to Kill

Given that clothes are necessary, there are basic ethical considerations that should inform our choices. When we buy designer-label clothing are we buying for reasons of beauty (this is a well-designed item) or for reasons of pride (this will impress others)? The seventeenth-century mathematician and Christian thinker Blaise Pascal noted that many of the upper-class fashions of his day displayed power rather than beauty. He wrote,

> It is not mere vanity to be elegant, because it shows that a lot of people are working for you. Your hair shows that you have a valet, a perfumer, etc. . . .
>
> The more hands one employs the more powerful one is. Elegance is a means of showing one's power.[8]

How much style is just a disguise for one-upmanship?

Designer labels, taking advantage of our craving for recognition and power, make us pay for the privilege. In 2010 the *Wall Street Journal* reported that True Religion's Super T jeans, identifiable by their oversized white stitching, cost around $50 a pair to make, were sold wholesale at $152 and retailed for $335. *Time* magazine revealed what we probably already knew, which is that an expensive pair of designer sunglasses offer no better protection than a pair bought for $50, sometimes considerably less. "If you're paying $300 for sunglasses, you're buying them to look cool and impress people," it concluded. "You're not buying them for the sake of your eyes' health."[9] At this point, buying clothes becomes a spiritual issue. If it's wrong to covet your neighbor's possessions it's presumably equally wrong to acquire possessions with the subsidiary aim of making our neighbors covet them.

Designer labels easily become contemporary idols, if by *idol* we mean something that encourages extravagant devotion. The prestige given to certain brands is out of all proportion to their usefulness and actual material value. Although the clothing has gained prominence because of the quality of its style, very often the reason people opt for designer labels is to communicate a message of privilege to other people: "Look at me. Not only do I have taste but I have a lot of money to spend on clothes." In previous ages the divide was between those who had breeding, education, property, manners and social standing, and those who didn't. Today it is more often between those who have money and fame and those who don't, and one of the most effective ways of signaling status is through showing off your Gucci, Armani, Cartier or Louboutin.

From Sweatshop to Catwalk

A related ethical issue is that of the working conditions under which some clothing is made. In order to make higher profits Western labels and stores have their clothes made as cheaply as possible in countries where there is no minimum wage, health and safety regulations or trade unions' protection. Newspaper investigations in 2007 found that a range of clothes designed by model Kate Moss for Topshop were being made in Mauritian sweatshops where workers were shipped in from Bangladesh, India and Sri Lanka to work seventy-hour weeks for the equivalent of 62 cents an hour. Tommy Hilfiger had clothes made in American-owned Saipan because it allowed him use "Made in the USA" on the labels even though Saipan had no minimum wage laws.

When Bono and his wife, Ali Hewson, founded the Edun clothing label in 2005, they committed themselves to providing work for African manufacturers in fully protected environments. They also committed themselves to four principles that exemplified Christian principles: Respect for the people who make the product. Respect for the community where it is made. Respect for the materials used. Respect for the consumer who buys the clothing. It's a small revolution, but a revolution nonetheless.

Fashion should be an enjoyable pursuit involving imagination, variety, choice and opportunities for celebration and self-expression. Too often it becomes dictatorial. It works to breed dissatisfaction and insecurity in order to sell new collections. It encourages pride, arrogance and greed. It educates people to find their identity in what they wear rather than in who they are. Fashion models set standards of body shape that few are able to emulate. Why do catwalk models almost always maintain a stony-faced, haughty, jaded look as though they are defying anyone to do or say anything that would impress them? It would seem that fashion houses are keen to identify their product with people who look superior and standoffish rather than people who look cheerful and content. Alexander McQueen said, "I want people to be afraid of the women I dress."[10]

The Mind Made Visible

Aside from basic ethical questions it's good to be aware of what our clothes are telling others. It's not wrong to buy clothes because of their impact. The old saying that "first impressions count" is very true. We buy fine clothes because they reassure people that we're in charge, have taste and respect ourselves. A white shirt and necktie are not very practical clothes for men. A tie serves no useful purpose. However, their deeper value lies in the fact that if you can keep a white shirt looking white and pressed, and can keep a tie clean and neatly knotted, it reveals personal pride, self-control and consideration for others. To wear a dirty or torn shirt for an important meeting would suggest that you're not serious about the outcome.

Some Christians have resisted the dictates of fashion by not caring about their personal appearance, but this too communicates a message. Christians have often been not merely out of step with fashion but dowdy, boring and unadventurous. Their clothes suggest that they have no pride in their bodies, are content to be disconnected from the times they live in, don't value creativity or imagination and have no desire to provide aesthetic pleasure for those they meet. Sometimes it appears that some Christians are so uncomfortable with the sexual nature of their bodies that they try to conceal it lest anyone should become attracted. If, as James Laver believes, clothes are "the furniture of the mind made visible," what do shabby and dull clothes tell us about the minds that choose them?

I've known many young people who dismiss Christians as boring simply based on the way they look. This may not be fair, but it illustrates the point that it's assumed that our dress reflects who we are, and if we dress in a boring and outdated way there are many onlookers who will conclude that our faith must likewise be boring and outdated. If we dress in a way that suggests we're not happy with our bodies, they will think that we represent a faith that doesn't like the body. If we proclaim an exciting, vibrant, creative, liberating God and also declare that this God is living within us, isn't it realistic for people to expect this to make itself visible through our personal appearance?

It was the hippies who challenged the dull formality of Western clothing, and the repercussions are still being felt. In the era of "the man in the gray flannel suit" the emphasis was on people as part of the military-industrial machine where uniformity was seen as a great virtue.[11] The hippies found the machine concept dehumanizing and they instead stressed individuality and celebration. They favored natural fabrics over synthetic material, casual wear over formal attire, bright colors over dull shades, handmade over mass-produced, native cultures over advanced civilizations, beautiful objects over functional garments.

There is so much to commend in this approach. Although the Bible acknowledges the temptation to use clothes as tools on manipulation—Jesus said that the teachers of the law desired "to walk around in flowing robes and be greeted with respect in the marketplaces" (Mk 12:38)—it is not against "fine raiment." Joseph's father gave him an extraspecial coat (either of many colors or with long sleeves) that caused him to be envied by his brothers. Isaac presented Rebecca with "gold and silver jewelry and articles of clothing" (Gen 24:53). Jesus wore a tunic that was "seamless, woven in one piece from top to bottom" that involved more workmanship than a traditional garment (Jn 19:23-24).

It's perfectly in keeping with the scriptural outlook to have clothes that express our uniqueness, that are objects of beauty and that bring aesthetic pleasure by means of the feel of the fabric, the beauty of the design and the enhancement of the figure. Clothes can even have humor or make allusions to pop culture. When Jesus described God's way of clothing us he drew a comparison with the way in which he clothes "the flowers of the field," which he said were more gloriously dressed than even King Solomon (Mt 6:28-29). The way God clothes flowers is with beauty, delicacy and outrageous color.

Mixed Messages

The only warnings against clothes are against those that send out messages that are contrary to what we're called to be. Deuteronomy 22:5 calls for demarcations to be kept between the sexes: "A woman must not wear men's clothing, nor a man wear women's clothing." What's now referred to as "gender bending" may seem to be nothing more than a bit of an imaginative mashup, but it is usually rooted in moral relativism. The undergirding philosophy is that gender distinctions are unimportant. When Marlene Dietrich wore a man's top hat and tails in the 1930 film *Morocco*, she knew what she was doing, as did David Bowie when he wore a Michael Fish dress on the cover of the British release of his 1970 album *The Man Who Sold the World*.

The most specific command regarding dress comes in 1 Timothy 2:9-10. Paul directed the command to women, presumably because then as now women place more importance on clothes and jewelry, and spend more money on them, but it's applicable to men. The specific context was appropriate wear for worship, so Paul may have had in mind the potential for clothes to distract in a church gathering or the inconsistency of claiming humility before God in prayer and yet being anything but humble in dress. "I also want women to dress modestly, with decency and propriety, adorning themselves, not with braided hair or gold or pearls or expensive clothes, but with good deeds, appropriate for women who profess to worship God."

The overall thrust of the command is that our attractiveness should principally reside in who we are and what we do, not in what we wear. *Modesty* has two meanings. One is having a moderate estimation of who we are, and the other is being decent and observing propriety. Muslims from Asia or Africa coming to the West are often shocked by what they see as the sexually arousing nature of the way a lot of women dress. The stage wear of female singers such as Madonna, Beyoncé and Rihanna has become increasingly erotic. Commentators point out that it sends the message to young girls that the only sure way of getting attention is to be alluring. When in 2011 the *Daily Mail* interviewed girls outside British clubs who were wearing micro-miniskirts and six-inch "hooker heels," the most common reason girls gave for dressing in "stripper chic" was that it boosted confidence by making them the center of attention. One male onlooker commented that he liked girls dressing this way "because you get to think whether you want to sleep with them later."[12]

Some of these styles have been directly influenced by pornography and prostitution. There are girls who openly boast about this connection. "It does make me feel more confident," says one. "I'm a slut, but it's OK to be a slut as long as you use protection."[13] In her 2011 video for her song *S&M*, Rihanna wore a dress emblazoned with the words *whore* and *slut*, intentionally trying to deprive the terms of their moral connotations. Psychologist Dr. Linda Papadopoulos, who has done research into the sexualization of girls, says,

> We are inheriting more from the porn culture than we realize— everything from fake nails to fake tans. Porn has become mainstream. The sad thing is that the confidence of these girls has become directly proportionate to how they look. It doesn't come from what they have achieved or what skills they have learned. It comes from how much attention and looks they get from men.[14]

It's possible to be sexually attractive without revealing large expanses of body and deliberately trying to stir lust, just as it's possible to be fully appreciative of someone's sexuality without being led into temptation.

We can't ignore the fact that one of the primary functions of clothing is to make ourselves attractive, particularly to partners or prospective partners. We want to show others that we respect and care about ourselves. We naturally want to draw the eye away from our weaker physical characteristics and draw it toward those aspects we are more proud of. It's no good reasoning that because we want people to accept us for who we are we're more likely to be successful if we leave ourselves looking exactly the way we look without the help of shampoo, comb, brush, soap, toothpaste and other enhancements. The Bible is realistic when it reports that people chose partners who were "fair to look upon."

It's also undeniably true that when we're young we want to enjoy the way we look, because we know that we're not going to look that way for long. It's no good waiting until you're fifty to experiment with hairstyles, because by that time there won't be that much hair to experiment with. Hipsters and trousers with narrow legs look comical on someone with a spreading waistline, and so it's best to enjoy them while you can. Youth is worth celebrating because it's a unique period between childhood and full adulthood, when your body is at its best and responsibilities are minimal. The danger comes when we worship at the fount of youthfulness and see it as a goal rather than a stage.

The word translated *decency* in 1 Timothy 2:9-10 is translated as "sensibly" in the Revised Standard Version of Scripture, "prudently" in the Modern Language Bible and "shamefacedness" in the King James Version. *Shamefacedness* doesn't mean "ashamedness." In the biblical use it means "bashfully," in other words in a slightly shy way rather than pompously or arrogantly. The point of a lot of fashion clothing is the exact opposite. The point is to intimidate and exert power over others. Think of the implicit violence contained in language such as "power dressing," "stunning" and "dressed to kill." Think of Alexander McQueen's comment, "I'm not big on women looking naïve. There has to be a sinister aspect, whether it's melancholy or sadomasochist."[15]

The words translated "with propriety" is "seemly" in the RSV, "becoming" in the Modern Language Bible and "sobriety" in the KJV. The New Testament Greek word suggests moderation and self-control. Clothes that are unseemly, unbecoming or unsuitable draw attention for attention's sake. The request that clothes not be expensive must be partly for the same reason but also partly because wasteful spending is an insult to the poor. How can we justify extravagance in a world of poverty, hunger and sickness?

Something Beautiful for God

There is no specifically Christian way of dressing, but there are Christian considerations about dress. We need on the one hand to avoid dressing in a way that that makes it appear that we are ashamed of who we are, take no delight in aesthetics and have a low view of the body, and on the other to avoid wearing clothes designed to encourage sinful pride in ourselves or lust and envy in others. Above all, we need to avoid adopting fashions that say things contrary to what we truly believe, and that involves tuning in to what Alison Lurie called "the language of clothes."[16] Lady Gaga does this. She says that she's "a true academic" when it comes to her style and fashions. "There's nothing I've ever put on my body that I didn't understand where it came from, the reference of it, and who inspired it. There's always a story or a concept that I'm telling."[17]

We should encourage Christians involved in the fashion industry to design clothes that are exciting and beautiful and that can be produced in ethical ways. We should encourage them to come up with concepts that are informed by their view of the world in ways that they're maybe not even aware of. That's what the Shakers did with their furniture design in the eighteenth and nineteenth centuries. Drawing from their religious beliefs they felt that furniture should be simple, elegant, useful and of high quality. What they made was uncluttered and had clean lines. It continues to inspire the world of design. It's not the only way to make furniture inspired by biblical principles, but it's one way. "Don't make something unless it is both necessary and useful," they said. "But if it is both necessary and useful, don't hesitate to make it beautiful."

Questions for Reflection or Discussion

- Are you aware of wearing clothes that tell a story? If so, what are you telling others about yourself?

- Do you feel in control of the story your clothes tell, or is necessity or fashion doing the talking for you?

- Is there any inconsistency between being proud of your body and yet concealing most of it beneath clothing?

- What does the increasing acceptance of nudity tell us about our culture?

- C. S. Lewis claimed that we are "more ourselves" when clothed. Do you think he was right?

- Do we buy designer clothing because it is better made, more economical, more flattering to the figure or for other reasons?

- Is "ethical fashion" a contradiction in terms?

- If we dress in a dull and boring way, does it show that we are (1) lazy, (2) poor, (3) humble, (4) ashamed, or (5) dull and boring?

- Often performers from church backgrounds defend wearing erotic stage costumes by saying that they're celebrating the body that God blessed them with. Is this a reasonable defense?

- Monks and Puritans wore sober clothing to express humility. Cardinals and bishops often wear rich and colorful clothing to express beauty. Can we be both humble and beautiful at the same time?

General Books on the Meaning of Fashion

Barnard, Malcolm. *Fashion as Communication*. London: Routledge, 2002.

Barthes, Roland. *The Language of Fashion*. London: Berg, 2006.

Bolton, Andrew. *Alexander McQueen: Savage Beauty*. New York: Museum of Modern Art, 2011.

Davis, Fred. *Fashion, Culture and Identity*. Chicago: University of Chicago Press, 1994.

Laver, James. *Costume and Fashion: A Concise History*. 5th ed. London: Thames & Hudson, 2012.

―――. *Modesty in Dress*. Abingdon, UK: Heinemann, 1969.

Lurie, Alison. *The Language of Clothes: The Definitive Guide to People-Watching Through the Ages*. Boston, MA: Holt, 2000.

Svendsun, Lars. *Fashion: A Philosophy*. London: Reaktion, 2006.

Five Suggestions for Action

- Read interviews with fashion designers in order to discover their influences, ideas and intentions.

- Check through the clothes in your wardrobe and work out what your favorite items are saying about you and your view of the world.

- If you're a designer, create clothes that are beautiful, elegant, enhancing, ethical and useful. Be governed by an excitement about doing right rather than a fear of doing wrong.

- If you're a designer, imagine that there are styles of clothing inspired by your beliefs that haven't yet been contemplated and that could be as unique and inspiring as the chairs of the Shakers or the fugues of Bach.

- Enjoy your clothing as an expression of who you were made to be rather than a purely functional requirement for warmth, protection and covering.

8

Ever-Greater Thrills

The Search for Sensation

†

When we talk of human fear we first of all talk of fear of death, then maybe fear of the unknown, the dark, pain, loneliness or the loss of loved ones. We rarely talk about fear of boredom and yet so much is driven by that fear. We crave change, movement, excitement and novelty because we can't stand being bored. A lot of popular culture is consumed in order to alleviate boredom. If we find the day becoming too tedious, we listen to music, turn on the TV, check Facebook, play a game or maybe even go shopping.

One of the effects of boredom is that we find ourselves alone with our thoughts and questions. We may ponder our mortality, review mistakes we've made or wonder about the purpose and direction of our lives. Some time ago entertainments were commonly called "diversions" because not only did they divert minds away from the hardships of life but also from the roiling mass of ideas produced by self-reflection. Until the eighteenth century the word *amusement* meant something that deceived or cheated. One of the reasons Puritans disapproved of many recreations was that they believed such things could be used to smother the work of the Holy Spirit in producing consciousness of sin. In *A Practical Exposition of the 130th Psalm* (1668) John Owen wrote, "There are also other ways whereby sinful souls destroy themselves by false reliefs. Diversions from their perplexing thoughtfulness pleases them. They will fix on something or other that cannot cure their disease, but shall only make them forget that they are sick."

Also writing in the seventeenth century Blaise Pascal observed, "The sole cause of man's unhappiness is that he does not know how to stay quietly in his room."[1] Pascal believed that people invented diversions to avoid the big questions of life. "You would only have to take away all their cares, and then they would see themselves and think about what they are, where they come from and where they are going. That is why men cannot be too much occupied and distracted, and that is why, when they have been given so many things to do, if they have some time off they are advised to spend it on diversion and sport, and always to keep themselves fully occupied."[2] Maybe T. S. Eliot was thinking something similar when he wrote in the Burnt Norton section of his long poem "The Four Quartets" that humans can't bear much reality.

We all need entertainment in our lives because too much self-absorption, drudgery or inactivity reduces our capacity for enjoyment. The ideal life would have a rhythm of tedium and excitement. Too much inactivity and repetition and we would be in a state of ennui. Too much excitement and we would become satiated. For the sake of our emotional stability we need to be able to cope with both. Hence the old saying "All work and no play makes Jack a dull boy. All play and no work makes Jack a mere toy."

Extravagant Expectations

Two pertinent questions are whether popular culture has become so pervasive that it allows little time for reflection, and whether we are embarked on an increasingly fruitless search for ever-bigger thrills. The comedian Russell Brand comments, "I've noticed from my participation in popular culture that it functions to prevent synaptic connections happening in our minds so we can't think properly."[3] Daniel Boorstin said that we suffer from extravagant expectations. "We expect too much of the world," he wrote in The Image. "Our expectations are extravagant in the precise dictionary sense of the word—'going beyond the limits of reason or moderation.' They are excessive."[4]

One of the great values of popular culture is that it can help "take our minds off things." We need that sort of relief. Any survey carried out to discover what makes a happy marriage will find that "humor" rates highly. Why so? What have wisecracks, puns and leg-pulls got to do with marital harmony? The answer is that humor creates a buffer. If marriages consisted only of intense discussions about things that "really matter," it would be like two bones engaging each other without the benefit of cartilage. Humor relaxes the facial muscles, lightens the mood, dispels anger and neutralizes conflict. It provides space.

In a similar way what we sometimes call "the daily grind" is brightened by entertainment. Seeing a film won't cure depression but it will give temporary relief and can help put things into perspective. Music won't reduce the workload but it can make it more enjoyable. There are suggestions in the Bible that music was played during the construction of buildings (2 Chron 34:12-13) and that songs were sung in the vineyards (Is 16:10). When Saul suffered anxiety his first thought was "to search for someone who can play the lyre" (1 Sam 16:16). This was how David first came into Saul's life. David took his harp and played. "Then relief would come to Saul; he would feel better, and the evil spirit would leave him" (1 Sam 16:23).

But when entertainment is used either to evade the questions and problems of life or becomes the central purpose of life, then it is occupying a position for which it was never intended. For many people the reality of life as described by God is regarded as fantasy, and the fantasies of life as concocted by the entertainment industry are regarded as reality. The writer of Ecclesiastes was a wise man who concluded that life was empty, repetitive, fruitless, boring and without meaning. Having exhausted the possibilities held out by reason and knowledge, he sought consolation in the realm of experiences. If he couldn't get answers to questions, maybe he could at least shield himself from the logic of his conclusions. He tried madness, folly, pleasure, intoxication, food, beauty, possessions,

music, sex and consumerism, but they only led him back to his
original conclusion:

> When I surveyed all that my hands had done
>   and what I had toiled to achieve,
> everything was meaningless, a chasing after the wind;
>   nothing was gained under the sun. (Eccles 2:11)

The Engineering of Thrills

Although there have always been forms of popular culture, diversions
and amusements for the masses, the technological developments that
have taken place in the twentieth and twenty-first centuries have meant
an increased capability for maximizing sensation. In just over one
hundred years we have gone from saucy Mutascope machines to
hardcore online pornography in HD, from silent black and white films
to 3D color movies and computer generated imagery, from kaleido-
scopes to video games. The roller coaster, carousel and Ferris wheel
have given way to amusement park rides that push human fear to an
extreme. Brendan Walker, the world's first "thrill engineer," believes
that the future of these rides exists in psychological stimulation: "The
human body is a limiting factor," he admits. "There are only so many
Gs it can take before it blacks out. So, to make rides scarier, we're having
to move towards mental stimulation, playing on real human fears."[5]

When I first saw a rock band, the musicians had two small speakers
and no stage lighting. One of the last times I saw a band play, the stage
set was 167 feet tall and contained 200 tons of equipment, including a
cylindrical video screen of 411,000 pixels onto which film of the band
was projected. The show was streamed live on YouTube. Sound levels at
rock concerts regularly peak at around 115 decibels, higher than the
recommended level to avoid hearing loss and only ten decibels below
the pain threshold. When The Who recorded their album *Quadrophenia*
the playback sound went up to 160 decibels, the equivalent of the noise
made by Concorde on takeoff. Guitarist Pete Townshend subsequently
suffered hearing loss and now has to wear aids in both ears.

Rather than a straightforward listening and viewing experience, rock concerts have become sensory assaults where you are dazzled visually, aurally and physically. You can often feel your body vibrate with the impact of the bass guitar, and the volume can leave your ears ringing for days after. It's difficult to see how much more could be loaded on the senses of a concert audience.

In every area of popular culture the search is on to outdo whatever it was that came immediately before. Audiences become satiated with familiar forms, and when that happens the experience that once alleviated boredom itself becomes boring. Producers are then forced to find things that are louder, longer, faster, higher and, always, more sensational. The mantra of the true adrenaline junkie is "Too much is not enough."

When reality TV ceased to entertain just through the novelty of unscripted drama, participants had to be manipulated into extreme behavior through injecting stress factors designed by people with psychological training. TV shows such as *Jackass*, *Dirty Sanchez*, *Toyko Shock Boys* and Brazil's *N. O. I. A.*, which featured people performing dangerous, crude, ridiculous and self-injuring stunts, had to constantly push the boundaries not only of human endurance but also of public taste to maintain their "edgy" reputations. It underlines the truth that the writer of Ecclesiastes learned: "The eye never has enough of seeing, / nor the ear its fill of hearing" (Eccles 1:8).

There are still movies that gently stir the deepest emotions and songs that encourage reflection, but there is a constant temptation to stir up the most readily accessible feelings and to do it within as short a time as possible. When we use phrases like *knocked out, pumped up, doubled up, nail biter* or *white knuckle*, we're describing an immediate physical response to a concert, a movie or a comedy show. When *Travel and Leisure* magazine reviewed new theme park rides in 2008, they recommended, "The kind with G forces that will knock you silly and massive free-fall drops that will have you involuntarily laughing and praying for your life."[6]

The Selling of Experiences

As well as chasing ever-greater thrills, popular culture is constantly extending its reach into our lives. Early twenty-first-century technological developments have meant that it's possible to be in permanent phone contact, to listen to music anywhere at any time of day, to share photographs and film footage instantaneously, and to look up information electronically from handheld devices. For a documentary TV series six British teenagers were sent to live in various Amish communities in America.[7] On the first program one of the girls complained that it was a "bit too quiet" for her and that she kept thinking about what she'd be doing at home on her laptop or her phone. One of the boys said much the same thing. He said that even when he was on his own at home in Britain there would always be a TV on in the background. In other words, they both found it difficult to be alone either with nature or their own thoughts. A world without commercially produced popular culture was disorientating.

Many engineers of popular culture products regard "immersive experience" as the ultimate end product. The goal is that consumers will not just feel that they are buying something but they are totally wrapped in it. Emily Brown and Paul Cairns in their 2004 study "A Grounded Investigation of Game Immersion" found that there were three levels to participation in games. The first was engagement, the second was engrossment and the third was total immersion. At the final level the gamer is "cut off from reality" and experiences "detachment to such an extent that the game was all that mattered."[8] The Disney Cruise Line offers programs for children that enable them to enter the worlds of Disney characters: "Parents select programs to create a customized experience for each child."[9]

In 1998 Joe Pine and Jim Gilmore coined the phrase *the experience economy* to describe the economic reality of the West.[10] Their argument was that economies begin with commodities, move to goods as they begin manufacturing, create services and then, finally, sell experiences. They gave the example of coffee. The commodity (enough coffee beans to make a cup of coffee) would cost 2-3 cents. After the beans had been roasted, ground and packaged, they would cost maybe 10-15 cents as goods. Bought as a drink from a coffee stand (a service industry) the price could rise to 50 cents or a dollar. However, a coffee drinking "experience" at Starbucks could cost 3-5 dollars. What is bought from Starbucks is more than a mere cup of coffee. It's an experience signaled through everything from graphics, décor and seating, to sounds, smells and branding.

What Pine and Gilmore found is that we want to buy experiences. For example, we don't just want to "go shopping," we want a shopping experience. Meeting that need are stores that incorporate design elements of movie sets, theater stages and theme parks. Some individual stores and shopping malls are so full of sensation that they become tourist destinations in their own right. We're enticed to cross their thresholds not in order to acquire goods but to imbibe the atmosphere, and while we're imbibing we'll no doubt feel sufficiently warmed to start spending. When Prada opened its New York store in 2001 its promise was "an ongoing experiment to enhance the shopping experience through interactive technology."[11]

Restaurants such as Hard Rock Cafe and Planet Hollywood sell regular food, but customers are willing to pay more because they feel that the music, memorabilia, décor and visual projections give them an experience of the entertainment industry. Planet Hollywood's website promises "the world's one and only dining experience inspired by the glamour of Hollywood."[12] Hard Rock Cafe offers "a special experience to its devoted, ever-expanding clientele."[13] Themed restaurants become tourist spots that people want to visit and return with a souvenir T-shirt, baseball cap or mug, rather than places to buy good food.

The Disneyfication of Destination

Even destinations are packaged and themed. Travel companies are keen not just to sell transport, food and accommodation but "authentic experiences," something complicated by the fact that customer expectation is often based on fiction or a golden period from the past. Safari parks in Kenya and South Africa house their guests in canvas tents that are decked out with the hunter's paraphernalia of the 1920s because despite the fact that gaming is outlawed, travelers still want the experience they saw in *Out of Africa* or read about in a history book. Beale Street in Memphis hasn't been "the home of the blues" for over a half a century, and yet it has been redeveloped, keeping the old fascias, to provide visitors with a safe upmarket replica of what was a seedy, disreputable street best known for music, prostitution, gambling and crime.

Travelers now have to determine whether what they are witnessing is a genuine expression of contemporary indigenous culture or something that has been tailored to fit their expectations. Just as Disney can create a New York street right next to a Parisian boulevard in a corner of a reclaimed swamp in Florida, so it's possible to create replicas of the way things used to be on the very sites where they used to be.

Disneyland, built on the site of an orange grove in Anaheim, California, and Las Vegas, built in the Mojave Desert, Nevada, are the most potent examples of the manufacturing of experience. The whole point of both attractions is to draw the visitor into carefully created fantasy worlds that combine nostalgia, mythology, fairy tale and idealized versions of history. Everything is controlled to create the illusion of places where the normal consequences of life don't pertain. It's possible to stay in Las Vegas for days and never emerge into the sunlight. The abbreviated version of Walt Disney's avowed goal was "to make people happy."

Pine and Gilmore make the point that these experiences always offer the prospect of transformation, and they say, "Consciously . . . or not, all enterprises promote a worldview. Transformation issues cannot be avoided."[14] When we extract commodities from the earth, we transform the earth. Every time something is sold to someone the buyers are transformed into users. Services turn clients into recipients.

Experiences transform guests into participants in the encounter, whether the long-term effects are deleterious or therapeutic.

And transformations turn aspirants into "a new you" with all the ethical, philosophical, and religious implication that phrase implies. All commerce involves moral choice.[15]

The ultimate transformation experience is Christian conversion. We are told that anyone who undergoes it is turned into "a new creature" and is headed toward a "new creation." This experience has two main aspects. It usually begins with a conviction of sin and an apprehension about death. When this feeling of sinfulness and this fear of death is removed by God, the convert feels charged with new life. John Newton put the experience well in his hymn "Amazing Grace":

'Twas grace that taught my heart to fear,
And grace my fears relieved;
How precious did that grace appear
The hour I first believed.[16]

The very same action of grace that produces the fear, removes the fear.

Roller Coaster Psychology

The thrills offered by popular culture often mimic this pattern of fear and resolution. Explaining the psychology of theme park rides the magazine *Popular Mechanics* said, "Thrill rides are designed to trick our bodies and brains into thinking we are in mortal danger. It's the same trick that causes an exhilarating surge in our adrenaline levels."[17] Bill Linkenheimer, president of the American Coaster Enthusiasts, says, "People like to experience fear. . . . You know you aren't REALLY putting yourself in danger. But it's a way of going out of control at crazy speeds without risking your life."[18]

Commentators have speculated as to why such leisure activities have become so popular. One explanation is that it's because we are living at a time of unparalleled personal safety. Life expectancy is longer, regulations protect us from accidents, and we no longer worry about plagues or operations without anesthesia. Yet, the argument goes, we were designed for lives of risk and consequence. When we have no real danger we pay to have it delivered as an "experience."

This is sometimes offered as an explanation for the rise in extreme sports and adrenaline holidays. We have become so used to protective clothing, safety surfaces and the cosseted nature of tourism that we crave life-and-death decisions. Rock climbers, base jumpers, big wave surfers, skydivers and free runners all dice with the unpredictable as do adventurers who motorcycle across barren deserts or sail down crocodile infested rivers.

Could it also be a substitute for the natural fear of death and judgment, and the rewarding joy of salvation? People involved in extreme sports frequently speak of their need to maintain a spark in their lives. In an article titled "What Makes Us Seek Out Fear?" in the magazine *Intelligent Life*, journalist Deidre Fernand quoted one practitioner of coasteering (traveling along a coastline by swimming and rock climbing without using surfboards or boats) as saying, "When we master our fears, the reward is huge. Everything is heightened. I feel good for days." Another interviewee, a teacher by occupation, said, "I have to take these risks to feel fully human, fully alive. It's about joy and intensity." It's hard to read quotes like these and not to think of the words of Jesus such as, "I have come that they may have life, and have it to the full" (Jn 10:10) and "My peace I give you" (Jn 14:27).

Even though these people speak of overcoming fear and receiving joy, it's significant that the reward tends to last for only a few days before it needs to be replenished. But at least they are confronted with their mortality and get a sense of the wonder of human experience. Others use the experiences offered by popular culture simply to muffle the voice of conscience and block out thoughts of a spiritual nature.

The Peace of God

Although God can speak through the earthquake and the whirlwind, there is a special connection between his voice and tranquility. Jesus calms the storm; David says that God leads him "beside quiet waters." In the parable of the sower and the seed it is the "worries of this life and the deceitfulness of wealth" that "choke the word" (Mt 13:22). Jesus' recommendation for praying is to "go into your room, close the door" (Mt 6:6). The "noise" of popular culture can rob people of the quiet time necessary to think about ultimate issues. I am reminded of a poem by Sydney Carter, author of the well-known hymn "Lord of the Dance," in which he says brewing a cup of tea or taking Alka-Seltzer will kill haunting fears and questions.

Churches are not immune from trading in experiences. It's possible to give people uplift through light, sound and waves of communal enthusiasm instead of through doctrine and contemplation, to get them to think religion is exciting because of slick presentation rather than because of the challenge of discipleship, to give them worship experiences rather than worship opportunities. The church should be a place where those frazzled by sensation can come for rest rather than be faced by even more artificially induced thrills.

Excitement, unlike joy, tends to arrive suddenly and disappear just as quickly. It then demands constant top-ups. The things that Jesus promises are much deeper rooted, but last longer. Despite what people may think, he never promises his followers happiness or excitement, but joy and peace. He doesn't even promise adventure or transcendent experiences, but truth and abundance. He doesn't promise a safe passage through life, but the Holy Spirit as comforter. The conclusion isn't that we shouldn't partake in the normal thrills that life offers, but it does suggest that we shouldn't make them our goal, and should always regulate them so that they don't jam the sound of the still small voice of God.

Questions for Reflection or Discussion

- What are your favorite methods for coping with boredom?

- Have you ever been on a thrill ride? Has it tempted you to go for an even bigger thrill?

- Think of some stores you have visited recently that were as much about offering you a shopping experience as offering you products to buy. Did the environment have any effect on the way you spent your money?

- Have you ever been to a tourist destination and felt unsure whether you were experiencing the real thing or an exact replica of the real thing in the place where the real thing once stood?

- Do you think it is a coincidence that extreme sports and adventure travel have become more popular at the same time that life in the West has become safer and more controlled?

- Do you think people ever use manufactured excitement and nonstop entertainment to avoid confronting the big questions of life?

- Is there a substantive difference between excitement and joy?

- What are some of the ways that the church gets in on the act by offering experiences and excitement rather than enlightenment and peace of mind?

- Can you think of instances when people you know have spoken of having their lives transformed by thrilling experiences?

- Have music shows become more sensational and overwhelming during your concert-going life? Do you think they have to reach a point where a limit is reached and a return to simplicity is the only way forward?

General Books

Brymer, Alan. *The Disneyization of Society*. London: Sage, 2004.

Pine, B. Joseph, II, and James H. Gilmore. *The Experience Economy: Work Is Theater and Every Business a Stage*. Boston: Harvard Business School Press, 1999.

Postman, Neil. *Amusing Ourselves to Death: Public Discourse in the Age of Show Business*. New York: Viking, 1985.

Ritzer, George. *Enchanting a Disenchanted World*. Newbury Park, CA: Pine Forge Press, 2005.
Walker, Brendan. *The Taxonomy of Thrill*. London: Aerial Publications, 2005.

A Christian View

Winter, Richard. *Still Bored in a Culture of Entertainment: Rediscovering Passion and Wonder*. Downers Grove, IL: InterVarsity Press, 2002.

Website

Thrill Laboratory: www.thrilllaboratory.com/index.html

Five Suggestions for Action

- Spend a day without TV, radio, movies, mp3 player, iPad, computer or cell phone, and see what you learn about yourself, your thought processes and your dependence on media.

- When you pray, spend some time listening for God rather than always conducting a one-sided conversation.

- The next time you experience boredom, face up to it rather than run away from it. Learn from it rather than avoid it.

- Indulge yourself in some simple entertainment such as storytelling, folk music or a garden swing.

- On your next vacation, go off the beaten track and find somewhere untainted by the tourist industry.

9

Comedy

Laughs, Lies and Truth

✝

Humor is a great tonic. The act of laughing relieves tension, relaxes muscles, increases blood supply, oxygenates the body, boosts the immune system and releases the endorphins that help alleviate pain. Socially it strengthens relationships, defuses conflict, enhances teamwork and makes people appear more attractive. To return to Ecclesiastes, there is a time "for every activity under heaven" and that includes "a time to weep and a time to laugh; / a time to mourn and a time to dance" (Eccles 3:1, 4).

Humor can also help us see the world in new ways. A joking comment can put a problem into perspective. Gentle joshing can prevent us from taking ourselves too seriously. Caricature and impressionism can prick pomposity. Parody can expose weakness in style and argument. Satire can make us aware of prejudices, phobias, untested views and faulty logic. Observational comedy, where quirks and mannerisms are highlighted, brings people together by making them aware of shared but rarely discussed similarities.

Some Christians have argued that the Bible reports Jesus weeping but never laughing or smiling. They have drawn the conclusion that we should avoid jesting. But equally there is no mention of him bathing, cleaning his teeth, washing his clothes or scratching an itch. The lack of specific information proves nothing. Others have found that, taken in context, many of the stories Jesus told were humorous. We have become so familiar with the block of wood in the eye, the camel in the throat and the lamp beneath the bed that we miss the element of incongruity that his audience would have noticed. There is humor elsewhere in the Bible that uses hyperbole, irony, wit, pun, satire, paradox and epigram.

The Bible speaks of laughter in four different ways. There is the laughter of sheer joy. When people who love each other gather there is laughter. Good news produces smiles. There is the laughter of disbelief. When Abraham is told that his hundred-year-old wife is about to get pregnant, he laughs. So does his hundred-year-old wife! Then there is the laughter of scorn. Jeering, sneering and mocking involve laughter. Finally there is the laughter produced by incongruity. Humans behaving like gods are always laughable. God is portrayed laughing in the Psalms at the ridiculous idea that humans think they can take him on and win. We too laugh when people act as Masters of the Universe and then slip on a banana skin.

However, the argument that Jesus is portrayed as essentially soberminded has a point. Life in a fallen world is a serious business. We can't afford to make jokes about everything because not everything is funny. Flippancy treats life as if it is has no ultimate significance. C. S. Lewis, in the voice of the senior devil Screwtape, said that flippancy, if practiced over a long period, gave people the "finest armour plating" against God. "It is a thousand miles away from joy; it deadens, instead of sharpening, the intellect."[1] Cynicism is spiritually corrosive because it's an attitude that can't see the good in anything or, if it sees it, attributes bad motives. As the nineteenth-century novelist George Meredith commented, "Cynics are only happy in making the world as barren to others as they have made it for themselves."[2] Also, no Christian should use humor to demean people, vent hatred or degrade God's gifts. Paul says that "obscenity, foolish talk or coarse joking" shouldn't even be named among Christians (Eph 5:3-4), but, significantly, his corrective is "thanksgiving." I suspect this is because the humor he warns us to guard against is always belittling, ungrateful and self-serving.

There are many different types of comedy. Straightforward jokes ("A man goes into a bar . . .") usually depend on taking an audience along one level of thought and then suddenly plunging them to a level they weren't considering. Observational comedy ("Have you noticed the way that people . . .") uses the shock of recognition and often the exposure of thoughts or behavior usually kept secret. Satire ("You wanna know why they call it the American Dream?") holds public figures, institutions, habits and belief systems up to ridicule.

The Clues of Comedy

The comedy a culture produces shows what it values, despises and believes. It will reveal its concerns and also what never even crosses its mind. It will show you what it considers to be sacred and inviolable as well as what it thinks is fair game to be mocked and ridiculed. It will let you know how caring or vicious a society has become. Comedy is so sensitive to the zeitgeist that very little of it survives the age it was created in. Standup routines that made people howl in 1975 will seem perplexingly boring and unfunny to a twenty-first century audience. Taboos alter, morals change, language develops, fears switch locations and the dynamics that once made the jokes so powerful disappear.

All forms of comedy are based on assumptions about the world. The now old-fashioned standup routines about adulterous sex, drunken nights, nagging wives and domineering mothers-in-law were written and performed by men who clearly felt that adultery and drunkenness weren't activities worthy of condemnation, and that women should know their place. Routines that play with language ("If I melt dry ice can I swim without getting wet?"—Steven Wright) actually confirm the meanings of words rather than undermine them, just as nonsense verse confirms the validity of sense (if we lived in a truly nonsensical world nonsense poems wouldn't be funny).[3]

It's difficult to generalize about trends in humor because of national and regional variations, but overall comedy has become more intelligent, socially conscious and affected by trends in the other arts, but also more vicious, sexually explicit and keen to break taboos. Fifty years ago comedians were people who had left school at an early age and were working hard to make money. Today they are more likely to be people with degrees who regard comedy as a sensible career choice. Bill Maher has a BA in English from Cornell, Conan O'Brien graduated magna cum laude from Harvard, Jon Stewart majored in psychology at the College of William and Mary in Virginia, Stephen Colbert studied performance at Northwestern University. Some of the best-known British comedians since the 1960s are Oxbridge graduates: Peter Cook, Dudley Moore, the Monty Python team (John Cleese, Terry Jones, Eric Idle, Graham Chapman, Michael Palin), Rowan Atkinson, Sacha Baron-Cohen, Al Murray, Sue Perkins, David Baddiel, Richard Herring, Stephen Fry, Hugh Laurie and Jimmy Carr.

The higher education has produced comedy familiar with psychology, physics, sociology, theology, linguistics and political theory. Ricky Gervais, who studied philosophy at University College London, is a campaigning atheist and an Honorary Associate of the National Secular Society in Britain. In his one-man shows he deals with science, evolution and biology. The premise of his 2009 film *The Invention of Lying* is that consistent truth telling would make life impossible and so lies are necessary. The biggest of the lies, according to Gervais, is religion. Another British comic, Robin Ince, who studied English and drama at the University of London, has organized shows involving comedians, musicians and scientists. In 2008, in conjunction with the Rationalist Association, he put on "Nine Lessons and Carols for Godless People" (a parody of the Anglican Church service for Christmas), featuring comedians along with evolutionary biologist Richard Dawkins and particle physicist Brian Cox.

Comedians now see what they do as art and so draw influences from other art forms. Comedians like Lord Buckley in the 1950s were inspired by improvisatory jazz. They would "riff" on themes in the same way that instrumentalists would riff on melodies. The dialogue in *Monty Python's Flying Circus* owed a lot to the absurdist theater of writers like Samuel Beckett, Harold Pinter and Edward Albee. George

Carlin benefited from exposure to beat poetry. Shows such as *Google-whack* by Dave Gorman develop from firsthand research and involve PowerPoint presentations.

Taking It to the Edge

Prior to the early 1960s official censorship kept TV and radio free of anything "obscene" or "likely to corrupt or deprave." Comedians were arrested for using obscene language. This didn't mean that they were any purer, but it did mean that they tested the boundaries in a playful rather than an aggressive way. It's sobering to realize that no one had said the F-word on British TV until 1965, when theater critic Kenneth Tynan said it during a live broadcast. It resulted in four motions in the Houses of Parliament and an apology from the BBC. Eight years would pass before it was used again.

Today a typical edition of the BBC TV's *Thick of It* uses the F-word over forty times in a half-hour edition, and the comedy show employs a "swearing consultant" whose job it is to make the obscenities more creative and memorable.[4] There is now an attitude among some comedians that comedy isn't really doing its job unless it's pushing the envelope. The argument is that comedy needs to be edgy. But what happens when what lies beyond the edge of good taste is actually anti-human? And anyway, who decreed that humor must constantly push back the barriers of acceptability to remain vibrant?

Christian audience members need to decide how long to stay around if the humor becomes degrading or hateful. Of course, in any situation where we put ourselves in the way of art or argument we're going to have to face things that challenge or offend. Not everything that upsets us has to be avoided. But humor is more dangerous because it has a subtle way of winning us over or wearing us down. We may even find ourselves laughing at things that we profoundly disagree with.

The Comic as Social Critic

Forms of comedy that emerged in the 1950s and 1960s with performers like Lenny Bruce and Mort Sahl put worldviews at the forefront. The standup routines of people like Jack Benny, Bob Hope, George Burns and Milton Berle were designed simply to produce mirth. There was no higher purpose. They told jokes and measured their success by the length of the laughs. Bruce and Sahl, however, wanted to use laughs to force people to see the world in a different way. Bruce said,

A comedian of the older generation did an "act" and he told the audience, "This is my act." Today's comic is not doing an act. The audience assumes he's telling truth. . . . When I'm interested in a truth, it's really a truth truth, 100 percent. And that's a terrible kind of truth to be interested in.[5]

Bruce and Sahl took comedy from the nightspots and into the music clubs. Rather than playing resorts and hotels, they played on college campuses. They adopted the concerns of the emerging counterculture: civil rights, censorship, politics, recreational drugs, war, sex. They didn't do jokes about honeymooning couples, wedding nights, physical deformities or racial stereotypes. This was a new, radical, philosophical, political comedy that, despite its bad language and libertarian attitudes, had moral concern at its core. It spawned a strain of comedy that is so widespread today that even if comedians joke about subjects such as deformity and race (as in, for example, *South Park*) we assume that it's intended as irony.

George Carlin, who started as a conventional standup comic, believed that at different times in his career he had been a jester, a philosopher and a poet. The jester told jokes. The philosopher told jokes, but the jokes were based on sound ideas and were illuminating. The poet told jokes that had a strong worldview but were delivered in brilliant and memorable language. He felt that he had finally arrived as a performer when he became a jester-philosopher-poet. "I love the jokes but the jokes are there to decorate the ideas," he explained. "The ideas are (about) what I don't like in this country and what I'm disenchanted by in my fellow humans. Those are my ideas. But I found that I had this ability to be really good with language, to use graceful combinations of words and runs and rhythms."[6]

Live comedy is vibrant today. The Edinburgh Festival Fringe, the world's largest arts festival, has seen comedy shows increase almost tenfold since 1982. There are now more comedy venues in New York than there were in the whole of America in 1975. The beginning of the British "alternative comedy" movement was marked by the opening of the Comedy Store in 1979, and today the most popular comedians in the country play the largest venues possible and often outsell rock bands.

Skewed Views

Comedians, especially those who write their own material, usually see things differently from the rest of the world. That's what attracts us to them. They make connections that other people don't make, hear potential meanings of words that other people don't hear and note inconsistencies in behavior that other people don't see. At their best they refresh our perspectives by introducing us to possible ways of thinking that convention, repetition and social rein-forcement have blinded us to. At their best they make us less slavish to received opinion.

All of this would lead anyone to think that Christians were perhaps better qualified than most to produce comedy. Doesn't the Christian see the world in a different way? Doesn't the Christian have the equipment to spot contradictions and inconsistencies? Doesn't the Christian have the motivation to want to shake up accepted ways of viewing the world? Isn't the Christian suspicious of worldly authority, received opinion and popular views? Isn't it the Christian who has the most incentive to expose evil, falsehood and sham?

Yet comedy is largely deficient of Christians (and often Christians are largely deficient of comedy). My experience of comedy clubs in both Britain and America is that liberal secularism is the default outlook. Christianity, if it gets mentioned at all, is derided. Christ is a figure of fun. When George Carlin ridiculed organized religion on his HBO specials, the audiences would howl with approval. If there were jeers and walkouts they certainly weren't broadcast. It may be this attitude that has made Christians apprehensive about entering the profession.

What few Christians have done is to use comedy to highlight inconsistencies in the way that people like Lenny Bruce and George Carlin did. Instead of going on the offensive Christians either do jokes about church in a church context, Bible jokes as a warm-up for an evangelist or inoffensive comedy where the Christian influence is felt in the absence of swearing, blasphemy and references to sex and drugs rather than by the presence of anything. While the market leaders in comedy are creating material out of the hot issues of the day, Christians are known only for being meek and mild.

The most commonly used commendations on the webpages of Christian comedians are "clean" and "family friendly." Unfortunately this suggests that no humor can be found in any postpuberty experiences and that Christians are permanently stranded in childhood. It's hard to take on the ills of the world and the mess of our own sinful lives while remaining cute and uplifting. I accept that churches have responsibilities that don't apply to clubs and bars, but a Christian Lenny Bruce is unlikely to be house-trained. "We're nervous around the depiction or mention of Man's fallen nature or situations fallen Man gets himself into," says comedian and writer (and Lutheran) Susan E. Isaacs. "We don't like to look at unhealed wounds or sin that still exists in the world. We want our heroes to have no flaws. We want the evil to be entirely placed on the villain. We want everything to be resolved in the end. Actually, we want it to be resolved before it's even laid out!"[7]

Satire

In good hands satire can be the perfect weapon for challenging the dominant secular worldview. Humor is an effective way of shaking foundations, exposing weaknesses and challenging logic. It provides the opportunity to get people to see their assumptions from another point of view, or merely to see that they have assumptions. Webster defined satire as "the literary art of holding vices, follies, stupidities, abuses etc. up to ridicule and contempt." Also, it is "a literary manner which blends a critical attitude with humor for the purpose of improving human institutions or humanity." The aim is not to humiliate but to unsettle and to open people up to alternative ways of thinking. To refer back to the quote by Lenny Bruce, satire is obsessed by "truth truth."

Historically, many writers who have either been Christian or educated in a Christian environment have used literary satire. This is because satire is based on idealism. The satirist has a view of the way things should be and is angry that they're not this way. Christianity makes us aware of the gap between the way things are and the way God would like them to be. It's common to say that a satirist is a disappointed idealist, but a Christian employing satire would be an optimistic idealist.

One of the best-known satirists writing in English was Jonathan Swift (1667-1745), author of *Gulliver's Travels*, who was a doctor of divinity and became a priest in the Church of Ireland. His *A Modest Proposal*, a guide to ridding Ireland of its poor, is a classic piece of satire that is still studied in schools and universities. In the twentieth century G. K. Chesterton and Evelyn Waugh were both Catholics, and some of the key movers of Britain's satire boom in the 1960s had church foundations. C. S. Lewis, although not primarily a satirist, used satire in some of his writing, and *The Screwtape Letters* employed a technique known as ironic inversion.

Malcolm Muggeridge, a former editor of *Punch* who converted to Christianity, once told me,

> I try to point out the absurdities in people, including myself I hope. Mortal man conceives perfection but is forever imperfect, and this produces a form of disorientation. This is a very awkward situation that will be awkward until the end of time. I think laughter is as significant as inspiration. It is a sort of worldly, earthy form of inspiration. You can see this vision expressed in the great medieval cathedrals where you have a steeple climbing into the sky, giving a sense of reaching out, but also you have the funny faces of the gargoyles leering downwards.[8]

It's not enough merely to scoff at false beliefs. The most effective satire exposes the reasoning that produces bad conclusions. In *The Act of Creation*, the best book ever written about the process of comedy, Arthur Koestler says,

> The satirist's most effective weapon is irony. Its aim is to defeat the opponent on his own ground by pretending to accept his premises, his values, his methods of reasoning, in order to expose their implicit absurdity. . . . Irony purports to take seriously what it does not; it enters into the spirit of the other person's game to demonstrate that its rules are stupid or vicious. It's a subtle weapon, because the person who wields it must have the imaginative power of seeing through the eyes of his opponent, of projecting himself into the other's mental world.[9]

George Carlin

George Carlin was a virulent atheist. He had been raised by an Irish Catholic mother and educated by nuns. As he put it, "When I was a kid I was a Catholic, at least I was until I reached the age of reason." In one of his routines about religion and headwear, he said,

> One of the things they told us was that if a boy or a man went into a church he had to remove his hat in order to honor the presence of God. But they'd already told me that God was everywhere. So I used to wonder "If God is everywhere, why would you even own a hat?" Why not show your respect—don't even buy a hat.[10]

Carlin constantly used this approach to illustrate the folly of Christian belief. But he could also turn on some cherished secular ideas such as that of human rights. If there is no God, he reasoned, there is no such thing as "God-given rights."

> Hey folks. I hate to spoil your fun, but there's no such thing as rights. OK? They're imaginary. We made them up; like the Boogeyman, the Three Little Pigs, Pinocchio, Mother Goose. Rights are an idea. They're imaginary. They're a cute idea, but

that's all. Cute and fictional. But if you think you do have rights, let me ask you this. Where do they come from?[11]

In another popular routine Carlin attacked the proliferation of euphemisms in American English. "Americans have trouble facing the truth," he reasoned, "so they invent a soft language to protect themselves from it." He cited the example of soldiers' nervous response to warfare known as "shell shock" in World War I ("simple, direct"), "battle fatigue" in World War II, "operational fatigue" by the time of Korea ("We're up to eight syllables and the humanity has been completely squeezed out of the phrase") and then, during the war in Vietnam, to "post-traumatic stress disorder" ("The pain is completely buried beneath the jargon. This is language that takes the life out of life.")[12]

In the right Christian hands satire could similarly be used to expose weaknesses in secular-humanist reasoning or to draw attention to injustice, hypocrisy and prejudice. Christians get so used to being the object of attacks that they often don't consider the possibility of taking on the worldview of their attackers. They get so used to being harmless that they don't know how to inflict damage on false teachings. This doesn't mean scoffing at these people, belittling them or name-calling. It means carefully researching their beliefs (as Carlin did) and isolating flaws, inconsistencies and lapses of logic. The comedy in much of what Carlin did came from exposing what really lay beneath common assumptions and everyday language.

There may be problems on the way. Screenwriter Dean Batali (*That '70s Show*) says,

It's right for Christians to point out when the Emperor has no clothes, but if all we do is keep pointing that out then we are eventually just laughing at a naked man. Isn't it our responsibility to at least cover him up? The world has no such responsibility. They can keep on laughing, making more precise (and meaner) jokes at his expense.[13]

British comedian Milton Jones argues that Carlin and Bruce were successful largely because they were addressing the converted. In his view it would be difficult to tear down without exposing the source of your view and that would be considered preachy.

> Any writer who puts too much weight on a black and white message seems to test an audience's patience. The trouble is that laughter unites, but the gospel divides. I would love to be wrong about this but I imagine Jesus doing a stand-up set. It goes well for the first few minutes (stuff about Pharisees and hypocrisy) but then the mob boos him off when he starts talking about personal responsibility. Sure, he might pull some people in. But he won't get booked again.[14]

Most satire defining itself as Christian either laughs at godless humanism for already convinced church audiences or laughs at right-wing conservative Christians for the benefit of left-wing liberal Christians. The trouble with the former is that its unlikely to change attitudes and can lead to cheap-shot comedy that caricatures the opposition rather seeking to expose its flaws. The trouble with the latter is that this is a job that is already being carried out by most mainstream comedians who have no affection for evangelicals of any stripe.

When we say that laughter is a great medicine, an observation that has its roots in "A cheerful heart is good medicine" (Prov 17:22), we are generally thinking of its comforting and relaxing effects. It's like taking a cough medicine or a remedy to settle an upset stomach. It makes us feel better. But comedy can be an antibiotic that kills. This sort of medicine is disturbing. It does what Kenneth Tynan believed that Lenny Bruce did: "Others josh, snipe and rib; only Bruce demolishes. He breaks through the barrier of laughter to the horizon beyond where the truth has its sanctuary";[15] or what the nineteenth-century author William Makepeace Thackeray thought was achieved by humorists:

> The humorous writer professes to awaken your love, your pity, your kindness—your scorn for untruth, pretension, imposture— your tenderness for the weak, the poor, the oppressed, the unhappy. . . . To the best of his means and ability he comments on

all the ordinary actions and passions of life. . . . He takes upon himself to be the week-day preacher.[16]

Questions for Reflection or Discussion

- Why is a good sense of humor considered to be one of the most important characteristics when looking for a partner?

- Why was Jesus predicted to be a "man of sorrows"? Do you think this meant he never made a joke or laughed at incongruity?

- What makes cynicism such a corrosive form of humor? How is it different from satire or sarcasm?

- If it's true that comedy reveals what we cherish and what we despise, what do you think contemporary comedy tells us about the values of our society?

- Have you ever found yourself laughing at a point of view you actually hold to be true because a comedian led you there through a series of laughs?

- Should people who describe themselves as Christian comics be (1) meek and mild like the baby Jesus, (2) revolutionary and dangerous like the adult Jesus, (3) both, (4) neither?

- Can you imagine satire written and presented by a Christian and derived from Christian values? How do you think a largely secular audience would respond?

- British comedian Milton Jones says, "Laughter unites but the gospel divides." Is this true, and, if so, does it mean that comedy operating from a well-formed Christian view of the world is doomed to be marginalized?

- Should Christians lampoon the foibles of the church for a secular audience?

General Books about Comedy

Bruce, Lenny. *How to Talk Dirty and Influence People.* New York: Fireside, 1992.

Cohen, John. *The Essential Lenny Bruce.* New York: Ballantine, 1967.

Koestler, Arthur. *The Act of Creation.* New York: Arkana, 1989.

Books by Christians on Humor

Martin, James. *Between Heaven and Mirth: Why Joy, Humor and Laughter Are at the Heart of the Spiritual Life.* New York: HarperOne, 2012.

Taylor, Daniel. *Cynicism.* Downers Grove, IL: InterVarsity Press, 1983.

Trueblood, Elton. *The Humor of Christ.* New York: Harper & Row, 1964.

Websites

Christian Comedy Association: www.christiancomedyassociation.com

The Holy Observer: www.holyobserver.com

Lark News: www.larknews.com

The Wittenburg Door: www.wittenburgdoor.com

ChristWire: www.christwire.org

Five Suggestions for Action

- Why not have a creative heckle at a standup comic you disagree with? However, make sure it is creative, and don't do it unless you're prepared to be humiliated in return!

- Take a look at the premise of your favorite sitcom. What is the big joke behind all the little jokes?

- Study the tradition of the "holy fool" in Christian history.

- If you are a comedian, try to think of the inconsistencies in the worldview of your typical audience and think of ways of gently undermining them.

- Often comedians such as Lenny Bruce and George Carlin made quite sophisticated attacks on Christian belief. Use some of them as basis for a discussion on apologetics.

10

Advertising

The Hidden Persuader

†

Most of us have an ambiguous relationship with advertising. We have tourist photos of ourselves taken in Piccadilly Circus, London; Hachiko Square, Tokyo; or Times Square, New York, surrounded by massive digital and neon display boards and yet complain about the pollution of billboards on suburban streets. We admire the creativity of television commercials and yet get annoyed that our favorite programs are so frequently interrupted. This probably reflects a necessary balance of respect for an art form and skepticism about what we're being told, recognition that we need information about new products but concern that we are being harried or even deceived.

We tend to think of advertising as a recent phenomenon, a product of the modern more-frenzied world. This isn't so. Modern advertising is, of course, modern, but advertising itself is as old as civilization. People have always sold their products and skills to others, and once you've established a marketplace you have to draw attention to what you're selling by written and spoken words or by using signs. Jesus and Joseph presumably had to advertise their carpentry in some way, and Paul his tent making. There is no virtue or sense in making things for the use of others that you then never tell anyone about. That would lead to the sin committed by the person with the talents who buried them for safekeeping and therefore didn't maximize their potential.

The Roman city of Pompeii, which was drowned in volcanic ash in A.D. 79, was found to be full of examples of advertising from shop signs and political propaganda to trademarks and packaging. Tradesmen would use words like *quality* and *best* to set their product apart from that of competitors. The baths at Villa Julia Felix were promoted as being "good enough for Venus." There were at least 1,300 shops in Pompeii, each being identified with a visual sign indicating what was for sale. In some premises there may even have been a wall painting or mosaic depicting, for example, baking bread if it was a bakery or the picking and the crushing of grapes if it was a wine shop.

During times of widespread illiteracy advertising would be conducted primarily through visual images and street cries. The introduction of the printing press in the fifteenth century made handbills possible, and in the seventeenth century came newspapers. Signs in streets were still an important means of reaching people, and they were widespread enough for Charles II of England to announce, "No signs shall be hung across the streets shutting out the air and the light of the heavens."

It was at the end of the eighteenth century that the lithographic process made illustrated posters possible, and in the nineteenth century billboards began to appear in America. The first large outdoor poster in New York was to advertise a circus in 1835. By 1867 it was possible to lease boards. The invention of electricity, photography, film, radio, television and computer technology made the twentieth century increasingly different.

The first cinema advertisement (for Dewar's whisky) was screened in 1899. The first neon ad was for the vermouth Cinzano in Paris in 1913, when Jacques Fonseque erected letters three-and-a-half feet tall on the Champs-Élysées. Ten years later he sold two signs reading "Packard" to a car dealership in Los Angeles, the first neon advertising to appear in America. A year before, in 1922, the first paid-for radio commercial was aired on WEAF, New York. In July 1941 the first TV commercial (for Bulova watches) was screened on WNBT before a baseball game between the Brooklyn Dodgers and the Philadelphia

Phillies. It was a long time later, in September 1955, that British viewers got to see a TV commercial, this one for Gibbs SR toothpaste.

Developments in digital technology increased opportunities to reach people. The first clickable Web ad appeared in 1993 (for a now defunct Silicon Valley law firm); the first SMS text message was sent in 1994 (in Finland); and the first ads were sent by text in 2000. The invention of plasma and LED (light emitting diode) screens challenged the supremacy of both paper posters and neon. The future of OOH (out-of-home) advertising was digital. Falling revenues for print advertising led to the closures of some newspapers and magazines and the cutting of staff at leading publications.

So although the technology has changed, the advertisers of contemporary São Paulo, Los Angeles, Paris and Hong Kong are doing what the various painters and sign makers of Pompeii did in the first century. They are trying to arrest our attention and attract us to a particular product in the hopes that we will turn from being viewers or listeners into customers. Their challenge, as ever, is to hold our gaze long enough to impart information that will make us favorably disposed toward whatever is being sold, either by extolling its virtues or by giving us a good feeling we then associate with that product.

The Medium Shapes the Message

However, it's necessary to acknowledge that change of technology doesn't just mean the same message is transmitted in a different format. It also shapes the message. If I were living in Pompeii in the first century and heard someone shouting out the virtues of their fruit, wine, vegetables or perfumes, I would first of all take into account that person's reputation. Was he known to be honorable or dishonorable? Did they have a demeanor that encouraged trust? Additionally, there would be the immediate opportunity to ask questions or challenge statements. Painted signs that merely indicated "bread can be bought here" exerted no real powers of persuasion.

In the twenty-first century we generally have no idea who is talking to us through advertising. Is it the product designer, the company, the advertising agency or a skillful "creative"? Do they really believe what they're telling us or are they merely fulfilling a brief? We have no way of gauging their reputations or quizzing them. Also, advertising is more ubiquitous. We hear it on the radio and TV at home, it's in every publication we read, and it dogs us when we're online. "Cookies" enable interested parties to monitor our interests and online purchases so that advertisers can strategically target us.

True Communication

The primary question we should ask of advertising is, Is it true? This can be difficult to determine because very little contemporary advertising appeals to reason. In the nineteenth century many ads promised to cure whole ranges of physical ailments with a single pill. Today more and more countries are adopting strict advertising guidelines that forbid making false claims. This has been a positive development. It may not stop every lie but it provides a court of appeal for anyone who feels they have been misled.

Since 1962 the Advertising Standards Authority, a self-regulatory body established by the British advertising industry, has ensured that advertisements are "legal, decent, honest and truthful." In 2004 it banned advertisements by Apple Computer UK that claimed to have "the world's fastest computer."[1] The ASA found that this was unsubstantiated. Four years later an ad for the iPhone had to be removed for saying that the product could "access all the Internet." It didn't support plug-ins such as Adobe Flash or support Java, so this was deemed to be untrue. The cosmetic company L'Oreal, which had used actress Penelope Cruz in a campaign for mascara, was condemned because "it exaggerated the effect that could be achieved using the mascara on natural lashes."[2] A similar case against a L'Oreal campaign involving actress Julia Roberts and model Christy Turlington was upheld in 2011 because the photos of the stars were "not representative of the results that the product could achieve."[3]

Contemporary advertising doesn't work by supplying information that can either be verified or discredited, but by suggesting a mood, forging an association or implying the possibility of change. When the advertisers decided to promote Marlboro cigarettes by using tough-looking cowboys, they knew that the fear they needed to counteract was that smoking was dirty and unhealthy. They couldn't create a campaign saying that their cigarettes were clean and lengthened your life—that would have been too brazen a lie and would have drawn attention to its opposite—so they showed ruggedly healthy looking men smoking Marlboros against magnificent Wild West backdrops. The goal was to get people, mostly men, to associate smoking with power, hard work, good health and the outdoor life.

Henry Saffer and Frank Chaloupka offered a succinct summary of how cigarettes were promoted in their 1999 report "Tobacco Advertising: Economic Theory and International Evidence."

> Cigarette advertising is primarily designed to create various fantasies of sophistication, pleasure, social success, independence or ruggedness. These attributes become the product personality which advertisers expect will appeal to specific consumers. For a relatively small expenditure on tobacco, the consumer psychologically connects to the fantasy lifestyle and personality characteristics portrayed in the advertising. This process can induce individuals, who are not smokers, to try the product, for those who are smokers to smoke more, for those who might have quit, to continue, and for those who have quit to start again.[4]

The same is true for the advertising of other products. The ads rarely tell us what the product actually does but suggest that buying it will give us a higher standing among our peers, make us more attractive to the opposite sex or provide access to a more exciting lifestyle. They may also exploit our fears of being unfashionable, unpopular or out of tune with our times.

Favorable Feelings

Another way that advertising ingratiates is by creating a bond between the product and us. Advertisers recognize that most of us are commercials literate today and know that we are not so easily conned. They know that we're cynical and are as highly critical of new campaigns as we would be of new records or films. Therefore they seek to either amaze us by their artistry, so that the ads will become a talking point, or make us laugh so that we develop affection for what is being sold. In 1966 Marshall McLuhan predicted a world "where the ad will become a substitute for the product and all the satisfactions will be derived informationally from the ad."[5]

Filmed campaigns for cars have produced some of the most beloved commercials of modern times. The best have been so imaginative that they are genuine artworks. Again, the goal has not been to tell us something about the car in question—no mention of safety, space, miles to the gallon, carbon emissions—but to stun us with creative brilliance, maybe in so doing to plant the implication in our minds that the vehicle in question was made with equal commitment to precision, timing and all-round excellence.

These ads are normally based on a facet of the car that the manufacturers want emphasized. A campaign for the 2005 Volkswagen Golf GTI featured a dancer body popping to a remixed version of "Singing in the Rain" on a replica of the film set and with Gene Kelly's face superimposed over the dancer's face. The message was designed to show the car "as a classic that survives reinvention," and the slogan used was "The Original, Updated." But the main task of the campaign was to create a talking point. The BBC reported, "VW hopes its ad will be one of those that people want to watch again and again, and many websites discussing it talk with awe about its workmanship."[6]

A 2003 commercial for the Honda Accord known as "Cog" took seven months to create a two-minute sequence that showed all the car's components knocking into each other in one long domino chain. It was a painstaking production that cost £1 million and resulted first in awards and then in homage and parody. London-based style guru Peter York commented that it was "the water cooler ad conversation of the year."[7] In 2006 the same team made another Honda ad, this time for the Honda Civic, in which a choir spent six months learning to sing all the different noises a driver hears—crunching gravel, the echo of a tunnel, swishing windscreen wipers, even the sound of a pen skidding over a dashboard surface. Honda wanted to sell the experience of driving rather than the car. Its marketing communications manager said, "Honda's aim was not to produce a car that would just take you from A to B but to make sure you really enjoyed and had fun with every drive you took."[8]

Under increasing pressure not to target underage teens or to make false claims about the benefits of alcohol consumption, advertisers of beers, spirits and alcopops tend to employ humor and music that will resonate with young drinkers. Given that laughter, dancing, socializing and flirting are the high points of nights out, they're keen that their product be associated with such good times. Smirnoff, the vodka brand, gathered information from Facebook to find out what young people from fifty countries around the world considered made their nightlife special. Then, in 2010, based on its findings, it created the first Nightlife Exchange Project, where on one night fourteen of these countries had the best of their music, food, dance moves, fashion, bands and DJs swapped with another (the best of Australian nightlife in India, for example, and the best Indian nightlife in Australia). As the publicity announced, "Smirnoff believes great drinks are a key ingredient of original nightlife, and original nightlife calls for great drinks."[9] The Smirnoff campaign is clever in that it creates cutting-edge cultural events that the target market are likely to be keen to want to be a part of and which get a lot of publicity.

Foster's Lager, licensed to SABMiller in America, employed the communication management consultancy Naked and the social media monitor Attentio to find out "the conversation landscape around beer" so that it could identify its brand with whatever it was that beer drinkers associated with the joys of drinking. The research, carried out using a program designed by Attentio to intercept online chatter, found that the greatest number of people "referenced beer and comedy." Naked's verdict was that this was "an area really suitable for Foster's to build a great story and create cultural capital."[10]

Foster's did this in Britain by sponsoring comedy TV shows, making "laddish" commercials and, from 2010, sponsoring the high profile Edinburgh Awards, which have been described as being the Oscars of the world of stand-up. They have also funded comedy shows streamed only to their official website. The goal of all this is to firmly establish their brand of lager as inseparable from relaxation, laughter and good times. This is far more important than making an issue of flavor, calories or sugar content.

Manipulation

The analysis of online chatter raises the issues of manipulation and invasion of privacy. Although we accept the need for advertising, admire the more creative ads and may even have an affection for particular commercials or posters, most of us feel uneasy about having our personal choices tracked and monitored to accumulate data, and are repelled by the idea of being a target for psychological persuasion.

The landmark book on psychological advertising techniques was Vance Packard's *The Hidden Persuaders*, first published in 1957. In it he revealed something that wasn't widely known at the time—the fact that advertisers were using techniques developed through collaboration with psychological analysts, cultural anthropologists, social psychologists, sociologists and social scientists in order to tinker with people's minds. "Large-scale efforts are being made, often with impressive success, to channel our unthinking habits, our purchasing decisions, and our thought processes by the use of insights gleaned from psychiatry and the social sciences," he wrote. "Typically these efforts take place beneath our lack of awareness; so that the appeals which move us are often, in a sense, 'hidden.'" His main objection to this wasn't that it didn't work, but that it did work and "it has seriously antihumanistic implications."[11]

Advertisers in the late 1940s and early 1950s were faced with two apparently conflicting facts. The first was that people weren't buying enough goods to keep the economy expanding. There was not enough discontent. Men, for example, were perfectly happy with shoes and suits that they had been wearing for years. What advertisers had to create was "psychological obsolescence." They had to make consumers embarrassed at using clothes or products that were not the "latest thing." One American advertising executive of the period said, "What makes this country great is the creation of wants and desires, the creation of dissatisfaction with the old and outmoded."[12]

The second fact discovered is that consumers didn't buy in a rational way. They seem to be controlled more by irrational fears and desires than reasoning. For example, if questioned about what would constitute the perfect car, they would describe something small, compact and economical, and yet when it came to making a purchase they would buy something large, flashy and expensive. In other words, what people said wasn't always reliable, or, at least, it wasn't reliable unless interpreted by experts in psychology and social sciences.

In order to create the dissatisfaction needed to stimulate the economy and to play on the vulnerabilities of consumers, the advertisers started to employ motivational researchers to study the subsurface desires that controlled people—their needs, drives, guilts and fears. They introduced in-depth interviews, hidden cameras in supermarkets, focus groups, attitude tests, sociodramas, word association tests and a whole battery of psychological tools, many of which are now commonplace in the industry.

The motivational researchers also discovered that what held a lot of Americans back from consuming in even greater volume was guilt. The Puritan inheritance was stronger that imagined. The advertisers wanted people to indulge and be reckless, but the residual Puritan conscience urged moderation, sacrifice and consideration for the poor. Ernest Dichter, president of the Institute for Motivational Research, declared that "One of the main jobs of the advertiser . . . is not so much to sell the product as to give moral permission to have fun without guilt."[13]

Packard's argument that such techniques become antihuman bears consideration. One of the attributes of humanity that appears to be most precious to God is our ability to reason and choose and therefore be responsible for our actions. Of course, since the fall we have a natural bias toward sin, but nevertheless God still addresses people as being capable of making decisions. Forms of communication that attempt to bypass our critical faculties, wear down our consciences and act against our deepest convictions treat us as less than human. In *The Hidden Persuaders* Packard asks,

> What is the morality of playing on hidden weaknesses and frailties—such as our anxieties, aggressive feelings, dread of nonconformity, and infantile hangovers—to sell products? Specifically, what are the ethics of businesses that shape campaigns designed to thrive on these weaknesses they have diagnosed?[14]

Subliminal Temptation

An aspect he only briefly touches on, presumably because it was only in its infancy at the time, is subliminal advertising. He cites the example, reported in 1956, of an advertiser who had used images of ice cream flashed for fractions of a second during a film screening, which apparently had cinemagoers mad for ice cream during the interval. The theory was that information could be planted in the mind without the viewer even being aware of having seen it. This naturally raised the frightening prospect of brainwashing. (Subliminal advertising was outlawed in Britain, America and Australia in 1958.)

Yet other forms of what is in effect subliminal advertising are used. One of the most obvious is product placement. Companies vie to have their product, with logo in full view, used during the action of a movie. For the James Bond movie *Skyfall* (2012) the filmmakers Sony and MGM were given $45 million by the Dutch beer maker Heineken in return for having Bond drink their brew rather than his traditional vodka.[15] In 2008 *Vanity Fair* viewed the *Sex and the City* movie and noted the promotion of twenty-five designers, eight stores and services, eight places, seven gadgets, seven publications, seven snack outlets and five pharmaceutical goods.[16]

The power of product placement is that the viewer is more re-
laxed than when watching an advertisement and the goods that are
being subtly advertised benefit from the association with the fictional character. Companies like Calvin Klein, Samsonite, Revlon,
Rolex and Omega can draw on the fifty years of glamour accrued by
the Bond franchise. Although it's hard to believe that anyone would
consciously decide that Carrie Bradshaw's lifestyle could be theirs if
only they could afford a pair of Jimmy Choo shoes, that's apparently
what happens.

Advertising also subliminally promotes particular attitudes along
with its products, particularly in the area of sex and sexuality. For
example, if a couple was shown sharing a bed, it used to be that they
had to be shown wearing wedding rings. Now it would be considered
unsexy to allow them to wear rings because it would subtly introduce
concepts of responsibility and faithfulness that run counter to the
image of experimentation and carefree irresponsibility they want to
be identified with. Products such as soap, lipstick, moisturizer and
underarm deodorant are often positioned to look like sex toys.

Calvin Klein's campaigns for male underwear have an undisguised
homoerotic look. Unbelievably Klein has been able to take images
that would only have been available illicitly in the 1950s and have
them dominate Times Square. Although there are no words, the in-
your-face style of the billboards and the knowing allusion to gay porn
has clearly been used as a subversive tactic to make the homosexual
lifestyle attractive and acceptable. A Martian would see no difference
between it and a poster of an Olympic swimming champion, but a
savvy New Yorker would immediately note the references. A 1989
poll voted the first of these billboards, featuring athlete Tom Hinthaus,
as one of "10 pictures that changed America."[17]

Culture Jamming

Since the mid-1970s the culture jamming movement has been dis-
rupting advertising, most notably though "billboard modification."
Culture jammers try to use advertising against itself to expose what

they believe are questionable assumptions. This form of creative subversion is often very effective in reminding the public of the bigger issues at stake. One campaign involved replacing the skinny model in a Calvin Klein campaign with an anorexic girl vomiting in a toilet bowl with only the word *Obsession* left. This was potentially far more powerful than a series of newspaper articles linking eating disorders with advertising.

In another culture jamming exercise the Apple "Think Different" campaign was hijacked by superimposing a mug shot of Charles Manson over what would have been a portrait of John Lennon or Gandhi. The point was effectively and succinctly made. Thinking differently is not in itself a virtue. The simple replacement of an image revealed the vacuous nature of the slogan.

Culture jammers argue that advertising permeates almost every area of our life and that the industry behind it works tirelessly to get us to associate desire and identity with commodities. Advertising encourages us to believe that our needs for contentment and self-worth can be solved by spending money. The campaigns by organizations such as Adbusters and the Billboard Liberation Front are designed to counteract negative effects and ultimately to enable people to regain control of their culture.

Christians should share the disgruntlement of these organizations because we have a commitment to truth, a belief that people are not made whole and happy by possessions alone, and a desire that culture should be a shared expression rather than an imposed view. Some of their campaigns have the hallmarks of prophetic acts whereby false idols were exposed to the shock and disbelief of those who been educated into believing that objects of wood, metal and stone could solve their problems.

The delivery of the gospel stands as the model for all good communication. The Bible teaches us to engage people (as Jesus did with his parables), to fashion our message so that it's memorable ("The words of the wise are like goads" [Eccles 12:11]), to persuade (as Paul did with Agrippa) and to reason (as Paul did all the time). What we are never to do is to trick or deceive. In 2 Corinthians 4:2, Paul appears to defend himself against those who've accused him of doing this. William Barclay's paraphrase brings out his response: "But we have refused to have anything to do with hidden and shameful methods. We do not act with unscrupulous cleverness."[18]

Advertising is an area of popular culture that displays remarkable creative ingenuity along with the potential to manipulate and deceive. Many ads are brilliant examples of art put in the service of commerce, condensing complex ideas into a striking image and a few words. As creators we need to be truthful and respectful of those who we address. As consumers we need to be vigilant, careful not to admire creativity that uses our appreciation to sneak into our minds, and unafraid to fight back against the encroachment of advertising into every corner of our public and private lives.

Questions for Reflection or Discussion

- Do you see outdoor advertising as a blight on the landscape or a pleasant diversion?

- Has advertising affected what you buy? If so, in what way?

- Would the Christian values of honesty, truth and respect for human choice make it impossible to be successful in advertising, or could they transform advertising in a positive way?

- Do you think that monitoring online chatter for commercial use is an invasion of privacy or a way of giving us what we truly want?

- Describe an ad that attracted you because it was inventive, amusing or heartwarming.

- Describe an ad that repelled you because it was manipulative, deceptive.

- Can culture jamming be prophetic?

- Is breeding discontent ever justified?

- Should the church use the skills of advertisers to promote the gospel, or does advertising automatically devalue the message?
- Are some ads works of art equal to anything we put in museums and galleries?

General Books on Advertising

Key, Wilson Bryan. *Subliminal Seduction*. New York: Signet, 1974.
Lindstrom, Martin. *Buy-Ology: Truth and Lies About Why We Buy*. New York: Broadway, 2008.
Ogilvy, David. *Ogilvy on Advertising*. London: Pan, 1983.
Packard, Vance. *The Hidden Persuaders*. 1957. Reprint, Brooklyn, NY: Ig Publishing, 2007.

Websites

Adbusters: www.adbusters.org
Billboard Liberation Front: www.billboardliberation.com
ChurchAds.net: www.churchads.net

Five Suggestions for Action

- Take photos of ads that amuse, amaze or anger you.
- Be aware of how advertisers seduce, manipulate and deceive.
- Watch TV commercials for cars, and see how many stress economy, safety and practicality and how many stress speed, seductiveness and envy.
- Make a note of ads that use religious iconography or phrases. Decide whether they devalue religious currency or make it relevant to the modern age.
- Do some culture jamming of your own by defacing ads in a newspaper or magazine you own in a way that exposes the half-truths being told.

11

Technology

Rewiring Our World

†

Nothing has altered the landscape of popular culture more in recent memory than the digital revolution. To mention just a few examples, it has changed the way we correspond with each other, the means by which we consume music and film, our relationship with television and radio, our shopping habits, our access to archived knowledge, our control over photography, the way we bank and our research speed and capability. It created a new breed of entrepreneurs, many of them still in their twenties, and brands such as Apple, Amazon, Wikipedia, Tumblr, PayPal, Twitter, Google and Facebook.

Seemingly overnight many of the old landmarks of popular culture virtually disappeared. The invention of downloading and mp3 players ended the dominance of retail record stores, at one time one of the most important places for young people to congregate. Cell phones eliminated the need for payphone booths, or at least for many of them. Information available online reduced the circulations of magazines and newspapers, and as a result print advertising revenue plummeted. The invention of programs such as Pro Tools and music sites such as MySpace changed the way people made and shared music. Texting and emails meant a dramatic decline in the number of letters written and mailed through the postal system. While I was writing this chapter, Kodak, the photographic company formed by George

Eastman in 1889, filed for bankruptcy protection, a further victim of the switch to digital.

This revolution has also added a whole new range of activities (and verbs) to popular culture: *blogging, tagging, hacking, burning, capping, texting, spamming, trending, tweeting, trolling, googling, gaming.* It made possible fresh ways of being creative through sampling, citizen journalism, apps, computer graphics, photoshopping, flashmobbing, websites and CGI. Sixty years ago an artist trying to capture the essence of teenage life would perhaps have used an illustration of a couple jiving to music coming from a small record player or a transistor radio. Today the archetypal image of a teenager would be someone texting on a smart phone, playing a video game or listening to music with a headset.

Cyberspace has become such an important part of our lives in such a short time, and we have all become so dependent on it that serious concerns have been raised about the ability of an enemy to destroy our way of life by carefully calculated cyberattacks. In 2012 U.S. Defense Secretary Leon Panetta warned that hackers could bring down power grids, interfere with the control systems of chemical plants, derail trains and even damage military communications networks. He said that such attacks could "paralyze and shock the nation."[1]

On a personal level we have probably all experienced a sudden loss of information from corrupted files, computer viruses or the loss of a cell phone. These events make us wonder whether we are becoming too reliant on creating archives in highly vulnerable places. In the past the only way we'd lose our photographs, letters or address book would be though theft or fire, but now they can be wiped out by human error, computer malfunctions or anonymous attacks. None of us knows exactly where our emails are physically stored.

The revolution is still going on, and this makes my task in this chapter even harder. How is it possible to assess the impact of such a massive cultural change in the midst of that change (and while taking advantage of much of the technology I describe)? Anything said on the subject will necessarily be provisional, awaiting the verdict of further research and of history itself. Yet, as Christians, it's important that we do take a weather check, otherwise we could find ourselves inadequately prepared for the tsunami or the sunshine ahead. We are in good company, for the Christians of the early first and twentieth centuries were also living in a time of radical change and having to apply new teachings to a world that was altering beyond recognition.

Christians often try to hold back the future, hoping that by resisting change they can maintain a world that is less complex and therefore easier to understand, or they go with the flow, thinking that faith has nothing to do with computers or fashion or films. However, we should evaluate all new cultural trends in the light of Bible wisdom, discovering how the particular issues raised by the times open up the Scriptures in a fresh way or possibly direct us to parts of it that would not have had such pressing relevance to another age.

New Ways of Thinking

New technology, as well as replacing old technology, makes us act and think in different ways. When the printing press was invented in the fifteenth century it didn't merely speed up the exchange of ideas, it created a new type of thinking. Books were linear and visual; the act of reading, solitary and reflective. The society of books naturally led to individualism, rationalism and nationalism. It produced the Renaissance, the Reformation and the Enlightenment. Nicholas Carr, in an article for The Atlantic titled "Is Google Making Us Stupid?" echoed Marshall McLuhan's thought in saying, "Media are not just passive channels of information. They supply the stuff of thought, but they also shape the process of thought."[2]

The advent of downloading and home recording didn't just make things faster and easier; it totally altered the dynamics of record production, delivery and consumption. It made it more democratic (anyone can do it), but at the same time less special (everyone is doing it). Because recorded music no longer needed to take up physical storage space, it meant that no record had to be deleted from "the back catalog," but the availability of everything took the adventure out of seeking out obscure recordings and consequently removed a lot of the mystique, and therefore power, of popular music.

At the same time, listening to recorded music has become more private. The quality of reproduction on a top-of-the-range headset is almost studio quality, but the music has stopped being something that you would call your friends over to listen to. Listeners choosing tracks rather than buying entire albums has meant that albums are no longer viewed as cohesive units. It also means that people are less likely to know the social context of the music they listen to. My children have grown up appreciating the Beatles but may not know whether "Hey Jude" was released before or after "I Want to Hold Your Hand" or on what album "Lucy in the Sky with Diamonds" appeared.

The new media has altered sexual behavior. Flirtation online could be regarded as merely an update on older rituals such as hanging out on street corners, going to dances, writing to pen pals or responding to lonely hearts ads in newspapers. However, the Internet has been found to significantly change the way people meet, the number of people they approach, the degree of intimacy and the moral boundaries they are willing to cross. A British survey of almost nine hundred 16- to 24-year-olds found that 80 percent had used either a smart phone or a website for some form of sexual contact. The same percentage said that it was easier to be promiscuous online than off; 53 percent had used Web cams for cybersex, and a third of these had had cybersex with strangers.

In other words, the new technology is enabling relationships that couldn't have happened before. The carefully chosen images and fast responses give an immediate sense of intimacy, yet none of the normal social skills are engaged. People with tastes that would have previously been considered bizarre or deviant can quickly find similar people with similar tastes and therefore believe that their sexual quirk is normal. There are phone apps that link people who share a sexual preference and are in the immediate vicinity.

Social networking sites make it easier to stay in touch with a wide range of contacts but also make people conscious of having to turn

themselves into brands of a kind. Face-to-face meetings require that
we show more of ourselves, whereas online we can choose our best
face and only release information that enhances our appeal. Face-to-
face we accept an etiquette that (unless we're intoxicated) means that
we begin with small talk and generalities and slowly move on to spe-
cifics. Online there need be no such inhibitions. Messaging doesn't
lead to lulls in conversation or awkward moments.

Computers and the Counterculture

The digital revolution proper started in Northern California in the
1970s and 1980s, and was naturally embedded with some of the
values of that time and place. There is something incongruous about
personal computing being invented in the same area that produced
the hippie movement of the 1960s because hippies were as opposed
to the technological revolution as the Romantic writers had been to
the Industrial Revolution and for many of the same reasons. They saw
computing as the antithesis of the unfettered imagination and believed it would lead to individuals being reduced to statistics. Yet the
first computer geeks came from among these people. Instead of being
scared of the technology, many of them saw it as a tool that could ultimately bring about many of the changes that they'd thought they
could bring about through drugs, protests and alternative living.

One of the reasons that the hippie movement started in San Francisco was because some of the first large-scale experiments into the
effects of LSD (Lysergic Acid Diethylamide) took place at Menlo Park
Veterans Hospital. There was hope that the then-legal drug could be
used in treating mental health problems and even used as a "truth
drug" on captured enemies during war. In this way hundreds of young
people, many of them students from nearby Stanford University, took
LSD under controlled conditions as paid guinea pigs.

LSD profoundly altered the outlook of those who took it. One of
the major effects was of removing all sense of the individual self so
that the user felt one with everything. It then appeared that all divisions between self and others, the animate and the inanimate, had

merely been products of the rational mind. This led many to believe that pantheism was a more accurate portrayal of reality than the theism of Judaism, Christianity and Islam. Consequently the hippie movement adopted the religious language, symbols and ideas of Hinduism and Buddhism (*karma, nirvana, Tao, mantra, guru, chakra*, etc.) and had very little interest in monotheistic religion. Even after the trip was over, the experience left an indelible impression.

Some of the most significant breakthroughs in the digital revolution took place in Silicon Valley, a short drive from San Francisco. Even today the headquarters of a high percentage of the major players, including Apple, Netflix, Pixar and Google, are in the same relatively small area. Many of the earliest adopters of the new technology, the people who pioneered personal computing, grew up imbibing the San Franciscan countercultural spirit that had produced the Grateful Dead, light shows, the Free Speech Movement, head shops, free concerts, free clinics, communes, underground newspapers, organic food stores, vegetarianism, farmers' markets, peace protests and the ecology movement.

Steve Jobs, cofounder of Apple, was one such person. He rejected the Lutheranism of his childhood, but after taking LSD became seriously interested in both Buddhism and Hinduism. He visited India in search of a guru, became a vegetarian and had a Zen teacher, Kobun Chino. He was a big fan of the music of Bob Dylan and encouraged Apple employees to think of themselves as misfits and rebels. "I came of age at a magical time," he said. "Our consciousness was raised by Zen, and also by LSD." He said that his experience with the drug was "one of the most important things in my life."[3]

For many acidheads the model of interconnectivity promised by peer-to-peer sharing through computers rang true to the experience of oneness they'd had while tripping. The Internet was millions of individual minds joined together as one communal mind—cyberspace as cosmic consciousness. In 1992 the acid guru Dr. Timothy Leary, who had spoken at San Francisco's 1966 Be-In, said,

It's no accident that the people who popularized the personal

computer were Steve Jobs and Steve Wozniak, both barefoot,
long haired acid-freaks. It's no accident that most of the people
in the software computer industry have had very thoughtful,
very profitable and creative psychedelic experiences.[4]

Infamous for his 1960s slogan "Turn on, tune in, drop out," he
adapted this in the 1990s to "Turn on, boot up, jack in."

Also in keeping with the spirit of the counterculture was the fact
that the Internet couldn't be regulated or contained. It was virtually
impossible to police, crossed national and ideological borders, often
outwitted the traditional media, could be used to reveal military and
government secrets, made most forms of sexual censorship unen-
forceable, flouted copyright laws and could outmaneuver law enforcement agencies and security forces. Every form of traditional
authority was challenged.

John Perry Barlow, former student of comparative religion and
lyricist for the Grateful Dead, drew up the "Declaration of the Independence of Cyberspace" in 1996, which was addressed to the governments of the industrial world from a citizen of cyberspace, "the
new home of Mind." The declaration asked governments to restrain
from trying to interfere with cyberspace.

> Cyberspace consists of transactions, relationships, and thought
> itself, arrayed like a standing wave in the web of our communi-
> cations. Ours is a world that is both everywhere and nowhere,
> but it is not where bodies live.
>
> We are creating a world that all may enter without privilege
> or prejudice accorded by race, economic power, military force,
> or station of birth.
>
> We are creating a world where anyone, anywhere, may ex-
> press his or her beliefs, no matter how singular, without fear of
> being coerced into silence or conformity.
>
> Your legal concepts of property, expression, identity,
> movement, and context do not apply to us. They are all based
> on matter, and there is no matter here.[5]

Freedom of Information

From its earliest days one of the driving ideals of the Internet was the free sharing of data. Those who'd shared food on the streets of Haight Ashbury or who'd advocated free universities saw the possibility of realizing their dream of equal access to knowledge, news and data. Before the Internet a lot of information could only be acquired if you had money, contacts, memberships, subscriptions or happened to live close to well-maintained libraries and archives. This necessarily led to information haves and have-nots.

The development of search engines like Google and sites such as Wikipedia meant that facts could be checked almost instantaneously. Google's ambitious digitization project will mean that anyone connected to the Internet can have the sort of information that was previously only available to those able to visit London's British library, the Library of Congress in Washington, D.C., the New York Public Library or the Bodleian in Oxford. Jimmy Wales of Wikipedia said, "Imagine a world in which every single person on the planet is given free access to the sum of all human knowledge. That's what we're doing."[6]

Yet there is a downside. The opposition to hierarchies—the so-called flattening process—results in a loss of authority. One of the problems with Internet research is that often you can't be sure of the validity of information. The *New York Times* and the *Encyclopaedia Britannica* are meticulous with fact checking, but anyone can post information online. Newspaper and magazine columnists are usually people who've proved their worth through years of reporting and are responsible to editors and subeditors, but bloggers only have to have an opinion and a keyboard. They don't have to face the scrutiny of fellow journalists or even abide by press regulations.

In these and other ways the Internet promotes the idea of the wisdom of the majority. Wikipedia, for example, is entirely made up of contributions from nonpaid writers whose expertise can't be validated. Entries range from the masterful to the incoherent and opinionated. Google gives precedence to sites that get the most hits. As

Tim Challies writes in *The Next Story*, "Wikis measure truth by consensus, while search engines measure truth by relevance."[7]

Biblical Wisdom

The Bible has a more nuanced view. Yes, it believes in the significance of every individual, but it also believes that some are better qualified to lead, teach and interpret the times than others. It doesn't teach that the majority view is right or that all opinions are equally valid. In other words, the "foolish controversies" of Titus 3 are not equal to the "sound doctrine" of 1 Timothy 1:10. Although this refers specifically to spiritual teaching, I think it bears a wider application. We need to guard against the tendency of the Internet to inculcate us with relativism.

Similarly, the idea of oneness sounds very worthy. Isn't God in favor of harmony, unity and the human family? It's true that we should forgive, go the extra mile, love our neighbors as ourselves and seek to live peacefully with all. However, those who make unity their religion always do it at the cost of truth. If something in the Christian outlook is controversial or upsetting to others, they will abandon it for the sake of harmonious living. Jesus, promised as a Prince of Peace, was the most divisive individual in history. He said that he came not to bring peace but a sword (Mt 10:34).

The hippies of the 1960s wanted to change the world by making it more peaceful, tolerant, caring, healthy and ecologically responsible. They wanted everyday objects to be more beautiful, work to be more spiritually rewarding and people to be more important than money. Many of these good values have been incorporated into the thinking of new technology companies in a way that would have been almost unthinkable in the 1950s. Google's executive chairman, Eric Schmidt, said, "Our goal is to change the world. Monetization is a technology to pay for it."[8] When Steve Jobs tempted John Sculley away from PepsiCo to become president of Apple, he asked him, "Do you want to spend the rest of your life selling sugared water to children, or do you want a chance to change the world?"[9] Jimmy Wales said, "A big part of what motivates us [Wikipedia] is our larger mission to affect the world in a positive way."[10]

They are not people who've simply discovered a new way to print money; they want to use digital technology to transform lives. Many of them have adopted remarkably simple lifestyles and use their fortunes to relieve hunger, sickness and pain. There is something almost religious about their statements. The philanthropic arm of Google has put $45 million into renewable energy projects, and has also invested in developing technologies that can monitor the spread of diseases, detect environmental damage and rapidly trace survivors of major disasters. The Bill and Melinda Gates Foundation (motto: "All lives have equal value") has so far channeled over $26 billion of the Microsoft fortune to alleviate extreme poverty and poor health in developing countries and to improve poor education in America. We should all be grateful that these individuals and companies who've been blessed with so much money have chosen to use some of it to improve lives and preserve the natural world.

Yet at the same time that we welcome these improvements we need to be aware of the subtle ways in which our thinking may be changed by the new media. In the fourth century B.C., when writing was in its infancy, Plato worried that it would have a bad effect on people. Specifically he thought that people would no longer use their memories. If something could be inscribed there would be no need to memorize. We may look back and laugh at his concerns, but the fact is—he was right. We no longer rely on our memories in the way that people had to before the invention of writing. But what Plato couldn't see from his vantage point was all the benefits that replaced the lost ability to memorize. People developed analytical skills that would in earlier ages have been impossible. For the first time humans could monitor the development of their intellectual lives, speak to people not yet born, cross-reference, compare and contrast.

The same may be true of computer culture. Certain skills will be lost, but other skills will take their place. One of the most significant changes is the time people spend reading a single document. The Internet is set up to encourage people to follow links, pursue connections and become distracted. It's ideal for gossip and sound bites, but not so good for serious analysis, rumination or meditation. Skimming and scrolling don't allow for nuanced arguments to be effective. Writing in his book *The Shallows* Nicholas Carr reflected, "Once I was a scuba diver in the sea of words. Now I zip along the surface like a guy on a Jet Ski."[11]

The subtitle of *The Shallows* is *What the Internet Is Doing to Our Brains,* and Carr put forward a convincing argument that our brains are being rewired by constant use of the Internet. He points to recent neurological research showing that brain structure is not fixed, as was previously thought. "Virtually all of our neural circuits—whether they're involved in feeling, seeing, hearing, moving, thinking, learning, perceiving, or remembering—are subject to change."[12] New neural pathways are being opened up and old ones are falling into disuse. "With the exception of alphabets and number systems, the Net may well be the most powerful mind altering technology that has ever come into general use. At the very least, it's the most powerful that has come along since the book."[13]

Followers of Jesus are faced with the question of how reflection on Scripture and the study of theology will be affected. Will the surfing mind with its short attention span be sufficient for an exploration of "the deep things of God"? We need to be realistic. Most Christians for most of history haven't had Bibles or been able to read. There was no systematic theology in the sense that we know it before the twelfth century and no Bible concordance before the thirteenth century. Books aren't essential to spiritual growth. People have learned through songs, poems, images, plays, teaching, memorization, dialogue, stories, readings, catechisms and example. However, our failure to read won't be for the same reasons as earlier generations, because we have been blessed with print and paper. If we never pick up a book, it's not because there are no books to pick up.

Digital Literacy

We live in a culture where people probably read more than ever. Far more of us spend a large part of each day processing words. Look around on a bus or train and you see people engaged with texts. It's not the volume of what we read that is of concern but the way we do it. Relationships with people that are conducted in tweets of 140 characters or less can never be profound, and I doubt that a relationship with God that is conducted with a distracted mind can ever attain spiritual maturity. Believers of the pre-book era were not incapable of theological reflection. Illiterate church members of the nineteenth century could often quote long passages of Scripture, memorize hymns and pray in a language approaching great poetry in its intensity.

The Internet wants us to be restless. Its efficiency is measured in click-throughs not enlightenment. "Our goal is to get users in and out really quickly," said Irene Au, head of User Experience at Google. "All our design decisions are based on that strategy."[14] It also leads us to expect instant solutions. If we have a query, we can get an answer almost immediately. If we order a book, the purchase can be settled in seconds. It's easy to imagine how this could affect people's expectation of prayer, guidance and the solving of theological problems.

Computers, smart phones and music players have come to dominate our lives. In one sense they are just developments of the typewriter, telephone, camera and gramophone, but because they can accompany us wherever we go we devote more time to them. Instead of us using the technology, the technology uses us. We become addicted to trivial information, constant entertainment, instant news, updates, breaking news, gossip, rumor and scandal. Some people find it unbearable to be without Internet access.

Gaming

It's true that we are creatures of play, but we are also combatants in spiritual warfare, and people who are urged to redeem the time and press on to the higher calling of the Lord. If we are playing video or computer games, can we justify the hours in light of the needs of the world and our calling? As a planet we spend three billion hours a week playing games. A typical young gamer will rack up ten thousand hours of gaming by the age of twenty-one, only twenty-four hours less than they would spend in middle or high school if they had a full attendance record. Five million U.S. gamers play for more than forty hours a week. It's questionable whether anyone could play this much and also practice the pure religion advocated in James 1:27, which involves visiting orphans and widows in their distress and keeping ourselves from "being polluted by the world." I don't think we would need to engage in so many fantasy battles on screen if we were aware of the very real battles God asks us to get involved in.

The nature of games may also affect people's approach to what is real. The storytelling in games often involves different approaches that ultimately result in the same conclusion. Some have asked whether this acclimatizes players to the idea that in spiritual matters it doesn't matter which path you take. In *Halos and Avatars* Chris Hansen of Baylor University asks,

> Video gaming's multiple-path narrative style matches a pluralistic impulse. If we relate to the world through our stories, and our stories show us that we can play the game a different way every time and still come to the same resolution, then will the generation that experiences storytelling through this lens eventually come to accept that as reality?[15]

To be fair, Hansen's answer to his own question is that he doesn't think it will.

Others point out that games are generally about mastery, problem solving and winning, whereas the Christian life is about repentance, obedience and sacrificial living. If the life of Paul had been a game, he wouldn't appear to be a winner. Nor would Peter or John the Baptist. In some ways life *is* about mastery—mastery of temptations and the "sin that so easily entangles" (Heb 12:1), mastery of scriptural truth, mastery of our gifts—and there are problems to solve. We have an ultimate guarantee that we will win, but winning may not always feel like winning because there are paradoxes at the heart of the Christian life. We live by dying, we come in first by being last, and we gain by giving up.

Quiet Time

Reflection and meditation are an important part of the Christian walk. We need uninterrupted time when we do nothing but think about our mistakes and triumphs, our family and friends, our church and community, and the goodness and faithfulness of God. We need time to clear our minds to allow God to speak to us. We need time to store God's Word in our hearts and to see what combinations occur as new things learned react with old things learned. The "still small voice" may be imperceptible among the chatter of social networking.

It's easy to see how the new technology, if not controlled, can war against the meditative life. If I go for a walk alone, it can be a time to ponder, remember, assess past actions and make future plans. If I take the same walk with music, I can still ponder but I'm drawn into thoughts of lyrics, record production, musical styles and associations with particular periods in my life or moments in history. There are times when it's refreshing to do this, and times when in the course of work I need to do this, but there are also times when I'm being overindulgent or I'm choosing to avoid necessary rumination. Can gluttony for information be as bad for us as gluttony for food?

We are said to be living in the Information Age, yet it often feels as though we are drowning in facts, opinions and speculation. It's as if we've been blessed with unprecedented opportunities to communicate, yet with far less to say. Or possibly it's because capacity now exceeds what we actually need that everything is naturally thinned out. We have more celebrities but fewer heroes, more special effects but less effectiveness, more digital downloads but fewer classic songs, more opinions but less wisdom, more jokes but fewer laughs. It makes me think of Bruce Springsteen's song "57 Channels (And Nothin' On)," or T. S. Eliot's lines from "Choruses from 'The Rock'" (1934) where he mourned the life lost in living, the wisdom lost in knowledge and the knowledge lost in information.

It makes me think of the description of idols in Psalm 115:5:

They have mouths, but cannot speak,
   eyes, but cannot see.

Questions for Reflection or Discussion

- Does music mean something different to you than it did to your parents, and do you think this has something to do with the way it is now delivered?

- Does social networking make you more or less honest with your "friends"?

- Can you think of other hippyish elements to the ethos of the Internet?

- How has your life been made easier by the quantity of knowledge available online?

- How do you decide what information to trust on the Internet?

- Should we welcome or be wary of programs that promise to unify humankind?

- What effect do you think the availability of information and speed of access has had on your ability to reflect on wrestle with the Bible?

- Can a follower of Jesus justify spending forty hours a week playing games?

- Think of two ways the Internet has helped improve your spiritual life and two ways it has damaged it.

- Do you experience anxiety if your unable to check in online for twenty-four hours?

General Books

Auletta. Ken. *Googled: The End of the World as We Know It*. New York: Penguin, 2009.

Carr. Nicholas. *The Shallows: What the Internet Is Doing to Our Brains.* New York: W. W. Norton, 2010.

Isaacson, Walter. *Steve Jobs.* New York: Simon & Schuster, 2011

Kelly, Kevin. *What Technology Wants.* New York: Viking, 2010.

Markoff, John. *What the Dormouse Said: How the Sixties Counterculture Shaped the Personal Computer Industry.* New York: Viking Penguin, 2005.

McGonigal, Jane. *Reality Is Broken: Why Games Make Us Better and How They Can Change the World.* London: Jonathan Cape, 2011.

Turner, Fred. *From Counterculture to Cyberculture: Stewart Brand, the Whole Earth Network and the Rise of Digital Utopianism.* Chicago: University of Chicago Press, 2006.

Books Examining the Digital Revolution from a Christian Viewpoint

Challies, Tim. *The Next Story: Life and Faith After the Digital Explosion.* Grand Rapids: Zondervan, 2011.

Detweiler, Craig. *Halos and Avatars: Playing Video Games with God.* Louisville, KY: Westminster John Knox, 2010.

Websites

Hardcore Christian Gaming Association: www.christian-gaming.com; www.christcenteredgamer.com

"The Church and the Internet," Roman Catholic Church's Pontifical Council for Social Communications: www.vatican.va/roman_curia/pontifical_councils/pccs/documents/rc_pc_pccs_doc_20020228_church-internet_en.html

"Ethics in Internet," Pontifical Council for Social Communications: www.vatican.va/roman_curia/pontifical_councils/pccs/documents/rc_pc_pccs_doc_20020228_ethics-internet_en.html

Five Suggestions for Action

- Read Walter Isaacson's biography of Steve Jobs and learn of Jobs's fastidious concern for design, communication, motivation and relevance. There are many lessons in the book that can be applied to other areas of life.

- Build online communities around your special interests.

- Organize your searches of key websites so that you capitalize on your time spent online.

- Download free versions of literary and theological classics to your iPad. Never before have so many of humanity's greatest thoughts been so freely available.

- Watch TED lectures (www.ted.com) while ironing. There are hundreds of stimulating twenty-minute talks here that will massage your brain.

12

Photography

The Opening of the Eyes

†

Photographers teach us how to see the world. They not only draw our attention to things we might otherwise have overlooked but present a visual approach that often conditions our subsequent viewings. I frequently catch myself surveying a scene—a perfect combination of light, people and landscape—and thinking *I wish I had my camera with me*. Even though I'm not a professional photographer I have been trained by years of viewing high-quality photographs to know what makes a powerful composition.

This is largely to do with the age I was raised in. Photographic books are relatively inexpensive to buy, magazines and newspapers routinely carry award-winning work, printing quality is continually improving, and the Internet means that I can have immediate access to classic photos. My parents, due to the age they grew up in, weren't as familiar with good photographic art and would therefore have thought more in terms of "a nice picture" or "a good snapshot." In other words, I have learned to see in a different way because of photography. "The camera is an instrument that teaches people how to see without a camera," said the great documentary photographer Dorothea Lange.[1] In her book *On Photography*, the essayist Susan Sontag argued, "In teaching us a new visual code, photographs alter and enlarge our notions of what is worth looking at and what we have a right to observe. They are grammar and, even more importantly, an ethics of seeing."[2]

The things we might have overlooked if they weren't photographed range from insects in the Amazon basin and working conditions in Asian sweatshops to wars that are being fought in countries we perhaps can't even place on a map. They also include the fascinating details of life. Over recent years I have taken photographs of doors around the world—huge palatial doors and broken down barn doors, newly painted doors and weather-beaten doors, doors with "WELCOME" and doors with "WARNING." Although doors are "just" lumps of wood or steel, they represent so much more. They are flung open out of hospitality or slammed shut in anger; they protect our privacy and deter criminals. Our own front door is what we most anticipate the sight of when we are journeying home. The look of a door often suggests something of what has taken place behind it. I doubt whether my eyes would have alighted on these particular details if it hadn't been for photography. Pictures have opened up my imagination.

Similarly, I see more of the detail in nature. I notice the twisted roots of trees, the complex color contrasts created by peeling bark, the patterns of stretching branches and twigs. I wonder how much of this would have escaped my gaze if it hadn't been for the work of photographers over the years continually requesting that I pay attention, teaching me to see the glory in the dust.

To me the biblical worldview endorses such attention to detail. God cares about details and has to time to inspect, value and enjoy them. David's awe that the God who controls the planets and stars cared about him (Ps 8) was amazement at God's concern for detail. In his teachings Jesus would point to the seemingly insignificant—the mustard seed, the sparrow, a lost coin—to make the same point. From the Bible we learn that we can be taught lessons about diligence, patience and hard work by paying attention to the work practices of the ant. Jesus said, "The very hairs of your head are all numbered" (Lk 12:7). We gloss over the instruction to "consider the lilies" to get on to the bit about how God cares for us, but in itself it is advice about slowing down and focusing on precisely the details that a photographer helps to highlight. When he says, "Do you have eyes but fail to see?" (Mk 8:18), he is acknowledging our tendency to look but not see.

Ways of Seeing

Photography not only educates us in what to notice but also subtly informs us how to interpret what we see. Winston Churchill's image as the defender of the British Empire was greatly enhanced by a photograph taken in Canada in 1941 by Yousuf Karsh. Churchill was between important engagements, didn't really have time to pose for the camera and was consequently in a grumpy mood. He gave Karsh two minutes to capture his essence. The British Prime Minister sat down and glared into the camera with a cigar between his teeth. Karsh thought the cigar inappropriate, so he removed it. Churchill glared even harder and Karsh took his shot. The momentary anger at having to be photographed supplemented by his annoyance at losing his cigar captured his defiance and produced the portrait that would inspire millions.

Churchill later recognized the brilliance of what had been done, telling Karsh, "You can even make a roaring lion stand still to be photographed." Karsh titled his portrait "The Roaring Lion." He later said of his approach to distilling the essence of a subject,

> Within every man and woman a secret is hidden, and as a photographer it is my task to reveal it if I can. The revelation, if it comes at all, will come in a small fraction of a second with an unconscious gesture, a gleam of the eye, a brief lifting of the mask that all humans wear to conceal their innermost selves from the world. In that fleeting interval of opportunity the photographer must act or lose his prize.[3]

Another photo that has become iconic in a similar way is of a very different political figure from a different era: the head-and-shoulders shot of Marxist revolutionary Che Guevara wearing a beret, beard and military-style tunic taken by Alberto Korda in March 1960. This wasn't a posed portrait. Guevara was at a public meeting in Havana, Cuba, listening to a speech by Fidel Castro. Korda, a lifetime communist and a supporter of the Cuban revolution, spotted him on a balcony and took two photos because what he saw through his viewfinder summed up the guerilla leader's "absolute implacability." Guevara looked romantic, commanding, resolute and vaguely Christlike. Other pictures taken of him on the same day, wearing the same uniform, had nothing like the same impact. It has since become one of the most instantly recognizable photos in history, used on posters, T-shirts, books, albums and artworks. Korda recognized it as "the ultimate symbol of Marxist revolution and anti-imperialistic struggle."[4]

Because photographs usually don't involve verbal statements, people rarely think of them as having a point of view. The old saying "The camera never lies" implies that a photograph, unlike a verbal description given by a witness, is objective. All that a photographer needs to do is point and click and the truth is clearly recorded. But this isn't so. The camera will record what it sees but it's the photographer who chooses what the camera will see, how much of it will be seen, from what perspective the viewer will eventually look and which shots get printed or put online. The photographer and environmentalist Ansel Adams grasped this when he observed, "A great photograph is a full expression of what one feels about what is being photographed in the deepest sense, and is a true expression of what one feels about life in its entirety."[5]

Motivation

Photographers communicate how they see the world in five principal ways. It begins with motivation. Whatever it is that makes someone want to take photographs will have a telling impact on the work they produce. Some photographers want to alert the world to hidden beauty. Some want to highlight injustice. Photojournalist Henri Cartier-Bresson was interested in "the marvelous mixture of emotion and geometry, together in an instant."[6] The war photographer Donald McCullin said, "Seeing, looking at what others cannot bear to see, is what my life is all about."[7] Robert Frank spoke about trying to "see what is invisible to others."[8] Members of the paparazzi usually only have the aim of feeding the demand of celebrity hungry newspapers, magazines and TV channels.

Think of the difference between the mission statement of the early twentieth-century photographer Alfred Stieglitz, who said, "Photography is my passion. The search for truth is my obsession," and the goal of pop artist Andy Warhol, who said, "My idea of a good picture is one that's in focus and of a famous person."[9] Not surprisingly Stieglitz produced evocative photos of his life in New York, while Andy Warhol took celebrities to coin-operated photo booths or took Polaroid shots of them that revealed no character or depth. Warhol's approach was entirely in keeping with his philosophy of exalting the famous and admiring the mechanical more than the emotional, spiritual and intellectual. "Look at the surface: of my paintings and films and me, and there I am," he once said. "There's nothing behind it."[10]

War photographers risk their lives to keep the world informed about armed conflict. Thirty-six photographers and camera operators were either killed or abducted during the war in Iraq between 2003 and 2009. Often what they see has a deeply scarring effect on them. The South African photographer Kevin Carter, a passionate opponent of injustice, won the Pulitzer Prize for Feature Photography in 1994 for a photo he had taken in Southern Sudan of a child trying to crawl to a feeding center while a vulture looked on just a few yards away. It was an incredibly powerful image of human life reduced to carrion and affected public opinion, but some accused Carter of putting his art before the life of the child. Shouldn't he have dropped the camera and rescued the child? Later that year Carter killed himself. Part of his suicide note read, "I am haunted by vivid memories of killing and corpses and anger and pain, . . . of starving and wounded children, of trigger happy madmen."[11]

The commitment of the war photographer makes us all witnesses to suffering that we might have been able to avoid. It draws our attention to deeds that might otherwise have been carried out in darkness. It enables us to vote, pray, protest or support in a far more informed way. It reveals to us the extremes of the human condition in bravery, fortitude and self-sacrifice as well as brutality, cowardice and pain. The photojournalist and war photographer James Nachtwey has said that he would love to take everyone to a war zone to show them the pain caused by a single bullet or the damage done by a single piece of shrapnel:

> But everyone cannot be there, and that is why photographers go there—to show them, to reach out and grab them and make them stop what they are doing and pay attention to what is going on—to create pictures powerful enough to overcome the diluting effects of the mass media and shake people out of their indifference—to protest and by the strength of that protest to make others protest.[12]

Far removed from the battlefield are photographers who take risks to show the world the glories and delights of nature. Getting the perfect shot for magazines can be time-consuming and dangerous. Greg du Toit spent a total of 270 hours over a period of three months semi-submerged in a watering hole in Kenya to get never-before-seen shots of lions feeding. In doing so he almost died of malaria. To photograph an annual gathering of macaws in the Amazon basin, Frans Lanting had to drag a ton of scaffolding and a canoe through the jungle, and then spend twelve hours a day for a month in a space no bigger than an office desk atop a ninety-foot tower.

Wildlife photography has revealed creation in ways that no other generation has ever seen it. Underwater photography has exposed marine life previously known only to God. The growing concern to protect the environment owes a lot to the work of such photographers who can show both the glory and the destruction of nature.

Frans Lanting has said, "It's up to us as photographers to give voice to the natural world."[13] Giving voice to the natural world unwittingly gives voice to God because, as it says in Romans 1:20, "God's invisible qualities" are "understood from what has been made, so that people are without excuse."

Choice

Second, worldview conditions what the photographer chooses to photograph. As soon as a subject is chosen, a value has been assigned. The photographer is implicitly telling his or her audience that this image is worthy of our consideration. For every subject chosen, a number of other subjects or areas of life are rejected. Behind these choices will be a view of life shaped by religion, philosophy, background, social pressure or historical trends that will determine what is of significance. Ansel Adams once said, "We don't make a photograph just with a camera. We bring to the act of photography all the books we have read, the movies we have seen, the music we have heard, the people we have loved."[14]

The moment a photographer goes out to work with a camera a selection process is taking place. The retina picks up thousands of images but only a small fraction will be deemed worthy of preservation. The photographer is making constant assessments about such concerns as interest, value, originality, relevance, beauty, ugliness, shape, light and color. There isn't the time to shoot everything. The photographer's brain is constantly editing.

What people are attracted to tells us something about their spiritual condition. According to Proverbs 23:7, we are what we think. The notorious Weegee made his name by tuning in to police radios and arriving on the scenes of accidents, murders, violence and crime before law enforcement. His photos naturally honed in on death, destruction and the underbelly of New York. Diane Arbus had a fascination for the deformed and freakish. Louis Sass, a clinical psychologist from Rutgers University with an interest in modern art, summed up Arbus's interest as being in "deviant and marginal people . . . or of people whose normality seems ugly or surreal."[15] Referring to Arbus's work Susan Sontag said it was "a good instance of a leading tendency of high art in capitalist countries to suppress, or at least reduce, moral and sensory queasiness. Much of modern art is devoted to lowering the threshold of what is terrible."[16]

There's nothing wrong with photographing a murder scene, an accident, a deviant or an ugly person. These are part of the wider truth of the world. But how these things are portrayed and the attitude with which they are treated will communicate whether we think they are aberrations or just the way things are and should be. Robert Mapplethorpe, who gained attention for photographing homoerotic scenes as if they were as neutral as flower arrangements, once said, "Beauty and the devil are the same thing."[17]

Some visual artists will approach ugliness and decay with compassion and yet anger at the destruction that sin has made in the world; others will revel in it as if to say, "I told you so. This is life. Get used to it." The artist Francis Bacon, who used photos of raw meat, screaming mouths, skin disorders and forensic pathology as source material for his paintings, thought that images such as this showed the brute reality of a world without God. He told an interviewer that when he was seventeen he saw dog feces on a pavement and "I suddenly realised, there it is—this is what life is like. It tormented me for months. I think of life as meaningless; but we give it meaning during our own existence. We give this purposeless existence a meaning by ourselves."[18]

It would be revealing to find half a dozen photographers, each committed to a different worldview, and then set them the task of doing a one-day shoot of a particular city to see what differences emerged. I would expect to see a lot in common because of fundamental human values and experiences, but I would also expect to see differences because of personal outlook and interests. I wouldn't judge the Christian by the number of church spires photographed but the sort of people and places that caught his or her eye and how each subject was dealt with. The record of that day with a camera would reveal the concerns, priorities and passions of each photographer's heart.

Susan Sontag observed that initially photography was regarded as "impersonal seeing," but then people realized that "nobody takes the same picture of the same thing." The mindset of the photographer plays a vital role. A result of this understanding was that "objective image yielded to the fact that photographs are evidence not only of what's there but of what an individual sees, not just a record but an evaluation of the world."[19]

Treatment

Third, worldview is further communicated by the way the selected subject is treated. For example, someone photographing prostitutes could photograph them as if they were worthless, glamorous, enticing, revered, damaged or sinful yet capable of forgiveness and restoration. The eye behind the camera could be screwed up in disgust, leering with lust or wide-eyed through tender understanding. The "perfect shot" will be determined by the attitude of the beholder. As photographer Eve Arnold once said, "The instrument is not the camera but the photographer."[20] In a similar vein Susan Sontag commented,

> In deciding how a picture should look, in preferring one exposure to another, photographers are always imposing standards on their subjects. Although there is a sense in which the camera does indeed capture reality, not just interpret it, photographs are as much an interpretation of the world as paintings and drawings are.[21]

There are a few times in the Gospels where Jesus is reported to have looked at the crowds facing him and to have "had compassion" (Mt 9:36; 14:14; 18:27; 20:34). It's a description of how the heart links to the eye and how the visual stirs the physical. The world's great photographers are generally people who are moved by compassion. They empathize with their subjects and bring out all the beauty, suffering and

humanity. The German photographer, writer and filmmaker Wim
Wenders, when commenting on the war photography of James
Nachtwey, said, "The eye that looks through the lens is also reflected on
the photo itself. It leaves a faint, sometimes shadowy trace of the photographer, something between a silhouette and an engraving, an 'image'
not of his features, but of his heart, his soul, his mind, his spirit."[22]

"It's more important to click with people," said Alfred Eisenstaedt,
"than to click the shutter."[23] These photographs then reach out and
touch the viewer. I think of Walker Evans's photos of the victims of
the 1930s dustbowl in James Agee's book *Let Us Now Praise Famous
Men*. Even the title of the book (taken from the apocryphal book of
Ecclesiasticus) affirms the dignity of these economic migrants. Cartier-
Bresson said, "For me photography is to place head, heart, and eye
along the same line of sight. It's a way of life."[24]

In a world where a line or a crease in the face is seen as a blemish
that needs surgery or antiwrinkle cream, the photographer can show
that aging has its own beauty and that the scoring brought about by
care, suffering and laughter is worthy of respect. The Bible says, "Gray
hair is a crown of splendor," which could also be translated "a crown
of beauty" (Prov 16:31). Equally, those who are unsympathetic or
who have a low view of human life can make such erosion appear ugly
and disdainful. Eve Arnold once said, "The hardest thing in the world
is to take the mundane and show how special it is," and yet that is
precisely what great photographers can do.[25] Sylvester Jacobs, a photographer who is a Christian, said that with his work he was "intent
on finding traces of the divine in the human."[26]

Framing

A fourth way photographers show us how they see the world is in
how they frame their subjects. It's not just who is in the picture that
counts, but what surrounds them. When we see an image we immediately begin a process of interpretation. We read a picture as a story.
A person is usually captured in an environment, and viewers begin to
ask questions about the relationship between the subject and the

world that surrounds them. A CEO likes to be photographed behind a desk (usually a tidy desk) with family photographs behind and maybe some awards. These clues suggest status, commitment to family values, and professional achievements. The same CEO in dungarees eating a Big Mac would not exude power. It's for this reason that press photographers love the opportunity to catch high-profile people off-guard—the model without makeup pushing a supermarket cart, the politician yawning, the superstar with a mouth full of food.

The most immediate framing is decided by the photographer at the time of shooting—whether to zoom in or maintain a wide focus, whether to include surroundings or concentrate on the individual, whether to accentuate the facial features or go for a full body shot. But photographers, and editors, can crop pictures, and this can change the meaning. "The camera cannot lie," said Harold Evans, the highly respected former editor of *The Sunday Times* (London), "but it can be an accessory of untruth."[27]

There have been many examples of press photographs that have been audaciously cropped to make a political point. The advent of digital manipulation has increased the potential for altering the information in an image. This often involves removing unwanted people. A photo of President Obama used on the cover of the *Economist* showed him standing alone, head bowed, with the sea and an oil rig in the near distance. The story was about BP oil spillage. It appeared to show him pensive, isolated and possibly under pressure. The uncropped photo revealed that he was standing on a beach with two people beside him. One had been cropped out; the other had been digitally excised. The reason he had lowered his head was not out of remorse or because of the weight of his problems, but because the person next to him was short.

In 2009 Pulitzer Prize–winning photographer David Hume Kennerly complained in the *New York Times* about a photo he'd taken of former vice president Dick Cheney cutting up meat that had been used by *Newsweek* to illustrate a story about CIA interrogation techniques.

The Sept. 14th Newsweek cover line—"Is Your Baby Racist?"—
should have included a sub-head, "Is Dick Cheney a Butcher?"

Featured inside the magazine was a full-page, stand-alone
picture of former vice president Dick Cheney, knife in hand,
leaning over a bloody carving board. Newsweek used it to illustrate a quote that he made about C.I.A. interrogators. By linking
that photo with Mr. Cheney's comment and giving it such prominence, they implied something sinister, macabre, or even evil
was going on there.

I took that photograph at his daughter Liz's home during a
two-day assignment, and was shocked by its usage. The meat on
the cutting board wasn't the only thing butchered. In fact,
Newsweek chose to crop out two-thirds of the original photograph, which showed Mrs. Cheney, both of their daughters, and
one of their grandchildren, who were also in the kitchen, getting
ready for a simple family dinner.

However, Newsweek's objective in running the cropped
version was to illustrate its editorial point of view, which could
only have been done by shifting the content of the image so that
readers just saw what the editors wanted them to see. This
radical alteration is photo fakery. Newsweek's choice to run my
picture as a political cartoon not only embarrassed and humiliated me and ridiculed the subject of the picture, but it ultimately denigrated my profession.[28]

Closely related are instances where pictures have been set up. They
may tell a story that is broadly true but the actual event shown has
been stage-managed for maximum effect. Bodies are moved around,
mourners are told to grieve on cue, toys are placed in strategic positions and some events are even re-run for the cameras. The presence
of photographers in conflicts inevitably changes the nature of the
conflict because the participants realize the value of striking images
that will promote their cause. The famous photograph taken by Eddie
Adams in Saigon during the Vietnam war of Colonel Nguyen Ngoc

shooting a Vietcong prisoner in the head was carried out in the street rather than indoors only because the colonel thought the photographer would get a better angle.

Cases such as these raise questions of whether photography can be complicit in the inhumanity it chronicles. Many protests, demonstrations, rampages and acts of terrorism are put on for the benefit of the press. While covering riots in East Jerusalem, Italian photographer Ruben Salvadori took the opportunity to photograph his colleagues, and his pictures often showed masked men throwing rocks, burning flags and creating bonfires purely for the benefit of a crowd of photographers. "This is what we have to create if we want to sell," he said of a photo of a boy looking threateningly at the camera. "On the other hand though this pushes many photojournalists to seek and create this drama even when the situation lacks it." Salvadori's background in anthropology led him to conclude that such conflict was "a show in which the photographer is an actor and has a role."[29]

Presentation

Finally, photography communicates a worldview through the way it is presented. A photograph of a naked human body, for example, could mean totally different things depending on whether it appeared in a visual arts catalog, a health journal, a medical textbook, a guide for naturists, an A-Z of love making or a church magazine. The French semiotician Roland Barthes referred to the surroundings of text, caption, layout and even the title of the paper or magazine a "channel of transmission" and said that it represented "a complex of concurrent messages."[30]

In his 1986 essay "Photographs and Contexts" art critic Terry Barrett took the example of a Robert Doisneau photo of a man and a woman drinking wine in a Parisian cafe.[31] Doisneau loved the café culture of his home city and the couple had agreed to be photographed. It was first published as part of a photo essay on cafes in a magazine called *le Point*. However, shortly afterward it appeared, without Doisneau's permission, in a brochure about the evils of alcohol abuse. Later, again without Doisneau's permission, it was used in a French scandal sheet with the caption "Prostitution in the Champs Elysees."

The three different contexts produced three different meanings. Many years later it was framed and hung in a gallery of the Museum of Modern Art in New York. This context shifted the emphasis away from the couple and toward the genius of the photographer. It was also to be compared with other photographic art in the same gallery. Rather than a caption it was titled "At the Cafe, Chez Fraysse, Rue de Seine, Paris, 1958."

It was also included in a book, *Looking at Photographs*, where on the opposite page curator John Szarkowski gave his view on what he thought Doisneau had achieved. This was a specific interpretation based on his reading of the relationship between the man and the woman portrayed. "Most photographers of the past generation have demonstrated unlimited sympathy for the victims of villainous or imperfect societies, but very little sympathy for, or even interest in, those who are afflicted by their own human frailty," he wrote. "Robert Doisneau is one of the few whose work has demonstrated that even in a time of large terrors, the ancient weaknesses and sweet venial sins of ordinary individuals have survived. On the basis of his pictures one would guess that Doisneau actually likes people, even as they really are."[32]

Christian Photography

If the subject of Christian photography is mentioned, people assume that you mean photographs of church buildings, pilgrimage sites, weddings, christenings or Christian celebrities. Sometimes there are nature photographs that justify their inclusion by being given spiritual titles or Bible verses. An Internet search using the words *Christian* and *photography* soon yields pages containing the words *church graphics*. But truly Christian photography should not be defined by subject matter or usefulness to the church but by vision, attitude and truth. It's possible to take photographs of church events in an un-

Christian way by, for example, making a wedding look more like a Disney fairy tale than a spiritual union, just as it's possible to photograph a war in a Christian way, by being honest about suffering, courage, good and evil.

I don't know the personal spiritual beliefs of the celebrated war photographer James Nachtwey, but his philosophy of photography is informed by values of integrity, humility, compassion, sacrifice, humanitarianism and service that any Christian should be eager to hold. "If war is an attempt to negate humanity, then photography can be perceived as the opposite of war," he once said.[33] Speaking of the choice that often has to be made between alerting the world to suffering and exploiting the weak and bereft he said, "The worst thing is to feel that as a photographer I am benefitting from someone else's tragedy. This idea haunts me. It's something I have to reckon with every day because I know if I ever allowed genuine compassion to be overtaken by personal ambition I will have sold my soul. The only way I can justify my role is to have respect for the other person's predicament."[34]

I hope that one day websites devoted to Christians and photography will have quotes like that on them, and that when people think of a photographer who is a Christian they don't just think of someone who takes "nice" images of untarnished scenes but of someone who looks at the world in God's way with all of his passion, delight, anger, love and care. "I believe that all we really have to do is take a closer look. All we have to do is train our eyes to see not just the PHOTOGRAPH itself, but the ATTITUDE of the eye and the heart that took it," wrote Wim Wenders in a eulogy to Nachtwey. "Every look represents a certain attitude or state of mind, your gaze just as well, at any given time. Interest, boredom, disgust, indifference, sorrow, love, surprise, curiosity, hatred, cynicism, affection, respect, aversion, exhaustion, frustration . . . whatever guides our eyes is depicted along with the subject when a camera is lifted to the eye. There is no picture that wasn't taken with an attitude of some kind or other."[35]

Questions for Reflection or Discussion

- What photographs have meant the most to you and why?

- Do photographers have a duty to stop the violence or starvation they witness, or are their photographs the most effective long-term contribution they can make?

- Have photographs ever made you more socially conscious?

- Have photographs ever made you more conscious of beauty?

- Is it possible to take honorable photos of things that are ugly or destructive?

- Can the camera ever lie?

- In what ways can cropping a photo alter its message?

- Is it ever right to "stage manage" a photo in the cause of a greater truth?

- In what ways can the presentation of a photo alter its meaning?

- If Jesus had owned a camera, what are some of the things he might have photographed?

General Books on Photography and Images

Agee, James, and Walter Evans. *Let Us Now Praise Famous Men*. New York: Houghton Mifflin, 1941.

Berger, John. *Ways of Seeing*. London: Penguin, 1972.

Evans, Harold. *Pictures on a Page: Photo-Journalism, Graphics and Picture Editing*. 2nd ed. London: Pimlico, 1997.

Looking at Photographs: 100 Pictures From the Collection of the Museum of Modern Art. New York: MOMA, 1984.

Sontag, Susan. *On Photography*. New York: Farrar, Strauss & Giroux, 1977.

Websites

Southwestern Photojournalism Conference: www.swpjc.org, "This conference is for those who believe photojournalism to be a calling and the act of bearing witness to be important."

Photographers Gary Fong and Greg Schneider: www.christiansinpho tojournalism.org

Christians in Photography: www.christiansinphotography.com

Photomission: www.photomission.com. Supplies photos to "Christian publishing, designers, worship leaders and multimedia profes- sionals."

Five Suggestions for Action

- Spend a day photographing your village, town or city. Discover what your results tell you about your priorities.

- Collect some outstanding photos from magazines and newspapers and work out what makes them so effective.

- Buy or borrow from a library a book of Henri Cartier-Bresson's photographs. How does he capture the humanity of his subjects?

- Photograph the same scene or person from five different angles, each one of which will tell a different story.

- Visit a photography exhibition.

13

TV and Movies

The Image of the Faith

†

Up to now this book has been about a Christian understanding of popular culture, but now I turn to the subject of popular culture's understanding of the Christian. How are Christianity, the church and Jesus dealt with in films and on TV, and does it really matter? Are Christians misunderstood, vilified and persecuted by the media, or are they justifiably ridiculed? When the portrayals are unfair should Christians protest, or does that merely compound the idea that we are joyless, prickly and unable to see our flaws?

My own experience, and this seems to be borne out by research, is that the number of practicing Christians at decision-making levels in popular culture is disproportionately small. An internal BBC survey in 2011 found that only 22.5 percent of BBC employees identified themselves as Christians in a country where 71 percent identify themselves as such. A 2008 poll by the Anti-Defamation League in America found that 59 percent of respondents agreed with the statement "the people who run the TV networks and the major movie studios do not share the religious and moral values of most Americans." Lists of the "ten most powerful Christians in Hollywood" are notable only for the lack of power that Christians wield in that realm. This is despite the fact that, according to a Barna Group report in 2005, there are more evangelical Christians in Los Angeles than any other urban center in America.

Why should Hollywood be such a Christian-free zone? For almost
four decades the studios were ruled by the Motion Picture Production
Code, a list of rules drawn up to ensure a morality drawn from the
Bible informed the movies. It specifically protected religion from
scorn and religious leaders from being laughed at in their professional
roles. "No film or episode should throw ridicule on any religious
faith," it said. "Ministers of religion in their character as ministers of
religion should not be used as comic characters or as villains. Ceremonies of any definite religion should be carefully and respectfully
handled."[1] The man heading up the office, Will Hays, was a Presby-
terian, and every script ready to go into production was inspected.

At the same time the National Legion of Decency, a Catholic organization, was based in Hollywood and graded films as (A) "morally
unobjectionable," (B) "morally objectionable in part" or (C) "condemned."[2] No Catholic was supposed to see the condemned films.
Later the Protestant Film Commission, part of the National Council
of Churches, reviewed films for the faithful, organized awards to
promote what it considered to be good filmmaking and advised on
such biblical epics as *The Greatest Story Ever Told*.

All three organizations were swept away by the changes of the
1960s. The swing toward relativism meant that no religion could be
privileged over another; the mood for free speech meant that no one
was free from criticism, attack or parody, and the "new morality"
meant that Christian principles about personal behavior were regarded as hang-ups or guilt trips. The offices of the National Legion
of Decency and the Protestant Film Commission both closed down in
1966. The Motion Picture Production Code was dropped in 1968.
Andrew O'Hehir, writing on Salon.com, said, "It's only oversimpli-
fying a little to say that pop culture went in one direction and the
evangelical population went in another and despite a long process of
reconciliation, it's still not clear that they speak the same language."[3]

That Hollywood was subject to the code and treated religion with
respect for so long disguised the fact that the studios weren't full of
religious people. The creative industries attract people who are natu-

rally skeptical and experimental, and who like to make things up as they go along in their lives as well as in their work. This is as true today as it was then, the only difference being that they are now free to openly express their doubts or distaste. Brad Pitt, raised as a Southern Baptist, is fairly typical of a Hollywood person who found religion "stifling" and cast aside whatever faith he had when he entered the acting profession. "When I got untethered from the comfort of religion, it wasn't a loss of faith for me, it was a discovery of self," he said in an interview. "I had faith that I'm capable enough to handle any situation. There's peace in understanding that I have only one life, here and now, and I'm responsible."[4]

Those who enter the entertainment industry as Christians frequently find their faith eroded by a combination of antagonism from others, compromise and the demands of a busy schedule. It's easy to find people who became actors or directors with grand visions of changing the world, only to find themselves unexpectedly enchanted by the world they'd come to change. The people they'd been taught to fear weren't as bad as they'd been portrayed. When you're rewarded with money, acclaim and critical approval, it can be hard to rock the boat by making controversial Christian statements.

An additional reason for Hollywood's secularism is that for many years Christians were not encouraged to go into film because it was considered worldly at best, ungodly at worst. We were called to come out from the world and be separate, and that included not working in such fields as film, television and secular music. In his 1947 book *Movies and Morals* Herbert J. Miles wrote that movies "are the organ of the Devil, the idol of sinners, the sink of infamy, the stumbling block to human progress, the moral cancer of civilization, the Number One enemy of Jesus Christ."[5] These cultural expectations have meant that the movers and shakers in Hollywood are now almost exclusively non-Christian or ex-Christian. In 1998 a University of Texas poll of Hollywood actors, writers, producers and executives found that only 2 to 3 percent attended regular weekly services at a place of worship in contrast to 41 percent of the general public. In a recent list of "the twenty most influential people in Hollywood" I could find eight who'd expressed clear atheist or agnostic views, but none who'd expressed clear Christian views.

This doesn't automatically mean that the majority of people in the popular arts are overtly hostile to Christianity and are banding together to assault it, but I think it does mean that many of those with no Christian background have a poor understanding of the basics of the faith, and those who were raised in church but have rejected it tend to be irritated by believers and can use their work to exact revenge on whatever it was they didn't like.

The lack of Christian background is evidenced by the absence of convincing religious references in TV soaps, dramas and movies. Someone could argue that you never see people excusing themselves to go to the bathroom unless a bathroom scene is key to the action (a secret phone call is made, a witness is spotted) but the difference is that use of the bathroom is always functional and private whereas religious devotion is pervasive and has a public aspect. No one expects to see repeated scenes of Bibles read and hymns sung. That would be boring. But when such things are never mentioned reality is skewed. The characters in *Friends*, *Sex and the City* or *Two and a Half Men* drink, get drunk, party, listen to music, vacation, eat in restaurants, date, work, have sex, but they never do or say anything that would connect them to religion.

Not doing or saying anything spiritual may appear to be the most neutral of positions. That way you offend no major faith and keep the advertisers happy. But neutrality, in this case, is a vote in favor of a secular lifestyle where God is never mentioned, except as an expletive. It has the effect of making the audience feel that not belonging to a spiritual community, talking to God or having a spiritual discipline is normal. If a character came into one of these programs and said, "I'll see you after church on Sunday" or "I'll pray for you about that," it would seem outlandish.

The only dramas where churchgoing and faith are made to seem normal are on channels like True Movies and Hallmark, where they come in useful to evoke "traditional values" or nostalgia for more stable times. This is easy to do when dramas are set in the past (*Little House on the Prairie*) or in the Deep South, where it seems that "folk in them days" or "folk in them places" acted like this. Most influential contemporary dramas are set in places like London, New York, Los Angeles or Chicago, where churchgoing is lower than Belfast, Dallas, Grand Rapids or Rio.

Many influential creative people had religious backgrounds but subsequently either rejected them or have lived with permanent doubts. Sometimes, for such people, art becomes a refuge, a kind of alternative church where they can grapple with issues of identity, values, faith and a better world. For others art becomes the place where they can settle scores. I once asked Matt Groening, creator of *The Simpsons*, why so much of the satirizing of religion in the cartoon series was directed toward evangelical Christianity rather than to, for example, Islam. His answer was that many of the people who worked on the series were familiar with evangelicalism and so thought it fair enough to have a go at what they knew from experience rather that what they had only read about. "*The Simpsons* pretty much reflects the backgrounds of the people who make the show," he told me. "It's not about 'the other.' It's not about outsiders."

Stereotypes

When portraying church people, films and television tend to rely on stereotypes, largely because the writers rarely possess up-to-date knowledge of the contemporary church. Many people in the artistic community pass comment on the church, and what they have in mind is based on an impression formed in early childhood, very often in the countryside or from films. They would be scornful of someone who became a teetotaler because of a bad experience with one bar in one neighborhood many years ago, or because of a film that portrayed alcoholics committing crimes, but can reject church on an equally flimsy basis.

The most popular stereotypes are the dying church that has only a handful of (elderly and predominantly female) congregants; the very white, very middle class church where everyone is scrubbed clean and emotions are kept in check; and the dynamic urban black church where everyone is extremely joyful, emotional and musical, but where theology and philosophy are peripheral. Catholic churches seem preferable to Protestant churches, priests to pastors, perhaps because Catholic ritual is more visual and symbolic, and priests are distinguished by their clothing. In his study *Christians in the Movies* Peter Dans comments that Protestant church life has virtually disappeared from film "except for wedding ceremonies."[6] And, he could have added, graveside committals.

Rare in movies are portrayals of churchgoing as normal and the life of the church as vital to the community and the world. Contrast this treatment of the spiritual with the treatment of the physical. Think how matter-of-fact it is to see characters in kitchens preparing food or in restaurants eating it. Think how normal it is to see them jogging or lifting weights. Yet more Americans regularly attend church than a health club. It's likely that what we see in movies reflects the lifestyle of the community within which actors, directors, producers and screenwriters live rather than America as a whole.

Good and Bad

There are few good, memorable portrayals of ordinary Christians in movies or television drama. This may be because goodness isn't as dramatically compelling as its opposite. The things that make an unsuccessful spiritual life—anger, violence, hatred, infidelity, falsehood, deception, unpredictability, selfishness, pride—make good drama. It's frequently pointed out that in *Paradise Lost*, the epic poem by the Puritan writer John Milton, it's Satan rather than God who emerges as the most fascinating character. Simone Weil, the French writer, once observed that in real life nothing was so refreshing and sweet as good, and nothing so monotonous and boring as evil. "But," she added, "with fantasy it is the other way around. Fictional good is boring and flat, while fictional evil is varied, intriguing, attractive, and full of charm."[7]

This is a real problem. Drama depends on inconsistency, failure and unpredictability. If protagonists are such solid characters that they never err, they cease to be interesting because we know in advance how they will react. We know what will be revealed if they are tempted or put under stress. Of course, Christians make mistakes, but if someone is flagged as a believer and then behaves badly, the audience will immediately think *hypocrite* rather than *human*.

Religious Hypocrites

The other reason for the lack of believable Christian protagonists may be that the people who write the screenplays either can't conceive of such a person or don't want to make Christianity seem attractive. In British soaps Christians tend to be old, unstable, female or black. *EastEnders*, which is watched four nights a week by an audience of around ten million, has had five Christian characters in recent years; a seventy-six-year-old woman, two Nigerian girls, a female drug addict and a black Pentecostal pastor. The pastor, himself a former drug addict, went on to commit two murders.

In movies ordinary Christians, particularly evangelicals and fundamentalists, are routinely portrayed as gullible, stupid, repressed, weak, phony or self-righteous. Peter Dans comments, "Fundamentalist Christians have the distinction of having been almost uniformly portrayed negatively as charlatan preachers, unenlightened dupes, and more recently as mean-spirited hypocrites."[8] Justine Toh, a fellow of Australia's Centre for Public Christianity, argues that film promoted a lazy stereotype of Christians as "judgmental, harsh, ignorant, ultraconservative, uptight and hypocritical."[9]

Our instinctive reaction is to feel attacked and misunderstood. We want to accuse the filmmakers of unfairness. Yet, unfortunately, these portrayals are of recognizable failures and inconsistencies. The animated TV series *Family Man* and *South Park* mock God, Jesus and Christian doctrine, but *The Simpsons* more gently mocks the behavior of Christians—the uptightness of Marge Simpson, the veniality of Reverend Lovejoy, the well-meaning fussiness of Ned Flanders. These are things that genuinely bother people who look at Christian lives and attitudes as God's shop window. If the quality of the goods is so poor, it throws doubt on the Creator. If God's biggest fans are so unattractive, what does that say about God?

Ignorance

The criticisms of Christians appear to be multiple but boil down to three areas: ignorance, hypocrisy and repression. Christians are often shown as people whose beliefs fly in the face of all evidence. They dismiss science, ignore inconsistencies and trust in visions, signs and spiritual feelings rather than in common sense. Super-literalist Ned Flanders says that he does everything that the Bible says "even the stuff that contradicts the other stuff."[10] When Stewie Griffin of *Family Guy* finds himself in a parallel universe he's told, "In this universe Christianity never happened, which means that the dark ages of scientific repression never occurred, and thus humanity is a thousand years more advanced."[11] The superintendent of Springfield Elementary School in *The Simpsons* believes so firmly in the separation of church and state that he says, "God has no place within these walls, just like facts don't have a place in organized religion."[12]

The high school Christians in movies like *Saved!* (2004) and *Easy A* (2010) exist in an unreal world of sloganeering and hyped-up emotion apparently divorced from serious study and rational decision making. They seem to repeat phrases that have been drilled into them rather than speak from the heart. When Cassandra, the only Jewish girl at the school in *Saved!*, suddenly announces to Hilary Faye that she wants "a personal relationship with Jesus," Hilary responds, "Oh, wow. . . . Oh, I don't have all my equipment."[13] She can't respond to the question as a person with feelings and deeply held views, but only as a conveyer of prepackaged information. The documentaries *Hell House* (2001) and *Jesus Camp* (2006) show Christian leaders manipulating children through fear rather than teaching them to reason, appreciate and explore.

Hypocrisy

Christians are first shown to be judgmental, bigoted, harsh and uncaring; then they are shown as people who can't even live up to their own demanding standards. The brutal Warden Norton in *The Shawshank Redemption* loves to read the Bible and quote it while at the same time mistreating those under his care and pilfering money. Mrs. Carmody in *The Mist* blames her townspeople for bringing freak weather due to their sinfulness. Quinn, the only Christian in the early episodes of *Glee*, is president of the celibacy club, but gets pregnant by a classmate and then deceives her boyfriend into believing that he's the father.

In *Saved!* the "backslider" Mary emerges as the most honest and real character while the on-fire Christian Hilary Faye is self-righteous, and Skip, the pastor, has a bad marriage and churns out homilies not rooted in his own experience. When Skip tries to get Mary to toe the line, she asks the pertinent question "Why would God make us all so different if he wanted us to be the same?" Mary's doubts resonate more with the audience than such faux hipster quotes as Skip's "Let's get our Christ on. Let's kick it Jesus-style!"[14]

One of the most poignant scenes in *Saved!* comes when Hilary and her fellow believers attempt to drag Mary into their camper van to save her from Satan. After Mary has struggled free and accused her would-be captors of not knowing "the first thing about love," Hilary screams at her, "I am FILLED with Christ's love. You're just jealous of my success in the Lord" and hurls a Bible at her retreating figure. Mary picks it up and calmly says, "The gospel is not a weapon." Director and screenwriter Brian Dannelly based the movie on his experience of two years spent at a Baptist high school. He said, "Everything in the movie comes from either something I experienced, something I witnessed, or something I researched."

Repression

Christians are shown as joyless, mean-spirited and uptight. Unable to come to terms with the power of their own sexual desires, they seethe with resentment toward those who appear to be able to sin with impunity. The first type of repressed Christian is merely a bit boring and predictable; their worst sins are that they criticize others and seem unable to enjoy themselves. Angela Martin, head of accounting, is the one character identified as a Christian in *The Office*. Wikipedia describes her as "cold, condescending, judgmental and uptight," says that she "frowns upon any sort of superfluousness or inappropriateness in general" and has "little sense of humor and almost never smiles or expresses happiness." She's described by one her fellow workers as "that tight-ass Christian chick."[15]

The second type of repressed Christian is the one who has either been damaged by an over-strict religious upbringing or who is secretly attracted by the very sins he or she condemns. Either way these Christians are powder kegs of unfulfilled desires that turn into explosions of anger, hatred, violence, rape or murder. Matthew Winkler in *The Pastor's Wife* (2011) is a preacher who when at home is angry and abusive and gets his wife to dress as a hooker and watch pornography before they have sex. In *Crimes of Passion* (1984) the Reverend Peter Shayne, played by Anthony Perkins, feels called to rescue prostitutes, but his mission is a disguise for his love for illicit sex and feelings of violence toward strippers and hookers.

The fanatical moralist with a penchant for cleanliness, order and physical perfection but who seethes with hatred toward sinners perhaps because he (and it usually is he) is unable to come to terms with his own desires has become a cliché of modern cinema. These characters aren't always Christians, but they mouth condemnations of moral collapse that use biblical language. Travis Bickle in *Taxi Driver* wants to clear New York of depravity. Driving the streets alone at night in his cab he says, "Some day a real rain will come and wash all his scrum off the streets."[16] Colonel Frank Fitts in *American Beauty* tells his son that "this country is going straight to hell" and later complains "faggots" are "so shameless."[17] He's later revealed to be a closet homosexual.

Christian workers generally fare no better. Priests are abusers (*The*

Boys of St. Vincent, Deliver Us from Evil, Twist of Faith), church leaders are killjoys (*Footloose, Chocolat*), missionaries are Western imperialists (*The Mosquito Coast, At Play in the Fields of the Lord*), evangelists are con artists (*Elmer Gantry, Marjoe, Wise Blood, Leap of Faith*) and vicars are bumbling idiots (*The Princess Bride, Four Weddings and a Funeral*).

Biblical Epics

There have been movies based on the Bible since the dawn of cinema, but the 1950s and 1960s were the golden era of such epics as *The Ten Commandments* (1956), *King of Kings* (1961) and *The Greatest Story Ever Told* (1965) as well as *The Robe* (1953) and *Ben-Hur* (1959), which were set in biblical times. Largely noncontroversial, they fit the mood of prosperous postwar times during which there was much common agreement about values, and the Christianity of the West was favorably contrasted against the godlessness of communism.

But John Huston's *The Bible: In The Beginning* (1966) marked the end of that particular era. It coincided with the scrapping of the Production Code, the closing down of church outreach to Hollywood and the rise of the counterculture. The old certainties were being shaken, young people were questioning the values of the parental generation, and there was no longer an appetite for uncritical retellings of Bible stories. The next major biblical films were imaginative, skeptical and playful. *Godspell* (1973) was set in New York and featured Jesus as a clown; *Jesus Christ Superstar* (1973) showed him as a first-century celebrity who'd become a victim of his own publicity. Both films had rock soundtracks.

The Life of Brian (1979), while not strictly about Jesus, posited the suggestion that messiah worship was misguided and possibly the result of a collective delusion. It outraged a lot of Christians and evidenced a huge shift away from the reverence and respect that had surrounded previous biblical films. When Charlton Heston filmed *The Ten Commandments* he wouldn't take a phone call or drink from a paper cup while dressed as Moses. The announcement that Jeffrey

Hunter was to play Jesus in *King of Kings* drew the following comment from a minister writing in *Modern Screen*,

> Has an ordinary human being the right to portray Jesus Christ? In the past moviemakers have avoided showing the face of Christ on screen. But, in *King of Kings* the producers are going to show His face and body.
>
> And actor Jeffrey Hunter is taking the biggest risk of his life. Many people may say "How dare he, a divorced man, a man not only born with the taint of original sin but also a man who has led a man's life—how dare he portray the Son of God?" [18]

It has since become accepted not only for actors to play Jesus but to play God. In the film *Oh, God!* veteran actor George Burns played God as a supermarket manager in a sailor's cap, a role he reprised in another two films. In *Evan Almighty* God was played by black actor Morgan Freeman and in *Dogma* by female singer Alanis Morrissette. Shifting attitudes toward blasphemy can be seen by the fact that prior to 1966 there were only twenty-three movie portrayals of God. Since that year there have been 328.

Hollywood Jesus

It's said that every age re-creates Jesus in its own image. The Victorians favored "Gentle Jesus, meek and mild," but after the 1960s film-makers were reimagining him as a hippie (love, peace and sandals), a revolutionary (beard, conflict with authorities, arrest) or a rock star (big crowds, stunning tricks and a way with words). *The Last Temptation of Christ* (1988), although based on the 1953 novel by Nikos Kazantzakis, suited an age of skepticism and doubt. This was a post-Freudian Jesus caught up in self-examination. "I want to rebel against everything, everybody . . . against God," he says at one point. "If you look inside of me you see fear. That's all. Fear is my mother, my father, my God."[19] The director was lapsed Catholic Martin Scorsese. The screenwriter was former Calvinist Paul Schrader.

Mel Gibson's *The Passion of the Christ* (2004) was a surprise because it was both orthodox in its understanding of Jesus and a huge commercial success. Each decade can usually only tolerate around two new films about Jesus, and because the story is so familiar there is a pressure to present a unique interpretation that viewers will find intriguing—"Jesus as you've never seen him before." What was so unexpected about *The Passion* was that it was radical without being liberal, authentic without being sentimental, orthodox without being dull, new without being modern (or postmodern). Its one short-coming was that in making the violence more graphic than in previous Jesus films, it left the impression that Christ's sufferings for sin were primarily physical and visible rather than spiritual and unseen.

At the time of writing this book, the Dutch director Paul Verhoeven (*Robocop*, *Total Recall*) is planning a film, *Jesus of Nazareth*, that will present Jesus as an ethical teacher and political agitator whose birth was the result of a Roman soldier raping Mary. Verhoeven argues that Jesus died because his teachings were a threat to Roman dominance. "It's not about miracles," he said. "It's about a new set of ethics and an openness towards the world."[20]

The Passion of the Christ alerted Hollywood to an untapped mass of potential cinemagoers, the people who felt overlooked by the pre-dominantly secular outlook of commercial movies. There was a flurry of faith-based movies starting in 2006, but none of them duplicated Gibson's success, and the movement settled into films made by Christians, predominantly for Christians, and very often direct to digital. Because the whole life of these films takes place beyond the vision of the movie-going public, they don't contribute to the main cultural debate, aren't known by the average person and have no effect on cinematic history. Most of them are message-driven rather than story-driven. Although messages inevitably develop from great stories, great stories rarely grow out of messages.

Negative Portrayals

Negative images of Christians in popular culture confirm the nonbelievers' prejudice that Christianity is unattractive and therefore untrue.

They also make Christians feel uncomfortable with their social identity. When the group that you belong to is persistently derided, it can push you into wanting to disassociate. However, this derision itself doesn't warrant a campaign against Hollywood. One of the perils of our cherished freedom of expression is that people can say things about us that we don't like.

A more constructive response would be to look at the images purveyed to gauge how much truth they contain. There may be animosity and caricature in these portrayals, but there must also be recognizable faults. We have to face the truth that Christians often live up to their charmless reputation; they are ditzy, boring, gullible, harsh and given to irrational behavior. At the beginning of my life as a Christian I thought that "religious maniac" was an unfair description applied to sincere believers, but then I encountered people for whom this was an accurate description. The only question was whether their mania had led them to the church because they were needy or their beliefs were the cause of their irrational behavior.

Every time a leading evangelist is found guilty of financial irregularity, adultery, rape, drug taking or falsehood, it furthers the view that Christians are hypocritical, either because religion is a coverup for problems they haven't dealt with in their own lives or because their expectations for moral behavior are unachievable. Every time a preacher sets a date for the end of the world, it seems to prove that faith means losing a grip on reality. When an evangelical leader known for his condemnation of homosexual practice is found to be using male prostitutes and abusing those in his care, it confirms the belief that Christians don't hate sin or the sinner but their own concealed passions.

A Barna survey published in David Kinnaman's book *unChristian* found that young people outside the church found Christians to be antihomosexual, judgmental, hypocritical, out of touch with reality, old-fashioned, insensitive to others and boring. This was perhaps to be expected. More surprising was to find that churchgoers of the same age felt the same, only to a slightly lesser degree.

Our most powerful message is who we are. Imagine if the only

Christians that Hollywood writers knew were strong, assured, rational, caring, forgiving, loving, sincere, exciting, lively, wise and joyful people. Then they'd have far less excuse for portraying us in a negative light. In fact, to do so would then bring them into disrepute for failing to be observant. If our own houses were in order, others might listen more attentively. As Gandhi once said, "Be the change you want to see in the world."

Questions for Reflection or Discussion

- How do you respond to the statement "The people who run the TV networks and the major movie studios do not share the religious and moral values of most Americans"? What evidence would you cite to support your answer?

- Do you think that boycotts and protests against allegedly blasphemous productions bring about a change of attitude or merely give the productions a publicity boost?

- What were the advantages and disadvantages of the Motion Picture Production Code? Would cinema benefit from the reintroduction of the code?

- Why do you think the movie industry attracts those who are less religious?

- Why do you think the movie industry repels those who are more religious?

- Why is fictional bad more interesting than fictional good?

- Have you ever seen Christians portrayed in a bad light in a movie and yet thought it was totally accurate?

- Have you ever been embarrassed by a self-consciously "Christian movie" designed to win converts? If so, why?

- Should movies that mock Christ be considered blasphemous, and if so should we (1) campaign for them to be banned, (2) avoid watching them, (3) watch them to see what others are saying, (4) watch them but enjoy only the nonblasphemous bits or (5) something else?

• Do you think faith-based movies put out by Hollywood studios are a step toward reclaiming mainstream culture or toward making special movies for Christians and therefore toward dividing culture?

Books on Hollywood and Christianity

Black, Gregory D. *Hollywood Censored: Morality Codes, Catholics and the Movies.* Cambridge: Cambridge University Press, 1996.

Dans, Peter. *Christians in the Movies.* Lanham, MD: Rowman & Little-field, 2009.

Joseph, Mark. *Mel Gibson's Passion: The Story Behind the Most Controversial Film in Hollywood History.* Nashville: W Publishing, 2004.

Lindlof, Thomas. *Hollywood Under Siege: Martin Scorsese, the Religious Right and the Culture War.* Louisville: University Press of Kentucky, 2008.

Medved, Michael. *Hollywood vs. America.* New York: HarperCollins, 1992.

Pavelin, Alan. *Fifty Religious Films.* Chislehurst, UK: A. P. Pavelin, 1990.

Romanowski, William. *Reforming Hollywood: How American Protestants Fought for Freedom at the Movies.* New York: Oxford University Press, 2012.

Five Suggestions for Action

• Research the twenty most powerful people in Hollywood to see if you can discover their philosophical/religious worldviews.

• List the different types of Jesus that have been portrayed in film or on stage over the past fifty years and work out what they say about the times they were created in.

- If you are a filmmaker wanting to portray a Christian, be sure to search out inspiring role models that confound the stereotypes of weakness, gullibility and hypocrisy. Think of Sandra Bullock's portrayal of Leigh Anne Touhy in *The Blind Side* or Susan Sarandon as Sister Helen Prejean in *Dead Man Walking*.

- Work out what aspects of the life and teaching of Jesus speak most urgently to contemporary culture. Could there be a cinematic Jesus that was complete and faithful to Scripture yet angled to meet the specific questions and needs of our age? (The Gospel writers differed in emphasis without compromising truth.)

- Examine your own life to discover if there's a story worth telling.

14

What Should I Do?

Consuming, Critiquing, Creating

†

Christians quite rightly want to know what they can do when faced
with the issues surrounding something like pop culture. I hope this
book will have helped answer the question simply by highlighting
areas where the Bible and Christian tradition have something to say.
I'm aware that often there are no definitive answers and that I am,
like many others, still struggling to find out how things work while
in the middle of the very thing I am describing.

A lot of my findings, as you will have discovered, have come from
personal experience rather than academic study. I've always read as
much as I can, but the real learning has come from being involved in
popular culture and from discussions with friends, colleagues and
Christian leaders. When I was in my twenties I shared a house with
three other Christians—an architect, a film director and an advertising executive—and a lot of my education came from the discussions we'd have with each other during the evenings and on weekends.
I would thoroughly recommend living this way. We also all belonged
to a group committed to nurturing Christians in the arts and bene-
fitted from lectures, discussions, prayer meetings and festivals put on
by this group.

However, I'm aware that the "what should I do" question has a different answer depending on what your role is with regard to pop

culture. The majority of people are primarily consumers. They don't want to know how to make a movie, but how to watch and understand films. Some people are also critics. This may be in a formal position as a reviewer or in an informal position as a speaker, preacher or writer of letters to newspapers. Some people are either students or teachers. They need to deal with the latest ideas in cultural theory and may want to know whether the biblical worldview has something unique to contribute to this debate that could be seriously considered in the academic world. Some people are creators. Their reasons for asking the questions are because they want to know how to successfully and powerfully incorporate the biblical view of the world into what they produce as fashion designers, musicians, illustrators, web designers, journalists, comedians, photographers or filmmakers.

I believe that the overall most important thing is knowing what a biblical worldview is, because all of the arts and forms of communication just mentioned are dependent on ways of looking at the world rather than a single message. What usually makes a particular comedian, film director or novelist stand out is not that he or she has one thing to say and keeps repeating it over and over again, but that this person has a compelling vision of the way things are and the way things should be, which percolates through everything they make.

There is a problem with the Christian who "made a decision" while at camp when ten years old and who hasn't really pursued any theology beyond the Ten Commandments, the Seven Deadly Sins or the Four Spiritual Laws. These people can often be good at creating single-issue pop culture that could bring other people to make a similar decision, but when it comes to creating pop culture that touches on every area of life, they don't know how to do it in a distinct but perhaps not necessarily overt Christian way. They tend either to avoid the tough areas altogether or they unthinkingly absorb the values and outlook of the secular culture around them.

I come across a lot of people involved in the expressive arts who want to do something reflective of their Christian faith, but they're unsure how to proceed. Largely this is because the only Christian thing they know to do is to tell the gospel in some way, and yet they know that this isn't what's required by the *New York Times*, Chanel, Pixar or HBO, and neither is it appropriate to the level of discussion going on in popular culture. What they need is a biblical worldview that would enable them to look at such things as poverty, loneliness, pornography, architecture, fame and sexuality as God would look at them.

Consuming Discerningly

If you are primarily a consumer of pop culture, you want to know what to consume and how to consume it. As I hope I have already shown, there are some things better not consumed because of spiritual negativity or because they waste valuable time. What those things are will depend on the individual. Lists of approved and banned movies, books and such don't help people to develop their own powers of discernment. The important thing is to resist the pressure to consume something just because everyone else is doing so, and to realize that as one book title puts it, "ideas have consequences."[1] We're not taking ourselves very seriously if we think we're impervious to the influence of popular culture. "Can a man scoop fire into his lap / without his clothes being burned?" is the rhetorical question asked in Proverbs 6:27.

The other side of this is that there is a lot of popular culture that we'd be well advised to consume for the sake of our own enrichment as well as for enjoyment, enlightenment, pleasure and the connection it makes with the mind of our present age. Howard Jacobson, a Jewish novelist, recently wrote this in defense of fiction, and I think it can be applied to a lot of popular culture. "We are," he argued,

> if not exactly "saved" by reading, at least partially "repaired" by it: made the better morally and existentially. . . . We read to extend our sympathies, to see ourselves in others and others in ourselves, to educate our imaginations, to find liberation from the prison of the self, to be made whole where we are broken, to

be reconciled to the absurdity of existence, in short to be redeemed from flesh, the ego and despair.[2]

This means putting ourselves in the way of good "stuff"—movies, books, records, shows and exhibitions that have recommendations that suggest we'll be better, or at least better informed, for having seen, heard or read them. Rather than thinking of popular culture in terms of what we should avoid, maybe we should start thinking in terms of what we absolutely should consume.

The second part of the question is how we should consume. There is a temptation in our world to consume in a mindless mode. We might have to engage our critical faculties when reading *The Merchant of Venice* for an exam, but not when watching *Two and Half Men* with a pizza in our hands. Yet the danger of indiscriminate viewing is that we allow our values to be subtly shaped by a gentle but incessant nudging. Seeing bad behavior modeled and approved in a sitcom can have a more profound effect on us than a lecture advocating the same behavior.

We should always consume thoughtfully with our minds alert to the text but also to the subtext, to the words but also to the signs and symbols. We should have the biblical worldview so deeply ingrained in our consciousness that it's second nature for us to compare the way God looks at things with what we're being presented with. That's the value of the comment attributed to theologian Karl Barth about having the newspaper in one hand and the Bible in the other. The newspaper compels us to look in the Bible to make sense of our world, and the Bible compels us to look at the newspaper to apply what we know.

Critiquing Faithfully

The critic is a representative consumer. The only advantage critics have over the ordinary person who watches films or reads books is that they've hopefully seen and read a bit more, and are able to evaluate and compare with ease. At times ministers and other church leaders find themselves playing the role of a critic when informing an audience of something they think worth watching, or explaining the perspective of, for example, a new novel or film. Increasingly movie clips are being used in the pulpit, and it's important to remind viewers of the context, to explain the premise of the whole film and to accu rately report the view of the director or screenwriter.

When reviewing it's important to know who the target audience is. The target audience for this book, for example, is Christians who have some interest in the popular arts. I guess that the majority of my readers will be younger rather than older, evangelical rather than liberal. This allows me to make certain assumptions. I can talk about God, prayer and redemption and not have to explain what I mean by these terms. I know not everyone will agree with me, but I assume a certain set of shared values and a shared language within which we can argue. If I was doing the same book for a largely secular audience I wouldn't shed my opinions but I'd have to start in a different place, knowing the views of my readers would be quite different.

Sometimes I find myself writing for a general audience and at other times, as with my book *The Gospel According to the Beatles*, for an audience that will probably consist of both a secular and a religious component. I have to bear that in mind as I write. I wrote a biography of Johnny Cash for a similarly divided audience. If I were speaking to a group of Christians about Cash, I could talk of his conversion and expect my listeners (1) to consider it to be a good thing and (2) to know what *salvation* means and how a *saved* person is supposed to live. There is no reason for a general audience to be pleased that he became a Christian. Nor could I expect them to know what it involved.

I've written an obituary of the Christian singer and songwriter Larry Norman for a secular newspaper (*The Independent*) and an obituary of the Buddhist beat poet Allen Ginsberg for a Christian magazine (*Third Way*). I would have felt the same way about my subjects had the publications been reversed, but spent a bit more time in both cases carefully explaining who these men were, what values they represented and why they were worth listening to. Very often our duty is to explain Christian things to the secular world or secular

things to the Christian world. Sometimes we're called to explain the
secular world to itself or the church to itself. One of the best reviews
I ever got (meaning one of the reviews that most succinctly got what
I was trying to do) was when *People* magazine, reviewing my book
Amazing Grace: The Story of America's Most Beloved Song, said I had "a
hipster's eye and a parishioner's faith."

Some others of us might find ourselves studying popular culture at
school, college or university, or even lecturing on it. The challenges at
this level will be even greater because most of the approved schools of
thought on popular culture have deeply secular if not atheistic roots.
They don't accept that humans are made by God and have a spiritual
dimension. They don't acknowledge the power of sin or the importance of redemption. They don't believe in moral laws that transcend
cultures and periods of history.

Not all of these theories of culture are wrong in every way, by any
means, but it's obviously easier to totally buy into a particular approach than to carefully navigate all of them and then add the unique
insights that are possible only from a biblical view. When the economist E. F. Schumacher began developing the thoughts that he eventually published in his influential book *Small Is Beautiful*, he spoke of
"Buddhist economics." He was later asked why he did this, because
he was known to be a Roman Catholic with ideas influenced by the
Bible and authors like Thomas Aquinas, G. K. Chesterton and
Thomas Merton, and he answered that if he'd called it "Christian
economics," "nobody would have paid any attention."[3] His central
idea is that the West wrongly thinks that happiness is improved by
greater consumption and that workers are treated in a less than
human way in order to maximize profit. The subtitle of his book is
Economics as If People Mattered. It is a great example of religious principles being applied to an aspect of life usually dominated by purely
secular thinking.

C. S. Lewis is another example of someone highly regarded for his
literary criticism that spoke from a Christian standpoint, but not
always to a Christian audience. He once said that what we need is not

more books about Christianity but more books by Christians on other subjects with their Christianity latent. He added that our faith would be unlikely to be shaken by a book on Hinduism, but it might be if every time we read a book on geology, politics or astronomy the implications were Hindu. He might have added that a book on atheism might not shake us, but we might be shaken if every book we read on cinema, music or fashion was implicitly atheist.[4]

Creating Wisely

Last, we have the Christian who will definitely be a consumer and may also be a critic, a student and a teacher, but who is ultimately a creator. These are the people who want to design, make films, entertain audiences and write books, and who wonder exactly what their role is as Christians. Should they be evangelizing, creating work that can be safely consumed by fellow believers, entertaining the masses or simply making a living in as honest and honorable way as possible? Again I think the Christian worldview is the important factor, and I deal with this more thoroughly in my book *Imagine: A Vision for Christians in the Arts.*

As I said at the start of this book, Christians tend to think either that their faith is deeply personal and has nothing to do with their work beyond obvious ethical certain considerations, or that whatever form of popular culture they are involved in must somehow be used as an evangelistic tool. So we get Christians making highly dubious music who are happy to form a prayer circle before going onstage, as though that somehow redeemed it, and then Christians making faith films, religious comedy and inspirational fiction that doesn't trouble the main marketplace.

We need popular culture that is transformed by an alternative view. It's out there with everything else but is somehow different. It adds to the conversations that are going on between artist and artist, art and art, and public and art. A review on the *New Yorker* website by Mark O'Connell is an example of the effect that I think Christians should be striving for. He was writing about Marilynne Robinson, author of the novels *Housekeeping* and *Gilead*, and said that he loved her work for two main reasons. The first is the grace of her prose style, which he thinks got its grace from her vision. He said that her writing made him feel "what it must be like to live with a sense of the divine." The second is that it introduced him to a world that he would normally approach with "borderline hostility" and made him feel drawn to it. In conclusion he said, "She makes an atheist reader like myself capable of identifying with the sense of a fallen world that is filled with pain and sadness but also suffused with divine grace."[5]

What I love about his commentary is that it shows a contact between writer and reader. The fact that Mark O'Connell then wrote about his feelings added to the discussion. I also love the fact that he sees her prose style as a product of her vision and can see the harmony between the world, the way she reports on the world and the insights she brings to bear on the world she sees. "Robinson's moral wisdom," he wrote, "seems inseparable from her gifts as a prose writer."

Robinson is of course a writer of what is often referred to as "serious fiction," but people making films, writing songs or even doing comedy can achieve what O'Connell believes she achieved. The celebrated rock critic Greil Marcus was reviewing the album *Belle* by Al Green when he concluded that the record carried "a sense of liberation and purpose deep enough to make the sinner envy the saved."[6]

I think the secret of what a Christian creator of popular culture needs is contained in God's dealings with Bezalel, the first artist mentioned in the Bible. As we saw earlier in the book he was "filled . . . with the Spirit of God, with wisdom, with understanding, with knowledge and with all kinds of skills" (Ex 31:2-3). At first glance this list might seem like repetition, but I believe these are four distinct areas, and each one needs to be attended to. Yet having said they are distinct, they each inform the other—the knowledge helps create understanding, and understanding is a part of wisdom and so on. What O'Connell so loves about the writing of Marilynne Robinson is that understanding is reflected in her workmanship and inspired by her wisdom. It's all of a piece.

Workmanship is craft and technique, and it comes from education and practice. It should be unnecessary to state this but there are Christians who believe that they've been called to be writers or artists with such conviction that they think they can skip this stage. Just as God promises to give us the words to say if we're called to testify, they believe he can step in and overcome our lack of training. In fact, some have argued that by not training we are proving that it's all of God. Eager young people regularly turn up in Hollywood claiming to be on a divine mission to transform the film industry, but they don't even have the basic skill set necessary to make movies.

If God has gifted you, get the right training. Become as good as you can be. Don't despise the lessons that can be handed down by people who've been in your profession for years. So much toe-curling "Christian art" is made by people who think the only tutor they need is God, and they then regard criticism as a form of persecution. They have the attitude "They rejected Jesus so they're bound to reject me." But often the rejection is not because of the beliefs expressed but the shoddiness of the work. You don't have to study the history of film to know a bad film when you see one. The public is increasingly sophisticated in its understanding of what makes good popular culture.

A friend of mine who works in Hollywood recommends that anyone contemplating writing a screenplay should read a thousand scripts before starting. In his book *Outliers* Malcolm Gladwell puts forward the thesis that anyone wanting to excel in any area of art, sport or business needs to practice for 10,000 hours. The great Polish concert pianist Paderewski said, "If I don't practice for one day, I know it. If I don't practice for two days, my friends know it. If I don't practice for three days, everybody knows it."[7]

Knowledge can be both knowledge of your craft and knowledge of the world. This is basic information that anyone engaging with popular culture requires. It's different to understanding and wisdom because it's possible to be very knowledgeable and yet not to be able to make sense of that knowledge. It's possible to be well read yet foolish. Yet knowledge provides the raw material that understanding and workmanship can make something of.

It's vital to know all you can about the area of popular culture you are entering. The great innovators of the rock 'n' roll era—people like John Lennon, Paul McCartney, Bob Dylan, Mick Jagger and Keith Richards—were extremely well versed in pop, country, folk, blues and early rock 'n' roll before they ever recorded a single track of their own. They knew the origins of the music they went on to develop, and they knew where they stood in the historical continuum. Again, Christians often don't love or respect the art forms they enter. They see them as mere vehicles for what they want to say.

Coupled with this, it's necessary to know the world. In order to address the world you need to be familiar with its concerns, triumphs, failures and longings. You need to know its language because every nuance is important when communicating. You can learn about the world by traveling, reading, studying, talking to people, keeping your ear to the ground and taking a close interest in events as they unfold.

As Christians operating in the communications marketplace we not only need to know what we believe but how we can best present what we believe. We need to be aware of currently popular objections to our faith so that we can sharpen our responses when questioned. Also the more of the world we know the more we'll be stimulated. Artists that are always sparking are usually people who are responsive to new ideas and different ways of seeing things. Travel opens us up to new sights, sounds, smells and tastes. It introduces us to art, poetry, architecture, fabrics and colors that we otherwise would never have experienced. It broadens our horizons and enriches our palettes.

But knowledge isn't understanding. Understanding is what we do with the knowledge—how we analyze it, interpret it and make sense of it. We can do this by reading, keeping journals, taking courses and by having mentors and teachers. The Christian worldview isn't given to us automatically at the point of salvation. Some Christians go through their whole lives without developing it. It's something that takes time and effort.

Those who lead courses on the creative arts will stress the importance of vision. It's our unique way of seeing things that will transform what we do. It's possible to be highly skilled as a technician and to have acquired volumes of facts, but if you have no vision your work is likely to be pedestrian and mundane. People expect artists to take the pieces of information that we all have access to and present them in a new, refreshing and surprising way. None of us likes to be confused, lost or unable to make sense of the signs, and artists are among those people we look at to help us understand.

Finally, wisdom. I think it's a quality often lacking in popular culture. Maybe it's because we're so caught up in the idea of entertainment and so resistant to being lectured to in art. Maybe it's also because we're losing the spiritual and moral consensus that held sway until relatively recently, and so there's less commonly accepted wisdom. Several times the Bible uses the phrase "wise in their own eyes" and it's never as a compliment. When people are wise in their own eyes there doesn't need to be shared agreement over what is a good way to live. It's "different strokes for different folks" and "you have your truth and I have my truth."

Wisdom in craftsmanship would be that touch of genius that turns the ordinary into the extraordinary. It takes more than knowledge or understanding to write a song that remains popular for decades or to produce comedy that still makes us laugh a century later. Wisdom when creating helps us see that combination that no one else has seen or to take that risk that no one else has ever taken.

But wisdom is more than just being clever. I think it's a step beyond even knowledge and understanding. We've all known people, or at least known about people, who have a great understanding of their subject or even of human psychology and world politics, but nevertheless lived stupid lives. Maybe they couldn't control their passions. Maybe they were depressed by their own conclusions about life. Maybe they were so absorbed by their talent that they couldn't properly love anyone else.

Wisdom is an insight into living. It offers advice that proves to be true. It speaks from well-earned experience. I like it when poems, movies, novels, newspaper editorials and songs have a dash of wisdom along with the knowledge and understanding. It takes things to a higher level. People have a right to expect it of us because the Bible promises that "The fear of the LORD is the beginning of wisdom" (Ps 111:10; Prov 9:10).

So I would urge anyone to gain strength in the areas that Bezalel was strengthened so that we might find students and practitioners of pop culture who are workmanlike, knowledgeable, understanding and wise. I don't think we've yet seen a fraction of what we're capable of.

Notes

1 Leisure Pursuits: *Why We Should Care*

[1]Michael Cashman, quoted in Tom Geoghegan, "It Started with a Kiss," *BBC News*, June 26, 2008, http://news.bbc.co.uk/2/hi/uk_news/magazine/7475394.stm.

[2]George Orwell, "Boys' Weeklies and Frank Richards's Reply," *The Complete George Orwell*, www.george-orwell.org/Boys'_Weeklies_and_Frank_Richards's_Reply/0.html.

[3]Graham Greene, quoted in Grå Borup Nielsen, *Collected Essays* (Lanham, MD: University Press of America, 2000), p. 59.

[4]George Carlin, interview by Philip H. Farber, *Paradigm Shift*, http://users .bestweb.net/~kali93/carlin.htm.

[5]Pablo Picasso, "Pablo Picasso Famous Quotes," *Pablo Picasso*, www.pablo picasso.org/quotes.jsp.

[6]Will Galgey, quoted in Randeep Ramesh, "Britain Becomes Nation of Borrowers Spending Wildly on 'Experiences,' " *The Guardian*, April 8, 2010, www.guardian .co.uk/society/2010/apr/08/social-trends-ons-spending.

[7]Paul Schrader, "Beyond the Silver Screen," *The Guardian*, June 18, 2009, www .guardian.co.uk/film/2009/jun/19/paul-schrader reality-tv-big-brother.

[8]"Rolling Stone's Reasons to Get Excited About Hi Fi," *Stereophile*, May 16, 2010, www.stereophile.com/content/rolling-stones-reasons-get-excited-about-hi-fi-1.

[9]John Storey, *Cultural Theory and Popular Culture*, 4th ed. (Athens: University of Georgia Press, 2006), p. 3.

[10]Alexander McQueen, quoted in Andrew Bolton and Harold Koda, *Alexander McQueen: Savage Beauty* (New Haven, CT: Yale University Press, 2011).

[11]Marshall McLuhan, *The Mechanical Bride: Folklore of Industrial Man* (Boston: Beacon Press, 1967), p. 115.

[12]Jules Feiffer, "For the True Temper of a Nation, Turn to Its Comics," *Kingston Gleaner*, January 23, 1966, p. 5.

[13]Tom Wolfe, *The Kandy-Kolored Tangerine-Flake Streamline Baby* (New York: Picador, 1965), pp. xv-xvi.

[14]Robert Prechter, "Popular Culture and the Stock Market," August 1985, p. 5, www.socionomics.net/PDF/popular_culture.pdf.

[15]Personal email to author, July 13, 2012.

2 Popular Culture: *Defining the Term*

[1] Raymond Williams, *Keywords: A Vocabulary of Culture and Society* (New York: Oxford University Press, 1983), p. 87.

[2] Matthew Arnold, "Sweetness and Light," *Culture and Anarchy*, 3rd ed. (New York: Macmillan, 1882), sec. 7, www9.georgetown.edu/faculty/irvinem/theory/Arnold-Culture-Anarchy.html.

[3] Gilbert Seldes, *The Seven Lively Arts* (New York: Harper, 1924), p. 3.

[4] Quoteland.com, accessed December 4, 2012, www.quoteland.com/author/Marshall-McLuhan-Quotes/295/.

[5] Margalit Fox, "Ray Browne, 87, Founder of Pop-Culture Studies, Dies," *New York Times*, October 27, 2009, www.nytimes.com/2009/10/28/education/28browne.html?_r=0.

3 Working It Out: *Some Biblical Parameters*

[1] Percy Bysshe Shelley, letter to Thomas Jefferson Hogg, December 20, 1818.

[2] Percy Bysshe Shelley, "A Defence of Poetry," 1821, *Poetry Foundation*, www.poetryfoundation.org/learning/essay/237844?page=2.

[3] Max Weber, *The Protestant Ethic and the Spirit of Capitalism* (Mineola, NY: Dover, 2003), pp. 157-58.

[4] William Henry Davies, "Leisure," 1911.

[5] John Masefield, "Biography," 1914.

[6] Josef Pieper, *Leisure: The Basis of Culture* (San Francisco: Ignatius Press, 2009), p. 16.

[7] Ryan Duggins, "Confessions of an Online Porn Junkie," *Mail Online*, November 17, 2011, www.dailymail.co.uk/femail/article-2062466/Confessions-online-porn-junkie.html.

4 Cinematic Art: *The Story of Stories*

[1] See Andrew Fellows, "Movies and Apologetics" (audio), www.bethinking.org/culture-worldview/movies-and-apologetics.htm.

[2] Hortense Powdermaker, *Hollywood the Dream Factory* (New York: Arno Press, 1979), p. 12.

[3] Robert McKee, *Story* (New York: ReganBooks, 1997), p. 12.

[4] "The Mythology of Star Wars with George Lucas and Bill Moyers," PBS, 1999, http://vimeo.com/38026023.

[5] Christopher Vogler, *The Writer's Journey* (Studio City, CA: Michael Wiese, 2007), p. 1.

[6] Ibid., p. ix.

[7] Mary Henderson, *Star Wars: The Magic of Myth* (New York: Spectra, 1997), p. 198.

[8]Stanley Kubrick, interviewed by Eric Nordern in *"Playboy* Interview: Stanley Kubrick," in *Stanley Kubrick Interviews,* ed. Gene D. Phillips (Jackson: University Press of Mississippi, 2001), p. 73.

[9]"The Bible in Film," *Wikipedia.*

[10]Vincent Canby, "Network," *New York Times,* November 15, 1976, http://movies .nytimes.com/movie/review?res=EE05E7DF173CB82CA6494CC1B7799A8C68 96&pagewanted=print.

[11]Roger Ebert, "Network," *RogerEbert.com,* October 29, 2000, http://rogerebert .suntimes.com/apps/pbcs.dll/article?AID=/20001029/REVIEWS08/10290301 /1023.

[12]C. H. Dodd, *The Parables of the Kingdom* (New York: Charles Scribner's, 1961), p. 5.

[13]Mark Joseph, "The 'Passion' Playbook: The 10+ Commandments of the New Hollywood," *FoxNews.com,* December 5, 2006, www.foxnews.com/story/0,2933 ,234264,00.html.

[14]Charles Leavitt, interview by Denis Faye, "*Diamond* Scribe," *Writers Guild of America, West,* www.wga.org/content/default.aspx?id=3136.

[15]Ibid.

[16]Arthur Miller, *Timebends* (New York: Penguin, 1999), pp. 331, 338.

[17]Joan Didion, "Why I Write," *Oakland School for the Arts,* http://teachers.oakarts .org/~dsnyder/FOV1-0001FED4/S00AA8E2A-00AA8E2F.0/Why%20I%20 Write%20082812.pdf.

5 Journalism: *Reading Between the Lines*

[1]Andrew R. Cline, "Media/Political Bias," *Rhetorica,* http://rhetorica.net/bias .htm.

[2]James Parton, "Famous Americans of Recent Time," *Making of America,* p. 265, http://quod.lib.umich.edu/m/moa/ABK0774.0001.001?rgn=main;view=fulltext.

[3]Arthur McEwen, quoted in Daniel Boorstin, *The Image* (New York: Vintage, 1992), p. 8.

[4]Carl Bernstein, "The Idiot Culture," *New Republic,* June 8, 1992, pp. 24-25, www.carlbernstein.com/magazines_the_idiot_culture.pdf.

[5]Harry Blamires, *The Christian Mind* (Ann Arbor, MI: Servant, 1978), p. 20.

[6]Ibid., pp. 20-21.

[7]"Kate Hudson Cover Interview," *RedOnline,* www.redonline.co.uk/red-women/ cover-interviews/kate-hudson-red-cover-interview.

[8]"The Singer Escaped a Strict Christian Childhood to Find Fame," *Sunday Times,* March 25, 2012, www.thesundaytimes.co.uk/sto/comment/profiles/article 1001447.ece.

[9]Laura Craik, "Having a Ball: Is There Anything Natalia Vodianova Can't Do?"

London Evening Standard, June 24, 2001, www.standard.co.uk/lifestyle/esmagazine/having-a-ball-is-there-anything-natalia-vodianova-cant-do-6414976.html.
[10]"Keeping Up with Kim," *Cosmopolitan,* August 2011.
[11]Annabel Rivkin, "Rooney Vice Girl Helen Wood Talks Sex and Superinjunctions," *London Evening Standard,* June 24, 2011, www.standard.co.uk/lifestyle/esmagazine/rooney-vice-girl-helen-wood-talks-sex-and-superinjuctions-6414703.html.

6 Celebrity Culture: *The Game of the Fame*

[1]Joe McGinniss, *The Selling of the President* (New York: Penguin, 1970), p. 31.
[2]Ibid.
[3]Jarvis Cocker, quoted in Decca Aitkenhead, "Jarvis Cocker: 'Music Has Changed. It's Not as Central, It's More Like a Scented Candle," *The Guardian,* October 16, 2011, www.guardian.co.uk/music/2011/oct/16/jarvis-cocker-interview.
[4]Neal Gabler, *Life: The Movie* (New York: Vintage, 2000), p. 144.
[5]Daniel Boorstin, *The Image* (New York: Vintage, 1992), p. 45.
[6]Personal email to author, July 13, 2012.
[7]Malcolm Muggeridge, *Muggeridge Through the Microphone* (London: BBC Books: 1967), p. [#?]
[8]Bono, interview by Brian Williams, "Bono: 'This is a tipping point for Africa,'" *NBCNews.com,* May 23, 2006, www.msnbc.msn.com/id/12940132/ns/nbcnightly news/t/bono-tipping-point-africa/#.UIhxbG-jzSg.

7 Fashion: *The Language of Clothes*

[1]James Laver, *Style in Costume* (London: Oxford University Press, 1949), p. 6.
[2]John Henley, "The Rise and Rise of the Tattoo," *The Guardian,* July 19, 2010, www.guardian.co.uk/artanddesign/2010/jul/20/tattoos.
[3]I interviewed Westwood for the magazine *Over 21* in the 1980s and I cited this quote saying that she had made it in 1977.
[4]Robin Givhan, "Why Dole Frowns on Fashion," *Los Angeles Times,* August 8, 1996, http://articles.latimes.com/1996-08-08/news/ls-32243_1_fashion-industry.
[5]Alexander McQueen, quoted in Andrew Bolton and Harold Koda, *Alexander McQueen: Savage Beauty* (New Haven, CT: Yale University Press, 2011).
[6]Mary Quant, interview by Alison Adburgham, *The Guardian,* October 10, 1967, http://century.guardian.co.uk/1960-1969/Story/0,6051,106475,00.html.
[7]C. S. Lewis, *The Four Loves,* 2nd ed. (Orlando, FL: Mariner, 1971), p. 104.
[8]Blaise Pascal, *Pensées* 95 (New York: Penguin Classics, 1966), p. 54.
[9]Brad Tuttle, "How Fat Is the Markup on Designer Sunglasses?" *Time,* July 15, 2010, http://business.time.com/2010/07/15/how-fat-is-the-markup-on-designer-sunglasses.

[10]Jenna Sauers, "Met Manages Not to **** Up McQueen," *Jezebel*, May 5, 2011, http://jezebel.com/5799032/met-manages-to-not-fuck-up-mcqueen.

[11]See Sloan Wilson, *The Man in the Gray Flannel Suit* (Cambridge, MA: Da Capo, 2002).

[12]Toby Harris, quoted in Tanith Carey, "Why DO Young Women Go Out Dressed Like This?" *MailOnline*, November 30, 2011, www.dailymail.co.uk/news/article-2067391/Why-DO-young-women-dressed-like-We-meet-nightclubbers-unsettling-answer.html.

[13]Joanne Avery, quoted in ibid.

[14]Linda Papadopoulos, quoted in ibid.

[15]Alexander McQueen, quoted in "Alexander McQueen: Savage Beauty in the Costume Institute at the Metropolitan Museum of Art," *photoframd*, http://blog.photoframd.com/2011/05/03/alexander-mcqueen-savage-beauty-in-the-costume-institute-at-the-metropolitan-museum-of-art.

[16]See Alison Lurie, *The Language of Clothes* (Boston, MA: Holt, 2000).

[17]Lady Gaga, quoted in Anderson Cooper, "Lady Gaga on 'Mastering the Art of Fame,'"*60 Minutes*, February 14, 2011, www.cbsnews.com/stories/2011/02/10/60minutes/main7337078.shtml?tag=mncol;lst;10.

8 Ever-Greater Thrills: *The Search for Sensation*

[1]Blaise Pascal, *Pensées* 136 (New York: Penguin Classics, 1966), p. 67.

[2]Ibid., 139, p. 72.

[3]Russell Brand at The Secret Policeman's Ball, Radio City Music Hall, New York, March 4, 2012, www.youtube.com/watch?v=mmCLr9pSV6u.

[4]Daniel Boorstin, *The Image* (New York: Vintage, 1992), p. 3.

[5]Brendan Walker, interview by Nicola Isearch, "My Life in Travel," *The Guardian*, March 28, 2009, www.guardian.co.uk/travel/2009/mar/29/my-life-travel-brendan-walker-rollercoaster.

[6]Charles Runnette, "10 Scariest Thrill Rides on the Planet," *Travel and Leisure*, June 2008, www.travelandleisure.com/articles/10-scariest-thrill-rides-on-the-planet.

[7]See *Living with the Amish*, Channel 4, www.channel4.com/programmes/living-with-the-amish.

[8]Emily Brown and Paul Cairns, "A Grounded Investigation of Game Immersion," University College London Interaction Centre, p. 1299, http://complexworld.pbworks.com/f/Brown%2Band%2BCairns%2B(2004).pdf.

[9]"Disney Cruise Line Offers Immersive Experiences and Adventurous Activities for Kids of All Ages," *Disney Cruise Lines News*, http://dclnews.com/2012/07/disney-cruise-line-offers-immersive-experiences-and-adventurous-activities-for-kids-of-all-ages.

[10]B. Joseph Pine II and James H. Gilmore, *The Experience Economy* (Boston: Harvard Business School Press, 1999).

[11]Kyle V. Davy and Susan L. Harris, *Value Redesigned* (Norcross, GA: Greenway, 2005), p. 162.

[12]Planet Hollywood homepage: www.planethollywoodlondon.com.

[13]Hard Rock Cafe homepage: www.hardrock.com/corporate/history.aspx.

[14]Pine and Gilmore, *Experience Economy*, p. 183.

[15]Ibid.

[16]John Newton, "Amazing Grace," 1779.

[17]Seth Porges, "5 Theme Park Rides That Pushed the Limits of Common Sense," *Popular Mechanics*, December 18, 2009, www.popularmechanics.com/outdoors/sports/physics/4323692.

[18]"Scream Machines: the Science of Roller Coasters," *Carnegie*, September 30, 2000 to January 7, 2001, www.carnegiemuseums.org/cmag/bk_issue/2000/sepoct/feat4.html.

9 Comedy: *Laughs, Lies and Truth*

[1]C. S. Lewis, *The Screwtape Letters* (New York: Macmillan, 1961), p. 52.

[2]George Meredith, *The Works of George Meredith* (Whitefish, MT: Kessinger, 1897), 13:75.

[3]Steven Wright, "Steven Wright Jokes," *The Coffee Place*, www.thecoffeeplace.com/jokes/aaaaaatl.html.

[4]"Ian Martin, "The Thick of It's Swearing Consultant," *Guardian* Audio, July 9, 2007, http://blogs.guardian.co.uk/podcasts/2007/07/audio_ian_martin_the_thick_of.html.

[5]Lenny Bruce, quoted in Will Kaufman, *The Comedian as Confidence Man* (Detroit: Wayne State University Press, 1997), p. 107.

[6]Archive of American Television, George Carlin interviewed by Jenni Matz and Henry Colman in December 2007, www.emmytvlegends.org/interviews/people/george-carlin#. See part 3 of 7, 22 minutes and 22 seconds into interview.

[7]Susan E. Isaacs, personal email to author, May 23, 2012.

[8]Author interview with Malcolm Muggeridge, Battle, East Sussex, June 19, 1985.

[9]Arthur Koestler, *The Act of Creation* (New York: Arkana, 1989), p. 51.

[10]George Carlin, quoted in Sean Foley, "George Carlin on Religion," *Yahoo! Voices*, April 27, 2010, http://voices.yahoo.com/george-carlin-religion-5896236.html.

[11]George Carlin, *George Carlin . . . It's Bad for Ya!*, 2008.

[12]George Carlin, *George Carlin: Doin' It Again*, 1990.

[13]Dean Batali, personal email to author, May 15, 2012.

[14]Personal email to author, May 23, 2012.

[15]Kenneth Tynan, foreword to Lenny Bruce, *How to Talk Dirty and Influence People* (New York: Fireside, 1992), p. xii.

[16]William Makepeace Thackeray, *English Humourists* (London: Smith, Elder, 1867), p. 119.

10 Advertising: *The Hidden Persuader*

[1]Tony Smith, "Apple Rebuked Over G5 Speed-Lead Claim—Again," *The Register*, June 9, 2004, www.theregister.co.uk/2004/06/09/apple_uk_ad_slapped.

[2]"L'Oreal Rapped Over Penelope Cruz Mascara Ads," *Reuters.com*, July 5, 2007, www.reuters.com/article/2007/07/25/us-britain-loreal-idUSL2583702620070725.

[3]Mark Sweney, "L'Oréal's Julia Roberts and Christy Turlington Ad Campaigns Banned," *The Guardian*, July 26, 2011, www.guardian.co.uk/media/2011/jul/27/loreal-julia-roberts-ad-banned.

[4]Henry Saffer and Frank Chaloupka, "Tobacco Advertising: Economic Theory and International Evidence," Working Paper 6598, National Bureau of Economic Research, Cambridge, MA, February 1999, p. 2.

[5]Marshall McLuhan, "Future of Advertising" (1966), www.marshallmcluhanspeaks .com/prophecies/1966-future-of-advertising.php.

[6]Giles Wilson, "That's Me Singin' in the Rain," *BBC News*, March 4, 2005, http:// news.bbc.co.uk/2/hi/uk_news/magazine/4312217.stm.

[7]Peter York, "Click-start: Honda's Chain Reaction Is Poetry in Motion," *The Independent*, April 13, 2003, www.independent.co.uk/news/media/clickstart-hondas -chain-reaction-is-poetry-in-motion-594254.html.

[8]"The Power of Screams—Honda's 'Civic Choir' TV Campaign," *Car Pages*, January 14, 2006, www.carpages.co.uk/honda/honda-civic-14-01-06.asp.

[9]Fabrizio Galati, "Smirnoff Nightlife Exchange Project 2011," *Living Cool*, November 16, 2011, www.livincool.com/eventi/smirnoff-nightlife-exchange-project-2011.

[10]Simon Mcdermott, "Fosters Beer, Comedy and Cultural Capital," *Attentio*, April 12, 2011, http://blog.attentio.com/blog/2011/04/20/fosters-beer-comedy -and-cultural-capital.

[11]Vance Packard, *The Hidden Persuaders* (1957; reprint, Brooklyn, NY: Ig Publishing, 2007), p. 31.

[12]Ibid., p. 44.

[13]Ernest Dichter, quoted in ibid., p. 74.

[14]Packard, *Hidden Persuaders*, p. 233.

[15]Chris Hastings, "Vodka Martini, James? No Thanks, Mine's a Heineken," *Mail Online*, September 29, 2012, www.dailymail.co.uk/news/article-2210665/Vodka -Martini-James-No-thanks-mines-Heineken--just-28m-worth-product-tie-ins -Skyfall.html.

[16]Kate Ahlborn and Louisine Frelinghuysen, "*Sex and the City*: A Product-Placement Roundup," *VF Daily*, May 30, 2008, www.vanityfair.com/online/ daily/2008/05/sex-and-the-cit.

[17]"CK / Tom Hinthaus," *Iconic Photos*, http://iconicphotos.wordpress.com/2010/page/8.

[18]William Barclay, *The Letters to the Corinthians* (Louisville: Westminster John Knox, 2002), p. 230.

11 Technology: *Rewiring Our World*

[1]Leon Panetta, quoted in Jim Garamone, "Panetta Spells Out DOD Roles in Cyberdefense," U.S. Department of Defense, October 11, 2012, www.defense.gov/news/newsarticle.aspx?id=118187.

[2]Nicholas Carr, "Is Google Making Us Stupid?" *Atlantic*, July-August 2008, www.theatlantic.com/magazine/archive/2008/07/is-google-making-us-stupid/306868.

[3]Steve Jobs, quoted in " 'I Came of Age at a Magical Time'—Steve Jobs," *Lector: A Virtual Book Club*, February 23, 2012, http://lectorbookclub.com/2012/02/23/i-came-of-age-at-a-magical-time-steve-jobs.

[4]Timothy Leary, interview by Todd Brendon Fahey, "Timothy Leary: The Far Gone Interview," *Twentieth-Century Neuronaut*, September 28, 1992, www.fargonebooks.com/leary.html.

[5]John Perry Barlow, "Declaration of the Independence of Cyberspace," Electronic Frontier Foundation, February 8, 1996, https://projects.eff.org/~barlow/Declaration-Final.html.

[6]Jimmy Wales, "Wikipedia Founder Jimmy Wales Responds," *Slashdot*, July 28, 2004, http://slashdot.org/story/04/07/28/1351230/wikipedia-founder-jimmy-wales-responds.

[7]Tim Challies, *The Next Story* (Grand Rapids: Zondervan, 2011), p. 168.

[8]Eric Schmidt, quoted in Janet Lowe, *Google Speaks* (Hoboken, NJ: John Wiley, 2009), p. 150.

[9]Steve Jobs, quoted in "Top 10 Apple Moments: The Return of Steve Jobs," *Time*, www.time.com/time/specials/packages/article/0,28804,1873486_1873491_1873461,00.html.

[10]Jimmy Wales, quoted in "Wikipedia Talk: Prime Objective," *Wikipedia*, http://en.wikipedia.org/wiki/Wikipedia_talk:Prime_objective.

[11]Nicholas Carr, *The Shallows* (New York: Norton, 2010), p. 7.

[12]Ibid., p. 28.

[13]Ibid., p. 116.

[14]Irene Au, interview by Helen Walters, "Google's Irene Au: On Design Challenges," *Bloomberg BusinessWeek*, March 18, 2009, www.businessweek.com/innovate/content/mar2009/id20090318_786470.htm.

[15]Chris Hansen, "From *Tekken* to *Kill Bill*: The Future of Narrative Storytelling?" in *Halos and Avatars*, ed. Craig Detweiler (Louisville, KY: Westminster John Knox, 2010), p. 31.

12 Photography: *The Opening of the Eyes*

[1]Dorothea Lange, *Los Angeles Times*, August 13, 1978, quoted in *Dictionary.com Quotes*, http://quotes.dictionary.com/the_camera_is_an_instrument_that_teaches_people.

[2]Susan Sontag, *On Photography* (New York: Picador, 1977), p. 3

[3]Yousuf Karsh, quoted in "Yousuf Karsh," *Masters of Photography*, www.masters-of-photography.com/K/karsh/karsh_articles1.html.

[4]Ian K. Smith, "Cuba, 5 March 1960 / Alberto Korda," *New Statesman*, April 1, 2010, http://www.newstatesman.com/culture/2010/03/che-guevara-alberto-korda.

[5]Ansel Adams, *Ansel Adams: America* exhibition in the Bellagio Hotel, Las Vegas, *Wikiquotes*, http://en.wikiquote.org/wiki/Ansel_Adams.

[6]Henri Cartier-Bresson, *Aperture* 129 (fall 1992), cited in Ginny Felch, *Photographing Children Photo Workshop* (Hoboken, NJ: John Wiley, 2012), p. 19.

[7]Donald McCullin, *Unreasonable Behaviour* (London: Vintage, 2002), p. 4.

[8]Robert Frank, "Robert Frank: A Statement," *U.S. Camera Annual* 1958, p. 15, www.jnevins.com/robertfrankreading.htm.

[9]Alfred Stieglitz, quoted in "Alfred Stieglitz," *Masters of Photography*, www.masters-of-photography.com/S/stieglitz/stieglitz_articles2.html; Andy Warhol, quoted in "Biography for Andy Warhol," *IMDb*, www.imdb.com/name/nm0912238/bio.

[10]Andy Warhol, quoted in Arthur C. Danto, *Andy Warhol* (New Haven, CT: Yale University Press, 2010), p. 145.

[11]Kevin Carter, quoted in "Kevin Carter," *Wikipedia*, http://en.wikipedia.org/wiki/Kevin_Carter.

[12]James Nachtwey, "Statement from James Nachtwey (1985)," Icarus Films, http://icarusfilms.com/new2002/warp3.html.

[13]Frans Lanting, quoted in Kim Castleberry, "Bearing Witness," *Outdoor Photographer*, November 9, 2010, www.outdoorphotographer.com/locations/international/bearing-witness.html?start=1.

[14]Ansel Adams, quoted in Les Saucer, "Refining Your Vision, the Photographer's Journey," West North Carolina Foto Fest, www.wncfotofest.com/program.html.

[15]Louis A. Sass, *"Hyped on Clarity": Diane Arbus and the Postmodern Condition*, quoted in "Diane Arbus," *Exploring Photographic Practice*, December 1, 2010, http://exphotopractice-emily-bonner.blogspot.com/2010/12/diane-arbus.html.

[16]Susan Sontag, *On Photography* (New York: Picador, 1977), p. 40.

[17]Robert Mapplethorpe, quoted in "Robert Mapplethorpe Quotes," *SearchQuotes*, www.searchquotes.com/quotation/Beauty_and_the_devil_are_the_same_thing./145110.

[18]Francis Bacon, quoted in Megan Buskey, "Francis Bacon's Horror Show," *Intelligent Life*, http://moreintelligentlife.com/story/under-influence-despair.

[19]Sontag, *On Photography*, p. 88.

[20]Eve Arnold, quoted in "10 Minutes with David Chancellor," *This Is the What*, www.thisisthewhat.com/2012/05/10-minutes-with-david-chancellor.

[21]Sontag, *On Photography*, pp. 6-7.

[22]Wim Wenders, "Wim Wenders Presents the Dresden Peace Prize to James Nachtwey," *Time*, February 20, 2012, http://lightbox.time.com/2012/02/20/dresden-prize-to-james-nachtwey/#1.

[23]Alfred Eisenstaedt, quoted in "Alfred Eisenstaedt," Jewish Virtual Library, www.jewishvirtuallibrary.org/jsource/biography/Eisenstaedt.html.

[24]Henri Cartier–Bresson, quoted in Charles Chadwyck-Healey, "Line of Sight: the Head, Heart and Eye of Henri Cartier-Bresson," *Open Democracy*, November 23, 2004, www.opendemocracy.net/arts-photography/article_2238.jsp.

[25]Eve Arnold, quoted in Amanda Hopkinson, "Eve Arnold Obituary," *The Guardian*, January 5, 2012, www.guardian.co.uk/artanddesign/2012/jan/05/eve-arnold.

[26]Sylvester Jacobs, "Portrait of a Shelter" (London: Hodder & Stoughton, 1973).

[27]Harold Evans, *Pictures on a Page* (Belmont, CA: Wadsworth, 1978).

[28]David Hume Kennerly, "Essay: Chop and Crop," *New York Times*, September 17, 2009, http://lens.blogs.nytimes.com/category/essay/page/3.

[29]Ruben Salvadori, "Photojournalism Behind the Scenes" (video in Italian with subtitles), *Vimeo*, http://vimeo.com/29280708.

[30]Roland Barthes, "The Photographic Message," *A Barthes Reader* (New York: Macmillan, 1983), p. 194.

[31]Terry Barrett, "Photographs and Contexts," *At Education* 39, No. 4 (July 1986), http://www.terrybarrettosu.com/pdfs/B_PhotAndCont_97.pdf.

[32]John Szarkowski, *Looking at Photographs* (New York: Museum of Modern Art, 1973), p. 172.

[33]James Nachtwey, quoted in Kelly Knauer, *Time Goes to War* (New York: Time Books, 2002), p. 137.

[34]James Nachtwey, quoted in Richard Keeble, John Tulloch, and Florian Zollman, *Peace Journalism* (New York: Peter Lang, 2010), p. 168.

[35]Wim Wenders, "Eulogy for James Nachtwey at the Occasion of the Dresden Prize," *Burn*, February 11, 2012, www.burnmagazine.org/in-the-spotlight/2012/02/wim-wenders.

13 TV and Movies: *The Image of the Faith*

[1]"The Production Code of the Motion Picture Industry (1930-1967)," http://productioncode.dhwritings.com/multipleframes_productioncode.php.

[2]"National Legion of Decency," *Wikipedia*, http://en.wikipedia.org/wiki/National_Legion_of_Decency#Rating_system.

[3]Andrew O'Hehir, "Why Are Christian Movies So Awful?" *Salon.com*, April 12, 2011, www.salon.com/2011/04/13/soul_surfer.

[4]Brad Pitt, quoted in "Brad Pitt Says Christian Upbringing Was 'Stifling,'" *Fox News.com*, May 17, 2011, http://entertainment.blogs.foxnews.com/2011/05/17/brad-pitt-says-christian-upbringing-was-stifling.

[5]Herbert J. Miles, quoted in Robert K. Johnston, *Reel Spirituality* (Grand Rapids: Baker Academic, 2006), p. 57.

[6]Peter Dans, *Christians in the Movies* (Lanham, MD: Rowman & Littlefield, 2011), p. 9.

[7]Simone Weil, "Morality and Literature," quoted in Andrew Basden, "Real Life Versus Fiction," www.basden.demon.co.uk/xn/weil.html.

[8]Dans, *Christians in the Movies*, p. 9.

[9]Justin Toh, quoted in Shayne Looper, "Why on Earth This Preference for Sinners?" *Daily Reporter*, May 5, 2012, www.thedailyreporter.com/article/20120505/NEWS/305059942.

[10]Ned Flanders, "Memorable Quotes for *The Simpsons*," *IMDb*, www.imdb.com/title/tt0701131/quotes.

[11]Stewie Griffin, *Family Guy*, *YouTube*, www.youtube.com/watch?v=OZuAE2vRN-A.

[12]Superintendant Chalmers, "Sweet Seymour Skinner's Baadasssss Song," *The Simpsons*, April 27, 1994, www.snpp.com/episodes/1F18.html.

[13]"Memorable Quotes for *Saved!*" *IMDb*, www.imdb.com/title/tt0332375/quotes.

[14]Ibid.

[15]"Angela Martin," *Wikipedia*, http://en.wikipedia.org/wiki/Angela_Martin.

[16]Travis Bickle, "Memorable Quotes for *Taxi Driver*," *IMDb*, www.imdb.com/title/tt0075314/quotes.

[17]Frank Fitts, "Memorable Quotes for *American Beauty*," *IMDb*, www.imdb.com/title/tt0169547/quotes.

[18]"Dare I, a Sinner, Play Christ?" *Modern Screen*, January 1961, www.jeffreyhuntermovies.com/NewSite/InPrint/1961/modernscreen0161.pdf.

[19]Jesus, "Memorable Quotes for *The Last Temptation of Christ*," *IMDb*, www.imdb.com/title/tt0095497/quotes.

[20]Paul Verhoeven, quoted in Mike Fleming, "Paul Verhoeven Finds Backing and a Writer for Controversial Jesus Christ Movie," *Deadline*, June 19, 2012, www.deadline.com/2012/06/paul-verhoeven-finds-backing-and-a-writer-for-controversial-jesus-christ-movie.

14 What Should I Do? *Consuming, Critiquing, Creating*

[1]See Richard M. Weaver, "Ideas Have Consequences" (Chicago: University of Chicago Press, 1948).

[2]Howard Jacobson, "In Praise of Bad Boys' Books," *The Guardian*, October 5, 2012,

www.guardian.co.uk/books/2012/oct/05/howard-jacobson-bad-boys-books.

³E. F. Schumacher, quoted in Charles Fager, "Small Is Beautiful, and So Is Rome: Surprising Faith of E. F. Schumacher," *Christian Century,* April 6, 1977, p. 325, www.religion-online.org/showarticle.asp?title=1151.

⁴See C. S. Lewis, *God in the Dock* (Grand Rapids: Eerdmans, 1996), chap. 10 "Christian Apologetics," p. 93.

⁵Mark O'Connell, "The First Church of Marilynne Robinson," *New Yorker,* May 30, 2012, www.newyorker.com/online/blogs/books/2012/05/marilynne-robinson.html.

⁶Greil Marcus, "Al Green: *The Belle Album,*" *Rolling Stone Reviews,* February 23, 1978, www.rollingstone.com/music/albumreviews/the-belle-album-19780223.

⁷Ignace Paderewski, quoted in David Taylor, "Paderewski's Piano," *Smithsonian. com,* March 1999, www.smithsonianmag.com/arts-culture/object_mar99.html.

Author Q&A
with Steve Turner

What initially made you interested in studying the relationship between religion and culture?

It's the story of my life. My parents, who were both from nonreligious families, became Christians around the time I was born, so I grew up in a strong and enthusiastic Christian home. At the same time I was hearing these other voices coming from pop culture, especially in my teenage years, and it became important for me to understand each source of information in the light of the other. I needed to know how the values and views found in pop culture could be tested against the Bible and Christian theology and how ideas from the Bible and Christian theology could stick up for themselves in popular culture. I'm still doing this!

How has your career as a journalist shaped the way you view arts and culture?

All my writing—as a journalist, author and poet—has helped me understand the creative process. It has helped me identify with creative people. At the same time it has enabled me to have a front-row seat at many important cultural events and given me access to the people who make the culture. I count it as a great privilege to have been able to sit down with many culture makers and ask them how and why they do what they do. This has not only taught me a lot about the creative process as people have explained to me where they get their ideas, but it has also allowed me to hold people to account for the views embodied in their work.

How has working with cultural celebrities changed the way you, as a Christian, view the arts?

I don't think it has changed my views as much as it has deepened them. It has meant that I've been able to see films being made, albums being recorded, songs being written, publicity campaigns being planned, etc., and so I have greater knowledge of and appreciation for the process.

How has your experience as a critic and creator of culture affected the writing of Popcultured and other books?

I've been able to write books that have enabled me to dig deeper into aspects of culture that have intrigued me. I've written biographies of people who ask the big questions—people like Van Morrison, Jack Kerouac, Johnny Cash, Marvin Gaye—and those are the sort of people who interest me. I feel I should encourage that sort of questioning. I've also been able to explore the relationships between religion and music in *Hungry for Heaven* and faith and art in *Imagine*. Besides supplying information for readers, these books have allowed me to sort my own thinking out.

Why did you want to write the book Popcultured?

The reason for writing *Imagine* was that I was having so many conversations with Christians who were unsure how to reconcile their faith with their art. Was art something inferior that was best left behind, was it something that should be used as an "evangelistic tool" or was there a way of integrating faith with art that expressed the total person rather than only one aspect? *Popcultured* goes beyond the arts to examine the wider world of pop culture. As I have said, books are not only a way of sharing information but are also a way of finding out things I don't already know. I often found myself speaking about pop culture but had never examined the history and theory of it. This book gave me a great opportunity to learn new things and to try to pull together all the various thoughts I've had over the years. I enjoy being a commentator, but I think I'm most effective if I concentrate on the area of the world that I know best. Of course, as soon as you talk about culture you're talking about humans and the way they organize their lives, and that means you're commentating on life in general.

You write that the word culture means to play a part in "cultivating" people. How do you hope Popcultured will cultivate people?

I hope that *Popcultured* will add to the discussion going on amongst Christians about how we should understand, enjoy and contribute to our cultures. The situation today is far better than it was when I was young in that universities, colleges and schools with a Christian foundation now gladly run courses on popular culture. I've met many of the people who have designed these courses and have benefited from conversations with them. My book is not an academic book. It's a practicing writer's view. I don't get bogged down in theories. I hope that it will be helpful for those who consume culture (all of us), those who teach or review it, and those who make it. Above all, I hope it will help people achieve integrated lives in which they don't feel the need to switch off the popcultural side of themselves when they're in church or switch off the church side of themselves when they're in the cinema, club or concert hall.

You write that "popular culture constantly veers between authentic personal expression and commercial exploitation." How do you find the balance? And what combination of those two makes popular culture meaningful?

I don't think it's a case of finding a balance. There's nothing wrong with a toe-tapping tune and there's nothing wrong with a deeply confessional poem. Each has its place. Ecclesiastes 3:4 says that there's a time to dance and a time to mourn. If someone is exclusively into one or the other you might suggest that they try something new, but generally it's good to find pop culture that helps us relax and good to find pop culture that helps us think. I think it's a great achievement when pop culture manages to be both greatly entertaining and profoundly thoughtful at the same time. This happens with some of George Carlin's comedy, a musical like *Les Misérables*, a film like *Amadeus* and the songs of the Beatles.

What is your favorite cultural medium? Why?

As a creator I've spent time writing poetry, biographies and journalism. I also love photography and now supply images for all the travel stories I write. I've just returned from India where I took 2,500 pictures. Performing my poetry gave me a great empathy for actors, dramatists and stand-up comics. I've always loved contemporary dance and find it quite inspirational. The subject of a lot of my writing has been music, and that's certainly the art form I'm most associated with. But fashion, performance, spectacle, lighting and graphics all play a part in music, so I've come to appreciate all of these. I couldn't possibly tell you my favorite!

Who has been your favorite creator of popular culture that you've worked with personally? Why?

I suppose John Lennon and Paul McCartney. I interviewed John when I was quite young, and it was significant because he had loomed so large in my teenage imagination. I liked his way with words, the risks he took with his work and the fact that he constantly challenged received opinion. I've also interviewed Paul, but because I was the ghostwriter on Linda McCartney's book of '60s photos I got to know him much better. I had breakfast with him at his home in Sussex and he would sometimes sit in on my interviews with Linda and throw in some of his own memories. When I was about nineteen I wrote out Psalm 37:4 (in the version I had it read, "Delight thyself also in the Lord and he shall give thee the desires of thy heart") and beneath the verse I listed my desires. One of them was "meet the Beatles." The best thing about it is not meeting people who are famous but meeting people who've created such memorable work. I've written two books about the Beatles—one about their songs (*A Hard Day's Write*) and one about their beliefs (*The Gospel According to the Beatles*).

What is the number-one idea you want readers to take away from Popcultured?

That it's possible to understand pop culture using a biblically informed mind and that this doesn't lessen the appreciation but increases it. I used to think that if you started to think about culture Christianly it would either adversely affect your faith or adversely affect your enjoyment of culture. Now I see that it can make your faith more robust and useful and can also deepen your love of culture. We make culture because we are made by God, and however defiant and atheistic people are they cannot shake off the divine image. I would like the book to lead Christians in confidently contributing to the ongoing discussions about culture and within culture.

Name Index